Feiyue Basic Chinese

汉语初级教程

Student's Book 2

主编 林柏松

编者 李蓓 于岚

华语教学出版社
SINOLINGUA

First Edition 2014

ISBN 978-7-5138-0561-2

Copyright 2014 by Sinolingua Co., Ltd

Published by Sinolingua Co., Ltd

24 Baiwanzhuang Road, Beijing 100037, China

Tel: (86)10-68320585, 68997826

Fax: (86)10-68997826, 68326333

http://www.sinolingua.com.cn

E-mail: hyjx@sinolingua.com.cn

Facebook: www.facebook.com/sinolingua

Printed by Beijing Jinghua Hucais Printing Co., Ltd

Printed in the People's Republic of China

Preface

Feiyue Basic Chinese is a set of basic level Chinese textbooks intended for English-speaking undergraduate students, high school students and adults to learn Chinese. The Chinese name Feiyue means to fly forward, which serves as a metaphor for the progression that will occur in students' Chinese proficiency levels after actively working through these meticulously designed textbooks. Upon completion, the student will have learned about 1000 frequently used Chinese words and 800 characters; as well as a proficiency level expected to reach Intermediate Mid as rated by the American Council on the Teaching of Foreign Languages (ACTFL), and Level 1 of the Interagency Language Roundtable (ILR). *Feiyue Basic Chinese* and *Feiyue Intermediate Chinese*, which has already been published, will form a two-year textbook series that meets the basic needs of teaching and learning Chinese as a foreign language outside China.

There are 22 lessons in this set of textbooks for one academic year, with the content divided evenly into two books. Each book requires about 80 class hours to complete, or one semester in the U.S. school system. Each textbook has 11 lessons and each lesson requires approximately seven 50-minute class periods. The student book is accompanied by a CD of listening materials in MP3 format and a teacher's book, which provides the keys to all the exercises and the transcripts of all listening exercises. A glossary and a character list for 22 lessons in alphabetical order are also included. In addition to the printed copy, an Internet edition is also being planned which can be used online or downloaded to computers, cell phones or iPads.

Feiyue Basic Chinese textbook is a trinity of traditional textbook, workbook, and homework book. The same format is used for each lesson in the two books:

1. Lead-in: This section aims to activate students' related memories and bring out the subject matter and the key words of the lesson with four or five pictures associated with the lesson. Practice has shown that a few minutes' lead-in is an important stage for students before they learn a new lesson.

2. The text: Starting from Lesson 4, each lesson consists of a dialog and a narrative passage, the former helping students learn spoken Chinese and the latter, written Chinese. The lesson texts mirror all aspects of American students' real life with vivid and interesting scenarios and embody the principle of "a textbook reflecting real life". Both simplified and traditional characters are used to present the texts. This agrees with the reality that both forms of writing are used in overseas Chinese communities. Tips along the margin highlight the corresponding

text's communicative functions.

3. Vocabulary: Each lesson text is followed by a vocabulary list, in which new words are arranged according to the order of their appearance in the text, with both simplified characters and traditional characters listed side by side. In addition to pinyin transcription and precise English language explanation, the parts of speech and examples of usage for each new word are also provided. This prevents students from relying on English definitions of the new words as their only guide to word usage. A glossary of all lessons is provided at the end of each book for the convenience of word searching.

4. Exercises: A considerable amount of exercises in listening, speaking, reading, writing and translation follow each lesson text. Content questions and exercises on the use of words deepen students' understanding of the contents of the texts and usages of the key words. Such understanding lays a good foundation for the comprehensive use of language skills needed in the last part of the lesson, "Using the Language". Reflecting the principle to attach more importance in listening and speaking in foreign language teaching, this set of textbooks provides a significant amount of listening exercises, ensuring language input in large quantity and with high quality.

5. Phonetics: A special section of "Phonetics" is added to Lessons 1-7 in the attempt to help build a solid foundation on Chinese phonetics. Chinese initials, finals, tones, neutral tones, tone sandhi, retroflex ending "-r", and pinyin spelling rules are systematically introduced in this section with a great amount of practices and exercises, including the pronunciation and transcription of single syllables, multi-syllables, phrases, and sentences. One thing worth mentioning is this book's new teaching approach on the Chinese third tone, which is based on current research findings and successful teaching experience. The third tone is treated as a low falling tone when it is first introduced to students, thus effectively avoiding problems that foreign students often have in pronouncing the so called "half-third tone".

6. Chinese characters: Learning Chinese characters is a difficult yet important task for foreign learners of Chinese. Following the principle of "recognizing long form, writing in short form, and typing with pinyin," which is accepted by many overseas Chinese teachers, this set of textbooks introduces characters with the innovative character-component teaching approach. Each new character is introduced with an analysis of its components, which helps students learn the formation of Chinese characters. Students are required to hand-write all the one-component characters, which are considered the basic characters, so that they will gain a better understanding of the stroke order and character components to avoid producing "stroke-missing" characters. Since radicals are the most important components, we have selected 44 high frequency radicals from the texts of Book 2 to explain their origin and meaning. In order

to stimulate students' enthusiasm for learning characters, we have designed many fun exercises such as character formation games. Chinese composition used to be the bottleneck in teaching Chinese as a foreign language due to difficulties in writing and recognizing Chinese characters. Taking full advantage of computer technology, this set of textbooks provides a large amount of exercises for typing characters on the computer, in addition to writing characters by hand, to enhance students' skill in recognizing, reading and typing characters.

7. Language Points: This set of textbooks explains grammar in a simple, precise and practical way without trying to present a complete grammar system using complicated grammar terminology. The language points are selected with an eye on the special difficulties that English-speaking students often have in learning Chinese, and exercises are designed accordingly. Easy language points are introduced before more difficult ones and important language points are recycled with progression in spirals.

8. Using the Language: This is the teaching focus of the entire lesson. The aim is to develop students' abilities to use Chinese in the real world. Authentic materials related to each lesson's topic are used, such as store names, street signs, advertisements, handwritten notices and letters etc. The words and sentence structures in these materials are not confined to those taught in the texts. Therefore, this section not only helps students review what they have learned but also expands upon the lesson contents. The exercises in this section take a variety of forms that feature an integration of listening, speaking, reading and writing. The formats that American students often encounter in major tests such as the AP Exam and OPI Test are adopted in the designing of the exercises, such as multiple choice questions, situational role plays and writing essays based on pictures. The "Cultural Tips" of this section familiarizes students with the cultural knowledge and is thus of considerable reference value.

This set of textbooks is an attempt at applying new approaches to Chinese teaching and is by no means complete. We welcome feedback from fellow teachers and experts in the field so that we may further improve the textbooks. Thank you in advance for your help and support.

Patrick Lin
October 2013

目录

词类简称
Abbreviations for Parts of Speech

adj.	adjective 形容词
adv.	adverb 副词
a.v.	auxiliary verb 助动词
conj.	conjunction 连词
intj.	interjection 叹词
m.	measure word 量词
n.	noun 名词
nc.	numeral-classifier 数量词
num.	numeral 数词
ono.	onomatopoeia 拟声词
part.	particle 助词
pn.	proper noun 专有名词
pron.	pronoun 代词
pref.	prefix 前缀
prep.	preposition 介词
suff.	suffix 后缀
v.	verb 动词

第十二课 学中文
Lesson Twelve · Learning Chinese

一、导入 Lead-in

Exercise 1 📖 🗣️

Look at the pictures below and describe the activities in Chinese.

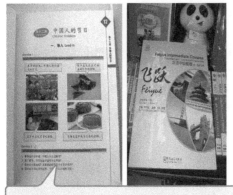

这学期我选了中文阅读和口语课。

我还选了中国功夫课。

周末中文学校有书法和画画儿课。

周末中文学校其实还是挺好玩儿的。

After learning this lesson, you will be able to:

1. Talk about your experience in learning Chinese language and culture at school.

2. Understand the wide range of Chinese cultural practices, such as Chinese paintings and kung fu.

3. Recognize the new characters in this lesson, and learn the common radicals 讠, 亻, 口 and 囗.

4. Use the structures 为了… and 不但 … 还 , and the verb complements 好 and 懂.

二、课文 Texts

课文（一） *Text (1)*

你选什么课？

飞跃——汉语初级教程学生用书　下册

简体版

Tom and Xiaohua are talking about taking Chinese courses for the new semester.

汤姆：小华，这个学期你选了几门中文课？

小华：我选了四门课，听力、阅读、口语，还有中国文化课。

Tips: how to ask about taking courses

汤姆：中国文化课都学些什么啊？

小华：什么都学，中国人的姓名、饮食、节日、风俗习惯等等。

汤姆：有中国功夫吗？

小华：有，比如太极拳什么的。

汤姆：那每门课是几个学分？

小华：三个学分，每周上六节课。

汤姆：考试呢？

小华：有期中考试和期末考试。平时有小测验。

汤姆：考试难不难？

Tips: talk about tests and quizzes

小华：我觉得不太难。

汤姆：我想将来去中国当一名英文老师，我也选一门中国文化课吧。

你選甚麼課?

繁体版

Tom and Xiaohua are talking about taking Chinese courses for the new semester.

湯姆：小華，這個學期你選了幾門中文課?

小華：我選了四門課，聽力、閱讀、口語，還有中國文化課。

湯姆：中國文化課都學些什麼啊?

小華：什麼都學，中國人的姓名、飲食、節日、風俗習慣等等。

湯姆：有中國功夫嗎?

小華：有，比如太極拳什麼的。

湯姆：那每門課是幾個學分?

小華：三個學分，每周上六節課。

湯姆：考試呢?

小華：有期中考試和期末考試。平時有小測驗。

湯姆：考試難不難?

小華：我覺得不太難。

湯姆：我想將來去中國當一名英文老師，我也選一門中國文化課吧。

(李荣光先生书法作品)

Kèwén (yī)   *Text (1)*

Nǐ Xuǎn Shénme Kè?

拼音版

Tom and Xiaohua are talking about taking Chinese courses for the new semester.

Tāngmǔ: Xiǎohuá, zhège xuéqī nǐ xuǎnle jǐ mén Zhōngwénkè?

Xiǎohuá: Wǒ xuǎnle sì mén kè, tīnglì, yuèdú, kǒuyǔ, háiyǒu Zhōngguó wénhuàkè.

Tāngmǔ: Zhōngguó wénhuàkè dōu xué xiē shénme ā?

Xiǎohuá: Shénme dōu xué, Zhōngguórén de xìngmíng, yǐnshí, jiérì, fēngsú xíguàn děngděng.

Tāngmǔ: Yǒu Zhōngguó gōngfu ma?

Xiǎohuá: Yǒu, bǐrú tàijíquán shénmede.

Tāngmǔ: Nà měi mén kè shì jǐ gè xuéfēn?

Xiǎohuá: Sān gè xuéfēn, měi zhōu shàng liù jié kè.

Tāngmǔ: Kǎoshì ne?

Xiǎohuá: Yǒu qīzhōng kǎoshì hé qīmò kǎoshì. Píngshí yǒu xiǎo cèyàn.

Tāngmǔ: Kǎoshì nán bu nán?

Xiǎohuá: Wǒ juéde bú tài nán.

Tāngmǔ: Wǒ xiǎng jiānglái qù Zhōngguó dāng yì míng Yīngwén lǎoshī, wǒ yě xuǎn yì mén Zhōngguó wénhuàkè ba.

生词（一）*New Words (1)*

	简体（繁體）	拼音	词性	解释 / 例子
1	学（學）期	xuéqī	*n.*	term, semester 上学期 / 下学期 / 一学年有两个学期。
2	选（選）	xuǎn	*v.*	select, choose 选课 / 选了几门课

	简体（繁體）	拼音	词性	解释 / 例子
3	听（聽）力	tīnglì	n.	listening ability; listening comprehension 听力课 / 练习听力 / 听力考试很难。
4	阅读（閱讀）	yuèdú	n.	reading 阅读课 / 阅读课本 / 阅读考试
5	口语（語）	kǒuyǔ	n.	spoken language 口语课 / 练习口语 / 口语要天天练。
6	文化	wénhuà	n.	culture 中国文化 / 西方文化 / 文化课
7	饮（飲）食	yǐnshí	n.	food and drinks 饮食习惯 / 注意饮食
8	节（節）日	jiérì	n.	festival 春节是中国人的节日。
9	风（風）俗	fēngsú	n.	folk customs 送圣诞礼物是圣诞节的风俗之一。 / 吃火鸡是感恩节的风俗。
10	习惯（習慣）	xíguàn	n.	habit 风俗习惯 / 生活习惯 / 早睡早起是好习惯。
11	等等	děngděng	part.	so on and so forth; etc. 我喜欢看电影、看电视、读书等等。
12	功夫	gōngfu	n.	kung fu; martial art skills 中国功夫 / 练功夫 / 功夫大师李小龙
13	太极（極）拳	tàijíquán	n.	taichi 打太极拳 / 练习太极拳
14	什么（甚麼）的	shénmede	part.	etc. 我喜欢看电影、看电视、读书什么的。
15	学（學）分	xuéfēn	n.	credit 学分制 / 修学分 / 转学分
16	考试（試）	kǎoshì	n./v.	take an examination 今天我们考试。 / 考试的时候不要说话。
17	期中	qīzhōng	n.	mid-term 期中考试
18	期末	qīmò	n.	end of semester 期末考试
19	平时（時）	píngshí	n.	at normal times 平时的小考 / 我平时不看电视，周末才看。
20	测验（測驗）	cèyàn	n.	test 生词测验 / 小测验
21	将来（將來）	jiānglái	n.	future 将来你想做什么？ / 孩子的将来很重要。

专有名词 Proper Noun			
汤（湯）姆	Tāngmǔ	pn.	Tom

Exercise 1 👂 🗣✳

Listen to Text (1) and answer the questions orally in Chinese.

1. What classes did Xiaohua select?

2. What is included in the Chinese Culture class?

3. What tests and quizzes do they have?

4. Why did Tom select Chinese Culture?

Exercise 2 📖

Read Text (1) and decide whether the following statements are true or false.

1. 汤姆想选一门中国文化课。	(　　)
2. 小华只有期末考试和小测验。	(　　)
3. 中文课有的是三个学分，有的是四个学分。	(　　)
4. 去中国教英文，最好学一点儿中国文化。	(　　)

Exercise 3 📖 ✍

Read the following dialogs aloud and complete the missing sentences using the English as a guide.

Dialog 1

A：约翰，这个学期你选什么课？

B：我想选听力、阅读和文化课。

A：＿＿＿＿＿＿＿＿＿＿＿＿＿＿＿＿＿＿。

（I want to select the culture course too.）

B：太好了，我们可以一起上课了。

Dialog 2

A：小华，你们周末中文学校都有哪些中文课？

B：＿＿＿＿＿＿＿＿＿＿＿＿＿＿＿＿＿＿。

(We have various kinds of Chinese courses, such as reading, listening, speaking, etc.)

A：你们有没有中国文化课，比如太极拳什么的？

B：当然有了！我们有太极拳课，也有中国书法课和画画课。

Dialog 3

A：你们学校一门课有几个学分？

B：＿＿＿＿＿＿＿＿＿＿＿＿＿＿＿＿＿＿。

(Many courses have three credits, but Chinese Culture has six credits.)

A：那我想选两门课，一门文化课，一门听力。

Exercise 4 ✑

Fill in the blanks with the given words.

测验　　考试　　选　　教　　风俗习惯　　中国文化

去年我去中国当了一年的英语老师。我到中国的时候，不会说中文。英语系的王老师 _____ 我中文，我教她英文。王老师教得很好。每个月给我一次大 _____，平时给我一些小 _____。我一边学中文，还一边看英文的关于 _____ 的书。这些书让我知道了中国的饮食和 _____。我还 _____ 了学校里的太极拳课。一年时间很快过去了。我离开中国的时候，已经会说不少中文了。

课文（二）Text (2)

简体版

周末中文学校

Jiang Xiaohua tells her classmates about her experience at her weekend Chinese school.

我爸爸妈妈都是从中国来的，而我是在美国出生的。在学校里，我跟同学们都说英文。回到家里，父母跟我说中文。所以，我能听懂简单的中文，可是，我不认识汉字。

为了让我学好中文，父母送我去了周末中文学校。开始的时候，我不喜欢周末还去上学。可是后来，我觉得周末中文学校其实还是挺好玩儿的。在那儿不但可以学习中文，还可以学习舞蹈、书法、画画儿等。自从高中开设了大学汉语先修课以后，我的很多美国同学都去周末中文学校学习中文。我很高兴，我又可以在周末中文学校和我的同学们在一起了。

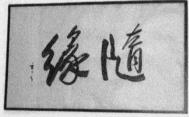

（李荣光先生书法作品）

第十二课　学中文

週末中文學校

飞跃——汉语初级教程学生用书 下册

繁体版

Jiang Xiaohua tells her classmates about her experience at her weekend Chinese school.

　　我爸爸媽媽都是從中國來的，而我是在美國出生的。在學校裏，我跟同學們都說英文。回到家裏，父母跟我說中文。所以，我能聽懂簡單的中文，可是，我不認識漢字。

　　爲了讓我學好中文，父母送我去了周末中文學校。開始的時候，我不喜歡周末還去上學。可是後來，我覺得周末中文學校其實還是挺好玩兒的。在那兒不但可以學習中文，還可以學習舞蹈、書法、畫畫兒等。自從高中開設了大學漢語先修課以後，我的很多美國同學都去周末中文學校學習中文。我很高興，我又可以在周末中文學校和我的同學們在一起了。

Kèwén (èr)　*Text (2)*

Zhōumò Zhōngwén Xuéxiào

拼音版

Jiang Xiaohua tells her classmates about her experience at her weekend Chinese school.

　　Wǒ bàba māma dōu shì cóng Zhōngguó lái de, ér wǒ shì zài Měiguó chūshēng de. Zài xuéxiào li, wǒ gēn tóngxuémen dōu shuō Yīngwén. Huídào jiā li, fùmǔ gēn wǒ shuō Zhōngwén. Suóyǐ, wǒ néng tīng dǒng jiǎndān de Zhōngwén, kěshì, wǒ bú rènshi Hànzì.

　　Wèile ràng wǒ xuéhǎo Zhōngwén, fùmǔ sòng wǒ qùle zhōumò Zhōngwén xuéxiào. Kāishǐ de shíhou, wǒ bù xǐhuan zhōumò hái qù shàngxué. Kěshì hòulái, wǒ juéde zhōumò Zhōngwén xuéxiào qíshí háishì tǐng hǎowánr de. Zài nàr búdàn kěyǐ xuéxí Zhōngwén, hái kěyǐ xuéxí wǔdǎo, shūfǎ, huà huàr děng. Zìcóng gāozhōng kāishèle dàxué Hànyǔ xiānxiūkè yǐhòu, wǒ de hěnduō Měiguó tóngxué dōu qù zhōumò Zhōngwén xuéxiào xuéxí Zhōngwén. Wǒ hěn gāoxìng, wǒ yòu kěyǐ zài zhōumò Zhōngwén xuéxiào hé wǒ de tóngxuémen zài yìqǐ le.

生词（二） *New Words (2)*

	简体（繁體）	拼音	词性	解释/例子
1	而	ér	*conj.*	whereas 他学中文，而我学英文。/ 他们喜欢中国饮食，而我吃不惯中国饭。
2	所以	suǒyǐ	*conj.*	therefore 我病了，所以不能上学。/ 我没有复习，所以没有考好。
3	听（聽）	tīng	*v.*	listen, hear 你能听懂中文吗？/ 我听不见你说什么。
4	懂	dǒng	*v.*	understand 我懂中文。/ 我能听懂他的话。/ 我能看懂这本书。
5	简单（簡單）	jiǎndān	*adj.*	simple 这一课很简单。/ 这次考试不简单。/ 他的生活很简单。
6	可是	kěshì	*conj.*	but 开始我不喜欢中文学校，可是后来喜欢了。/ 他说八点钟来，可是九点了他才来。
7	汉（漢）字	Hànzì	*n.*	Chinese character 你会写汉字吗？/ 日文和韩文里都有汉字。
8	为（為）了	wèile	*conj.*	in order to 为了学好中文，他买了一本新字典。/ 为了买到便宜的电脑，我一大早就去商店了。

简体（繁體）		拼音	词性	解释 / 例子
9	让（讓）	ràng	v.	let 为了让我学好中文，父母送我去了中文学校。/ 你可以让他给你买那本书。
10	上学（學）	shàngxué	v.	attend school 我早上七点上学。/ 他在美国上学，他太太在饭馆工作。
11	其实（實）	qíshí	adv.	actually 你说他是中国人，其实他是韩国人。
12	挺	tǐng	adv.	very 挺好 / 挺热 / 挺好玩儿
13	好玩儿（兒）	hǎowánr	adj.	fun, interesting 这个电子游戏很好玩儿。/ 那个刚开的购物中心很好玩，有商场、电影院、快餐厅什么的。
14	不但……还（還）……	búdàn… hái…	conj.	not only… but also 我不但会日文，还会中文。
15	舞蹈	wǔdǎo	n.	dance 看舞蹈 / 练习舞蹈 / 舞蹈家
16	书（書）法	shūfǎ	n.	penmanship, calligraphy 书法家 / 书法展览
17	画（畫）	huà	v.	draw, paint 画画儿 / 照猫画虎
18	画儿（畫兒）	huàr	n.	picture, painting 一张画儿 / 山水画儿 / 中国画儿
19	自从（從）	zìcóng	prep.	since 自从看了画展以后，他就喜欢上了画画儿。
20	高中	gāozhōng	n.	senior high school 上高中 / 高中生
21	开设（開設）	kāishè	v.	open; set up (a course in school) 学校开设了中文课。
22	大学（學）	dàxué	n.	university 上大学 / 大学生
23	汉语（漢語）	Hànyǔ	n.	the Chinese language 学汉语 / 我很喜欢汉语课。
24	先修课（課）	xiānxiūkè	n.	Advanced Placement Classes in high school 大学汉语先修课

Exercise 5 🎧 🗣

Listen to Text (2) and answer the questions orally in Chinese.

1. How is my Chinese?

2. What was I unhappy about in the beginning?

3. What activities are there in the Chinese school?

4. How did I later feel about the school?

Exercise 6 📖 ✎

Read Text (2) and fill in the following chart in pinyin and/or characters.

People	Origin/Birthplace	Language	Attitude	Action
爸爸妈妈				
我				

Exercise 7 👂

Listen to the following dialog and decide whether the statements below are true or false.

1. Xiaowen does not know Chinese at all.	( )
2. Xiaowen's mother wants him to be able to read books in Chinese.	( )
3. Xiaowen feels that he does not need to learn Chinese.	( )
4. There is no class for Chinese calligraphy at the school.	( )
5. Xiaowen does not like kung fu.	( )

Exercise 8 ✎

Fill in the blanks with the given words.

舞蹈　　中文学校　　听懂　　文化　　书法　　认识

　　我在美国一个学校工作。这个学校有很多中国来的老师。可是他们的孩子是在美国出生的。这些孩子能 _____ 一点儿中文，可是不 _____ 汉字。为了让这些孩子不忘记中文，一些老师办起了周末 _____。这个学校每个星期六上课。孩子们在这里学习中文，也学习中国 _____ 课，汉字 _____、中国 _____、中国画儿等。老师也教给孩子们一些中国功夫。

三、汉字 Chinese Characters

1. New characters in this lesson

序号	拼音	简 / 繁	部件	构词
1	cè	测（測）	氵＋则（贝＋刂）	测验 / 测试

2	dān	单（單）	单	简单 / 菜单 / 信用卡账单
3	dàn	但	亻+旦（日+一）	不但 / 但是
4	dǎo	蹈	𧾷+舀（爫+臼）	舞蹈 / 舞蹈课
5	dǒng	懂	忄+董（艹+重）	懂中文 / 听懂 / 看懂 / 懂了
6	dú	读（讀）	讠+卖（十+买）	读书 / 读报 / 早读
7	ér	而	而	而且 / 然而
8	fǎ	法	氵+去	书法 / 语法 / 办法
9	fēng	风（風）	几+乂	风俗 / 大风
10	fū	夫	夫	功夫 / 大夫 / 丈夫
11	gōng	功	工+力	功课 / 功夫 / 成功
12	guàn	惯（慣）	忄+贯（毌+贝）	习惯 / 惯用 / 惯常
13	Hàn	汉（漢）	氵+又	汉字 / 汉语拼音 / 汉文化
14	huà	化	亻+匕	文化 / 文化课 / 化学 / 变化
15	huà	画（畫）	一+田+凵	画画儿 / 图画儿
16	jiǎn	简（簡）	竹+间（门+日）	简单 / 简历 / 简化 / 简体字
17	jiāng	将（將）	丬+寽（夕+寸）	将来 / 将要 / 将军
18	kǎo	考	耂+丂	考试 / 考题
19	lì	力	力	听力 / 大力 / 力量
20	mǔ	姆	女+母	汤姆
21	nán	难（難）	又+隹	太难 / 难受 / 困难 / 难过
22	píng	平	平	平时 / 和平 / 水平
23	qí	其	其	其实 / 其他 / 其中
24	quán	拳	𢍏+手	太极拳 / 拳头 / 左右拳
25	ràng	让（讓）	讠+上	让我去 / 让他走 / 让开
26	shè	设（設）	讠+殳（几+又）	开设 / 建设
27	shí	实（實）	宀+头	其实 / 实在 / 老实
28	sú	俗	亻+谷	风俗 / 俗气
29	suǒ	所	戶+斤	所以 / 所有 / 所能
30	tāng	汤（湯）	氵+昜	汤姆 / 汤水

31	tīng	听（聽）	口＋斤	听说／听力／听话／听音乐
32	tǐng	挺	扌＋廷（壬＋廴）	挺好／挺大
33	wǔ	舞	無＋舛	舞蹈／舞蹈家／中国舞
34	xiū	修	亻＋攸	先修课／修理
35	xuǎn	选（選）	先＋辶	选课／选修课
36	yàn	验（驗）	马＋金	测验／试验／实验／验收
37	yǐn	饮（飲）	饣＋欠（⺈＋人）	饮食／饮料／饮水／饮品
38	yǔ	语（語）	讠＋吾（五＋口）	口语／语文／语法／语音／汉语
39	yuè	阅（閱）	门＋兑（丷＋兄）	阅读／阅读课／阅报

Exercise 1 ✎

Copy the following single-component characters with correct stroke order in the spaces provided.

dān	单	丶丶丷丷㣎旦单	
ér	而	一丆冂丙而而	
fū	夫	一二夫夫	
lì	力	刀力	
píng	平	一丆冈平平	
qí	其	一十卄卄甘甘其其	

Exercise 2 📖 ✎

Read the following sentences and choose the correct characters to fill in the blanks.

1. 你这个学期 _____ 了几门课？（选 远 先）
2. 我下午只有听力课，没有阅 _____ 课。（读 都 卖）
3. 我们有期中和期末两种 _____ 试。（考 靠 老）
4. 因为周末中文学校里有我的朋友，_____ 以我喜欢去那里。（所 听 析）

5. 这么 _____ 单的中文，我一听就懂了。（简　间　筒）

6. 中文学校里也教舞 _____。（滔　韬　蹈）

7. 这个学期，学校里开 _____ 了中国文化课。（没　舍　设）

8. 学习中文要学一点儿中国人的风 _____。（俗　舒　数）

2. Common radicals (1)

(1) 亻（人）dānlìrén, human

The radical 亻 is derived from the pictographic character 𠂉（人 human). The characters with this radical are usually related to people, or people's behaviors. The radical is always placed on the left side of a character, like 他 (he/him), 做 (to work), 住 (to live). When it is placed at the top or bottom of a character, it is written as 人, like 个 (measure word for people).

(2) 讠（言）yánzìpáng

The radical 讠 is simplified from the character 言, meaning speech. This radical is usually placed on the left side and occasionally in the middle of a character. When it is placed at the bottom, it is written as 言. Characters with the radical 讠 or 言 are usually related to language or words, e.g. 说 (to speak), 话 (speech), 请 (please), 谢 (to thank), 警 (to warn; alarm).

(3) 口 kǒuzìpáng

The radical 口 is derived from the pictographic character 𠙴, symbolizing a man's mouth. Thus, characters with this radical are usually related to the mouth or speech, e.g. 叫 (to call), 听 (listen to), 吃 (to eat), 吗 (question particle), 呢 (modal particle).

(4) 囗 fāngkuàng

The radical 囗 is simplified from the character 围 (wéi, to enclose). Thus characters with this radical are usually related to an enclosure or a boundary, like 国 (country), 园 (garden), 图 (map).

Exercise 3

Fill in the chart below by writing down as many characters as you can.

Radical	Meaning of the radical	Characters that you have learned containing this radical
讠		
亻		

口		
口		

四、语言点 Language Points

1. Question words indicating indefinite reference

We just learned the following sentence in this lesson:

我们<u>什么</u>都学，中国人的饮食、中国人的姓名、中国人的习惯等等。

In the sentence, the Chinese question word 什么 ("what") is used with 都, to indicate indefinite reference, meaning "everything, anything". Other question words, like 谁, 哪里/哪儿, 怎么, can also be used with 都 to indicate indefinite reference, meaning "anybody", "anywhere", and "any way", respectively. Here are more examples:

> (1) "她跟你说<u>什么</u>了？" "她<u>什么</u>都没说。"
>
> "What did she say to you?" "She did not say anything."
>
> (2) "长周末你想到<u>哪里/哪儿</u>去玩？" "去<u>哪里/哪儿</u>都行。"
>
> "Where do you want to go on the long weekend?" "Anywhere will do."
>
> (3) "明天<u>谁</u>要去滑雪？" "滑雪太冷了，<u>谁</u>都不想去。"
>
> "Who is going skiing tomorrow?" "It is too cold to ski, no one wants to go."
>
> (4) "你想<u>怎么</u>去？走路还是开车？" "我<u>怎么</u>去都行。"
>
> "How do you plan to go? Will you walk or drive?" "Any way is fine for me."

2. The verb complement 好

As we learned in previous lessons, a monosyllabic verb may become a compound word by adding another verb or adjective to it. The first syllable of the compound word indicates the action itself while the second one, which is called a *verb complement*, provides extra information such as the direction, the result, or the description of the action. In this lesson, we will learn 好 as a verb complement to indicate the result of the action.

> **Verb + 好 (well) → Verb Complement Compound**

学 + 好 → 学好 (learn something well)

想 + 好 → 想好 (think it over and make up one's mind)

说 + 好 → 说好 (talk and achieve an agreement)
做 + 好 → 做好 (finish doing something)
放 + 好 → 放好 (put something in a proper place)

(1) 为了让我学好中文，父母送我去了周末中文学校。
To help me learn Chinese better, my parents sent me to a weekend Chinese school.

(2) "后天就是长周末了，你们想到哪儿去玩儿啊？""还没想好呢。"
"The long weekend begins the day after tomorrow. Where do you want to go for fun?""I have not made up my mind yet. "

(3) 我跟他说好了，明天一起去滑雪。
I talked to him and we agreed to go skiing tomorrow.

(4) 你等我一下，我做好功课就跟你走。
Wait for me a while. I will go with you right after I finish my homework.

(5) "圣诞礼物都放好了吗？""放好了。我把圣诞礼物都放在圣诞树下了。"
"Have you put the Christmas gifts where they should be?""Yes, I put them under the Christmas tree."

3. The verb complement 懂

In this lesson, we will also learn 懂 as a verb complement to indicate the result of the action.

Verb + 懂 (understand) → Verb Complement Compound

听 + 懂 → 听懂 (listen and understand)
看 + 懂 → 看懂 (read and understand)

(1) 回到家里，父母跟我说中文。所以，我能听懂简单的中文。
Back at home my parents speak Chinese to me, so I can understand simple Chinese.

(2) 今天上午的听力课你能听懂吗？我听懂了一半。
Did you understand the listening class this morning? I understood half of it.

(3) 他认识汉字，所以他能看懂用中文写的电子邮件。
He can read Chinese characters, so he can understand emails written in characters.

(4) 我可以读懂玛丽给我发的短信。
I can understand the message that Mary sent to me.

4. The preposition 为了

The preposition 为了 introduces the purpose of an action or an event. It is often used in the following pattern:

> **为了 + a word/a clause, Subject + Verb + Object**

(1) 为了让我学好中文，父母送我去周末中文学校。
To help me learn Chinese better, my parents sent me to a weekend Chinese school.

(2) 为了妈妈，我要学好中文。
For my mother's sake, I should learn Chinese well.

(3) 为了上课不迟到，我今天早上六点一刻就起床了。
To be on time for class I got up very early, at 6:15.

(4) 为了买到便宜的圣诞礼物，我在网上花了很多时间。
To buy inexpensive Christmas gifts, I spent a lot of time online.

5. The adverb 其实

The adverb 其实 emphasizes what follows is true, meaning "actually, in fact, as a matter of fact".

(1) 后来，我觉得周末中文学校其实还是挺好玩儿的。
Later, I felt that the weekend Chinese school was actually pretty interesting.

(2) 你说他是中国人，其实他是日本人。
You said he was Chinese, actually he is Japanese.

(3) 那件衬衫她给你打了八折，其实还是很贵。
Actually, the shirt was still expensive even though she gave you a 20% discount.

(4) 其实她不是我的女朋友，只是我的同学。
Actually, she is not my girlfriend, only my classmate.

6. The 不但 ... 还 ... construction

The 不但 ... 还 ... construction has the same meaning as the expression "not only... but also..." in English. Note that 还 can be replaced by 而且 in this pattern.

(1) 在那儿不但可以学习中文，还可以学习舞蹈、书法、画画儿等。
There we can learn not only Chinese language, but also dance, calligraphy,

and painting.

(2) 这件大衣<u>不但</u>好看，<u>还</u>很便宜。
This coat is not only good-looking, but also inexpensive.

(3) 我喜欢夏天，因为夏天<u>不但</u>可以去野餐，<u>还</u>可以去露营。
I like summer because we can not only go picnicking, but also camping.

(4) 这个学期我<u>不但</u>选了中文口语课，<u>还</u>选了中国文化课。
This semester, I am taking not only Speaking Chinese, but also Chinese Culture.

Exercise 1 👂 ✍

Listen to four short dialogs and answer the questions in Chinese characters. Pay attention to the use of 听懂, 看懂, 做好, 想好.

Dialog 1 Question: 今天的课彼得都听懂了吗？	Answer:
Dialog 2 Question: 约翰今天的作业做好了吗？	Answer:
Dialog 3 Question: 小华的中文怎么样？	Answer:
Dialog 4 Question: 大卫想好了买哪件衬衫了吗？	Answer:

Exercise 2 ✍

Complete the following dialogs using 什么, 谁, 哪里 / 哪儿, 怎么 *based on the English given in the parentheses.*

Dialog 1

A：小江，我这儿有可乐、果汁，也有牛奶。你想喝什么?

B：_____。
(Anything is fine with me.)

Dialog 2

A：每年圣诞节的时候，哪些人喜欢圣诞礼物?

B：_____，男人、女人、老人，特别是孩子们。
(I think everyone likes Christmas gifts.)

Dialog 3

A：小雨，这个长周末你想去哪儿玩儿?

B：_____。你呢?
(I don't want to go anywhere. I want to rest at home.)

A：我啊，＿＿＿＿＿＿＿＿＿＿＿＿＿＿＿＿＿＿＿。(I want to go everywhere.)

　　我想去公园野餐，也想去山上露营，还想去电影院看电影呢。

Dialog 4

A：李文，我们明天怎么去中国城？坐地铁去还是开车去？

B：＿＿＿＿＿＿＿＿＿＿＿＿＿＿＿＿＿＿＿＿＿＿＿＿。

　　(Both are fine with me.)

Dialog 5

A：小王，今天放学后我们去哪儿做作业？去图书馆还是去咖啡馆？

B：＿＿＿＿＿＿＿＿＿＿＿＿＿＿＿＿＿＿。你想去哪儿呢？

　　(Anywhere is fine with me.)

Dialog 6

A：小林，你周末在家都做些什么？

B：＿＿＿＿＿＿＿＿＿＿＿＿＿，看书、做作业、上网、做饭什么的。

　　(I do everything.)

A：你还会做饭啊？会做什么饭？

B：＿＿＿＿＿＿＿＿＿＿＿＿＿＿＿＿＿，中国饭、日本饭、美国饭都会。

　　(I can make all kinds of food.)

Exercise 3 ✍

Follow the example and rewrite the following sentences using the 为了 ... construction to emphasize the purpose of the action.

Example:

我花了很多钱给家人买圣诞礼物。→为了给家人买圣诞礼物，我花了很多钱。

1. 我每个周末都去中文学校学中文。

＿＿＿＿＿＿＿＿＿＿＿＿＿＿＿＿＿＿＿＿＿＿＿＿＿＿

2. 李老师今天下班以后要留下来帮我补习。

＿＿＿＿＿＿＿＿＿＿＿＿＿＿＿＿＿＿＿＿＿＿＿＿＿＿

3. 明天有一个考试，我今晚要在图书馆复习到九点半左右。

＿＿＿＿＿＿＿＿＿＿＿＿＿＿＿＿＿＿＿＿＿＿＿＿＿＿

4. 星期六下午我和汤姆坐了一个小时的地铁去中国城看电影。

＿＿＿＿＿＿＿＿＿＿＿＿＿＿＿＿＿＿＿＿＿＿＿＿＿＿

5. 妈妈花了一上午的时间给我买了一件蓝色的衬衫。

＿＿＿＿＿＿＿＿＿＿＿＿＿＿＿＿＿＿＿＿＿＿＿＿＿＿

第十二课 学中文

6. 万圣节那天我要留在家里，给来要糖的孩子们发糖。

_____

7. 我和弟弟花了很多时间装饰我们家的圣诞树。

_____

Exercise 4 ✎

Complete the following sentences with the adverb 其实. Use the English in the parentheses as a guide.

1. 我以为他是英国人，_____。
(Actually, he is an American.)

2. 她告诉我说她很忙，没时间去看电影。我知道 _____。
(Actually, she is not busy.)

3. 小雨觉得这次考试很难，_____。
(Actually, this test is not very hard.)

4. 这件衬衫看起来很贵，_____。
(Actually, it's very cheap.)

5. 她看起来只有二十多岁，_____。
(Actually, she is already thirty five years old.)

6. 我们只知道他的英文很好，_____。
(Actually, his Chinese is also very good.)

Exercise 5 📖 ✎

Read the dialogs and rewrite the underlined sentences with the 不但 ... 还 ... construction.

Dialog 1
A：大卫，你怎么总喜欢上网买东西？
B：上网买东西又便宜又方便，不用花很多时间去逛商店。

_____

Dialog 2
A：王红，听说你老家的天气很好，是吗？
B：当然了。夏天不热，冬天不冷，很舒服。

_____

Dialog 3
A：哥，你觉得这双蓝色的球鞋怎么样？
B：挺好的，又好看又不贵，你就买吧。

_____

Dialog 4

A：比尔，小华有没有你的手机号码？

B：有。<u>她有我的手机号码，还有我姐姐的手机号码呢。</u>

Exercise 6 ✍

Translate the following sentences into English paying attention to the underlined parts.

1. 你喜欢哪一件衬衫，蓝色的还是黑色的？<u>其实</u>我两件衬衫都喜欢。

2. "我没有<u>听懂</u>他的话，你<u>听懂</u>了吗？""我只<u>听懂</u>了一半。"

3. <u>为了</u>明天的期中考试，我今天放学后在学校附近的咖啡馆学习了三个钟头。

4. 对于中国文化，他<u>什么</u>都想学，比如中国功夫、各种节日、风俗习惯什么的。

5. "小华，我还没有<u>做好</u>今天的作业，你<u>做好</u>了吗？""我早就<u>做好</u>了。"

6. "今天是星期六，你怎么七点钟<u>就</u>起床了？""<u>其实</u>我六点半<u>就</u>醒了。"

五、语言运用 Using the Language

Activity 1 🗩

Look at the following class schedule of Li Bing and talk about it. Ask each other at what time Li Bing attends a certain class.

New words: 历史 lìshǐ, history   文学 wénxué, literature

	星期一	星期二	星期三	星期四	星期五
8:00~8:50	听力	阅读	听力	阅读	听力
9:00~9:50	阅读	阅读	写作	阅读	写作

10:00~10:50	阅读	写作	阅读	写作	阅读
11:00~11:50	口语	听力	阅读	听力	阅读
2:00~2:50	文化	文化	口语	文化	口语
3:00~3:50	中国历史	中国文学	中国历史	中国文学	中国历史
4:00~4:50		中国功夫		中国功夫	

Activity 2 📖💬✳

Read the following photo descriptions and answer the questions orally in Chinese.

1

在中国，很多人喜欢书法。有人在公园的地上练习书法。

What is the man doing?

2

美国加州的一个小城市，每年都有一个文化活动。参加活动的美国女孩子都穿着中国的服装。

Who are they?

Why are they wearing Chinese dresses?

3

这是一所中学的中文教室。这个中学有各年级的中文课，也有大学中文先修课。

What Chinese courses does this school offer?

4

每年四月，加州中文教师协会 (association) 在旧金山举办一次中文比赛。这是参加比赛的学生们。

In what event are these students participating?

飞跃——汉语初级教程学生用书 下册

5	6
很多外国学生学了中国文化课以后，对中国画儿有了兴趣。他们到中国画店看中国画儿，学习怎么画画儿。 Where do international students go to learn about Chinese brush paintings?	李小龙是著名的功夫大师。他出演过很多部电影。 Who was this man? What was he famous for?

Activity 3 👂 🗨

Listen to the following conversation between a student and a teacher and answer the questions orally in Chinese.

1. Did David study Chinese before?

2. What Chinese cultural courses can he take?

3. What kind of course is Chinese 102?

4. How can he pass the final examination?

Activity 4 🗨

A. Students in a Chinese class should often practice writing Chinese characters. Look at the picture and tell your partner how many characters you can recognize. Note that some characters are simplified while others are traditional.

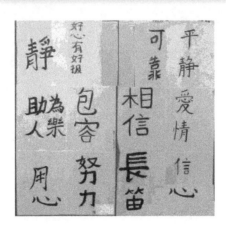

飞跃——汉语初级教程学生用书　下册

1

華語文教學中心
華語文博碩士學程

2

3

4

Activity 5 🗣

What do you say?

1. You want to state that you intend to take certain courses.
2. You wonder if a certain test is difficulty or not.
3. You want to list the contents of your Chinese program.
4. You want to say you can do something as well as someone else does it.

Activity 6 🗣

Role Play

You are a student on a study trip to China who will be taking language and cultural courses. Talk with a student who took those courses before to find out some information. Your partner will act as the student.

Sentences you may need to use:

请问你选过什么语言课和文化课?
一门课多少学分 (credit)?
……课一个星期有几节?
有晚上的课吗?
你觉得……课有意思吗?

Cultural Tip

In overseas Chinese communities, one can always find Chinese language schools aimed at helping the children of Chinese immigrants retain their parents' language. These schools are usually run by parents and former school teachers. They usually have class on weekends in addition to the children's regular schooling. Apart from Chinese language, the rudiments of calligraphy, art, kung fu, etc., may also be included in the curriculum.

第十二课　学中文

第十三课
Lesson Thirteen
中餐馆
Chinese Restaurant

一、导入 Lead-in

Exercise 1

Look at the pictures below and guess the meanings of the Chinese captions.

中国人喜欢在过中国新年（春节）的时候，全家人吃一顿团圆饭。

北方的饺子

甜酸肉

广东点心叉烧包

After learning this lesson, you will be able to:

1. Order drinks and foods in a Chinese restaurant, and pay the bill.

2. Talk about your experience of eating in a Chinese restaurant.

3. Recognize new characters in this lesson, and know the common radicals 氵, 冫, 饣, and 鸟.

4. Use 来, 着, 再, 又, reduplicated nouns, time expressions, and measure words correctly.

飞跃——汉语初级教程学生用书 下册

二、课文 Texts

课文（一）Text (1)

你们想喝什么?

簡体版

Li Wen and his classmates are eating in a Chinese restaurant on a Sunday morning.

李　文：你们想喝什么，红茶还是绿茶?

小　华：我喜欢绿茶。

Tips: a typical question asked in a restaurant

李　文：我也是。

汤　姆：我要一杯冰水。

马　克：我要一杯可乐。

李　文：服务员，请给我们来一壶绿茶，一杯冰水，一杯可乐。

服务员：好的。请稍等。

（一个服务员推着点心车过来）

汤　姆：这是什么?

Tips: a typical scene in a Cantonese restaurant

小　华：这是包子，这是饺子，那是春卷。怎么样? 每样要一碟吧。

马　克：好啊! 我还要一碗饭。

汤　姆：服务员，请给我们四双筷子。

服務員：好的。

（吃完以後）

李　文：你們收信用卡嗎？

服務員：收。

Tips: a common way to pay the bill in a restaurant

馬　克：我非常喜歡你們的點心。下次我還要再來，一邊吃點心，一邊練習說中文。

服務員：你的中文已經說得很不錯了。歡迎你們下次再來。

你們想喝什么？

Li Wen and his classmates are eating in a Chinese restaurant on a Sunday morning.

李　文：你們想喝什麼，紅茶還是綠茶？

小　華：我喜歡綠茶。

李　文：我也是。

湯　姆：我要一杯冰水。

馬　克：我要一杯可樂。

李　文：服務員，請給我們來一壺綠茶，一杯冰水，一杯可樂。

服務員：好的。請稍等。

（一個服務員推着點心車過來）

湯　姆：這是什麼？

小　華：這是包子，這是餃子，那是春卷。怎麼樣？每樣要一碟吧。

馬　克：好啊！我還要一碗飯。

湯　姆：服務員，請給我們四雙筷子。

服務員：好的。

（吃完以後）

李　文：你們收信用卡嗎？

服務員：收。

馬　克：我非常喜歡你們的點心。下次我還要再來，一
　　　　邊吃點心，一邊練習說中文。

服務員：你的中文已經說得很不錯了。歡迎你們下次再來。

Kèwén (yī) *Text (1)*

Nǐmen Xiǎng Hē Shénme?

　　　Li Wen and his classmates are eating in a Chinese restaurant on a Sunday morning.

Lǐ Wén: Nǐmen xiǎng hē shénme, hóngchá háishi lǜchá?

Xiǎohuá: Wǒ xǐhuan lǜchá.

Lǐ Wén: Wǒ yě shì.

Tāngmǔ: Wǒ yào yì bēi bīngshuǐ.

Mǎkè: Wǒ yào yì bēi kělè.

Lǐ Wén: Fúwùyuán, qǐng gěi wǒmen lái yì hú lǜchá, yì bēi bīngshuǐ, yì bēi kělè.

Fúwùyuán: Hǎo de. Qǐng shāo děng.

(Yí gè fúwùyuán tuīzhe diǎnxinchē guòlai)

Tāngmǔ: Zhè shì shénme?

Xiǎohuá: Zhè shì bāozi, zhè shì jiǎozi, nà shì chūnjuǎn. Zěnmeyàng?

Měi yàng yào yì dié ba.

Mǎkè: Hǎo ā! Wǒ hái yào yì wǎn fàn.

Tāngmǔ: Fúwùyuán, qǐng gěi wǒmen sì shuāng kuàizi.

Fúwùyuán: Hǎo de.

(Chīwán yǐhòu)

Lǐ Wén: Nǐmen shōu xìnyòngkǎ ma?

Fúwùyuán: Shōu.

Mǎkè: Wǒ fēicháng xǐhuan nǐmen de diǎnxin. Xià cì wǒ hái yào zài lái, yìbiān chī diǎnxin, yìbiān liànxí shuō Zhōngwén.

Fúwùyuán: Nǐ de Zhōngwén yǐjīng shuō de hěn búcuò le. Huānyíng nǐmen xià cì zài lái.

生词（一）New Words (1)

	简体（繁體）	拼音	词性	解释
1	茶	chá	n.	tea 红茶 / 绿茶 / 龙井茶 / 茶水 / 泡茶
2	红（紅）茶	hóngchá	n.	black tea 我喜欢喝红茶。
3	绿（綠）茶	lùchá	n.	green tea 你喜欢喝红茶还是绿茶？
4	冰	bīng	n.	ice 冰茶 / 冰水 / 冰山 / 冰河
5	水	shuǐ	n.	water 茶水 / 冰水 / 一杯水
6	服务员（務員）	fúwùyuán	n.	waiter, waitress 餐馆服务员 / 火车上的服务员
7	请（請）	qǐng	v.	please (do something) 请坐。/ 请给我们来一壶绿茶。
8	壶（壺）	hú	m./n.	pot 一壶茶 / 茶壶 / 壶嘴 / 壶把
9	稍	shāo	adv.	a little 请稍等 / 稍多给一点
10	推	tuī	v.	push 推车 / 把门推开 / 你推我干什么？
11	点（點）心	diǎnxin	n.	snack; dim sum 服务员推着点心车过来了。/ 唐人街有很多点心店。
12	过来（過來）	guòlai	v.	come over 他过来了。/ 你过来，我给你些点心吃。

简体（繁體）	拼音	词性	解释
13 包子	bāozi	n.	steamed bun with fillings 包包子 / 吃包子 / 肉包子 / 菜包子
14 饺（餃）子	jiǎozi	n.	dumpling 包饺子 / 吃饺子 / 饺子皮
15 春卷	chūnjuǎn	n.	spring roll 炸春卷 / 卷春卷
16 样（樣）	yàng	n.	kind, variety, type 这样的 / 那样的 / 什么样的？
17 碟	dié	n./m.	small plate 碟子 / 一碟凉菜
18 碗	wǎn	n./m.	bowl 一碗饭 / 一碗水
19 筷子	kuàizi	n.	chopsticks 一次性筷子 / 你会用筷子吗？
20 信用卡	xìnyòngkǎ	n.	credit card 信用卡很方便。
21 非常	fēicháng	adv.	unusually, very 非常好 / 非常美
22 下	xià	n.	next 下个月 / 下个星期 / 下一次
23 练习（練習）	liànxí	v.	practice 练习书法 / 练习画画儿
24 不错（錯）	búcuò	adj.	not bad; pretty good 你的作业写得不错。
专有名词 Proper Noun			
马（馬）克	Mǎkè	pn.	Mark

Exercise 1 🎧 🗣

Listen to Text (1) and answer the questions orally in Chinese.

1. What did Li Wen ask his friends?

2. What did they drink?

3. What did Tom ask the waiter to do?

4. How did they pay?

Exercise 2 📖 🗣

Read Text (1) and answer the following questions.

1. 他们几个人各要了什么喝的东西？

2. 服务员怎么送吃的？

3. 马克为什么还想去那家中餐馆？

4. 服务员说马克的中文怎么样？

Exercise 3 🎧

You will hear three statements followed by four responses. Choose the most logical response to the statement.

1. a. 有饺子吗？

b. 请给我们四双筷子。

c. 我要绿茶。小王你呢？

d. 服务员来了。

2. a. 好的，请稍等。

b. 筷子多少钱一双？

c. 饺子和包子一样一碟。

d. 你们收信用卡吗？

3. a. 我还要再练习。

b. 你们收不收信用卡？

c. 我非常喜欢你们的点心。

d. 我朋友说你们的春卷很好。

Exercise 4 ✍

Complete the following sentences using the measure words from the list below.

碟　　家　　次　　碗　　壶　　双

1. 为了练习中文，大卫周末常常去附近一 _____ 中国餐馆吃饭。

2. 他们要了两 _____ 饺子，一 _____ 饭，还有一 _____ 绿茶。

3. 服务员给他刀叉，可是他说："给我一 _____ 筷子吧。"

4. 欢迎你们下 _____ 再来我们餐馆。

课文（二）Text (2)

吃年夜饭

简体版

In her journal, Jiang Xiaohua talked about her experience of eating in a Chinese restaurant in Chinatown.

昨天是中国新年，我们全家到一家中餐馆吃年夜饭。那是中国城有名的餐馆，餐馆的里面和外面都有不少人在等。我们问餐馆的服务员要等多久，服务员说半个钟头左右吧。妈妈说不要等了，到别的餐馆去吧。爸爸说

飞跃——汉语初级教程学生用书　下册

今天到哪一家中餐馆都得等。
结果，我们在外面等了四十分
钟。

Tips: it's not unusual for a
good Chinese restaurant

爸爸点了三道菜：北京烤鸭、清蒸鱼、还有蒙古牛肉。
妈妈点了一盘饺子，她说，在她的老家北京，过年时家
家户户都吃饺子。爸爸让我和弟弟也点一个菜，我拿着
菜单看了半天，最后点了一个甜酸肉，弟弟点了一盘春
卷。我们点的菜味道都不错，不过结帐时才知道，四个
人一顿饭吃了一百二十多美元。

吃年夜飯

繁体版

In her journal, Jiang Xiaohua talks about her experience of
eating in a Chinese restaurant in Chinatown.

昨天是中國新年，我們全家到一家中餐館吃年夜飯。
那是中國城有名的餐館，餐館的裏面和外面都有不少人
在等。我們問餐館的服務員要等多久，服務員説半個鐘
頭左右吧。媽媽説不要等了，到別的餐館去吧。爸爸説
今天到哪一家中餐館都得等。結果，我們在外面等了
四十分鐘。

爸爸點了三道菜：北京烤鴨、清蒸魚、還有蒙古牛肉。
媽媽點了一盤餃子，她説，在她的老家北京，過年時家
家户户都吃餃子。爸爸讓我和弟弟也點一個菜，我拿着

菜單看了半天，最後點了一個甜酸肉，弟弟點了一盤春卷。我們點的菜味道都不錯，不過結帳時才知道，四個人一頓飯吃了一百二十多美元。

Kèwén (èr) *Text (2)*

Chī Niányèfàn

In her journal, Jiang Xiaohua talks about her experience of eating in a Chinese restaurant in Chinatown.

Zuótiān shì Zhōngguó xīnnián, wǒmen quánjiā dào yì jiā Zhōngcānguǎn chī niányèfàn. Nà shì Zhōngguóchéng yǒumíng de cānguǎn, cānguǎn de lǐmian hé wàimian dōu yǒu bù shǎo rén zài děng. Wǒmen wèn cānguǎn de fúwùyuán yào děng duō jiǔ, fúwùyuán shuō bàn gè zhōngtóu zuǒyòu ba. Māma shuō búyào děng le, dào bié de cānguǎn qù ba. Bàba shuō jīntiān dào nǎ yì jiā Zhōngcānguǎn dōu děi děng. Jiéguǒ, wǒmen zài wàimian děngle sìshí fēnzhōng.

Bàba diǎnle sān dào cài: Běijīng kǎoyā, qīngzhēng yú, hái yǒu Měnggǔ niúròu. Māma diǎnle yì pán jiǎozi, tā shuō, zài tā de lǎojiā Běijīng, guònián shí jiājiā-hùhù dōu chī jiǎozi. Bàba ràng wǒ hé dìdi yě diǎn yí gè cài, wǒ názhe càidān kànle bàntiān, zuìhòu diǎnle yí gè tián suānròu, dìdi diǎnle yì pán chūnjuǎn. Wǒmen diǎn de cài wèidao dōu búcuò, búguò jiézhàng shí cái zhīdào, sì gè rén yí dùn fàn chīle yìbǎi èrshí duō Měiyuán.

生词（二）New Words (2)

	简体（繁體）	拼音	词性	解释
1	昨天	zuótiān	*n.*	yesterday 昨天我跟朋友去饭馆吃饭了。
2	新年	xīnnián	*n.*	New Year 过新年 / 新年好！/ 新年快乐！
3	全	quán	*adj.*	all 全家 / 全班 / 全校学生 / 全家去吃年夜饭。
4	餐馆（餐館）	cānguǎn	*n.*	restaurant 中餐馆 / 西餐馆 / 餐馆老板
5	年夜饭（飯）	niányèfàn	*n.*	Chinese New Year's Eve dinner 年夜饭对中国人很重要。
6	有名	yǒumíng	*adj.*	famous, well-known 有名的学校 / 有名的书法家
7	外面	wàimian	*n.*	outside 学校外面有个公园。
8	久	jiǔ	*adj.*	long time 你在这儿住多久？/ 我学中文学了很久了。
9	钟头（鐘頭）	zhōngtóu	*n.*	hour 两个钟头
10	结（結）果	jiéguǒ	*conj.*	as a result 他没有好好学习，结果考试不及格。
11	分钟（鐘）	fēnzhōng	*n.*	minute 五分钟 / 一个小时有六十分钟。
12	点（點）	diǎn	*v.*	order 点菜 / 每次去饭馆他都点红烧肉。
13	道	dào	*m.*	(measure word for a dish) 点一道菜 / 这次宴会有十道菜。
14	菜	cài	*n.*	dish of non-grain food 我吃饭总是三菜一汤。/ 来来来，吃菜，别只吃米饭！
15	烤鸭（鴨）	kǎoyā	*n.*	roast duck 北京烤鸭 / 烤鸭很肥。
16	清蒸	qīngzhēng	*v.*	steam in broth 清蒸鱼 / 清蒸鸡
17	鱼（魚）	yú	*n.*	fish 鱼头 / 鱼汤 / 大鱼吃小鱼。
18	牛肉	niúròu	*n.*	beef 牛肉面 / 牛肉是红肉。
19	肉	ròu	*n.*	meat 肉菜 / 牛羊肉 / 肉包子
20	盘（盤）	pán	*n./m.*	plate 一盘菜 / 盘子 / 洗盘子
21	过（過）年	guònián	*v.*	celebrate the Chinese New Year 回家过年 / 过年很热闹。/ 过年要吃年夜饭。
22	时（時）	shí	*n.*	time; when 我去中国时看到了很多老朋友。

23	家家户户	jiājiā-hùhù		each and every family 家家户户都吃饺子。/ 这里的家家户户他都去过。
24	拿	ná	*v.*	hold in hand 拿起来 / 拿着 / 拿住
25	菜单（單）	càidān	*n.*	menu 有中文的菜单吗？/ 请拿菜单来我们看看。/ 让我们看看菜单。
26	甜	tián	*adj.*	sweet 又酸又甜 / 甜酸苦辣 / 甜菜
27	酸	suān	*adj.*	sour 酸菜鱼 / 酸辣汤 / 这种醋不太酸。
28	味道	wèidào	*n.*	flavor, taste 尝尝味道 / 味道好极了。
29	结帐（結帳）	jiézhàng	*v.*	pay a bill 用信用卡结帐 / 服务员，请结帐！
专有名词 Proper Noun				
	蒙古	Měnggǔ	*pn.*	Mongolia

Exercise 5 🎧

Listen to Text (2) and choose the correct answer for the following statements.

1. The restaurant they went to is

    a. a Sichuan restaurant.

    b. a famous restaurant.

    c. located in the suburbs.

2. The father insisted eating there because

    a. it is inexpensive.

    b. there was no restaurant which was not crowded.

    c. there were less people there.

3. At the restaurant

    a. only the father ordered food.

    b. the father and mother ordered food.

    c. everyone ordered food.

4. The writer thought that the food there were

    a. delicious and inexpensive.

    b. delicious but expensive.

    c. inexpensive but plain.

Exercise 6 📖 🗣

Read Text (2) and answer the questions orally in Chinese.

1. 江小华一家什么时候，在什么地方吃年夜饭？

2. 他们到那里的时候，那个地方怎么样？ 为什么？

3. 他们一家到别的餐馆去了吗？ 为什么？

4. 江小华的爸爸、妈妈、弟弟和她都点了什么？

5. 北京人过年的时候都喜欢吃什么？

Exercise 7

Fill in the blanks with the given words.

中餐馆　　新年　　结帐　　牛肉　　吃　　鱼

去年 ＿＿＿＿＿ 的时候，一个老朋友来看我。我请他到城里的一家 ＿＿＿＿＿ 吃饭。那家餐馆是新开的。他们的 ＿＿＿＿＿ 很好吃，我们点了清蒸鱼，还点了蒙古 ＿＿＿＿＿ 和甜酸肉。那家饭馆一点儿也不贵。两个人一共 ＿＿＿＿＿ 了一百块钱。因为是我请我的老朋友，所以我 ＿＿＿＿＿。

Exercise 8

Translate the following sentences into Chinese.

1. You could see many people were waiting for seats.

＿＿＿＿＿＿＿＿＿＿＿＿＿＿＿＿＿＿＿＿＿＿＿＿＿＿＿＿＿＿＿＿＿

2. We had to wait more than 20 minutes before we got into the restaurant.

＿＿＿＿＿＿＿＿＿＿＿＿＿＿＿＿＿＿＿＿＿＿＿＿＿＿＿＿＿＿＿＿＿

3. We ordered Beijing roast duck and a large plate of dumplings.

＿＿＿＿＿＿＿＿＿＿＿＿＿＿＿＿＿＿＿＿＿＿＿＿＿＿＿＿＿＿＿＿＿

4. Can you tell me where should I pay the bill?

＿＿＿＿＿＿＿＿＿＿＿＿＿＿＿＿＿＿＿＿＿＿＿＿＿＿＿＿＿＿＿＿＿

三、汉字 Chinese Characters

1. New characters in this lesson

序号	拼音	简 / 繁	部件	构词
1	bīng	冰	冫＋水	冰水 / 滑冰 / 结冰 / 冰雪
2	cài	菜	艹＋采（爫＋木）	三菜一汤 / 炒菜 / 点菜 / 大白菜
3	chá	茶	艹＋人＋木	早茶 / 红茶 / 龙井茶 / 茶水
4	cuò	错（錯）	钅＋昔（共＋日）	不错 / 错了

5	dié	碟	石＋枼（世＋木）	碟子／一碟凉菜
6	dùn	顿（頓）	屯＋页	一顿饭
7	fēi	非	非	非常好／非常美
8	gǔ	古	古	蒙古／古时候／古代／古书
9	hú	壶	士＋冖＋业	茶壶／一壶水
10	hù	户	户	家家户户／户口
11	jiǎo	饺（餃）	饣＋交	包饺子／饺子皮／虾饺
12	jié	结（結）	纟＋吉（士＋口）	结账／结果
13	jiǔ	久	久	多久／很久／长久
14	juǎn	卷	龹＋㔾	春卷／菜卷
15	kǎ	卡	上＋卜	信用卡／卡片
16	kǎo	烤	火＋考（耂＋丂）	烤鸭／烤鸡／烤肉
17	kuài	筷	𥫗＋快（忄＋夬）	筷子／木筷子／公筷
18	liàn	练（練）	纟＋东	练习／练武／晨练
19	lǜ	绿（綠）	纟＋录（彐＋氺）	绿茶／绿灯／绿色／绿草
20	mǎ	马（馬）	马	马克／牛馬／白馬
21	měng	蒙	艹＋冖＋一＋豕	蒙古
22	ná	拿	合＋手	拿好／拿着／拿住
23	pán	盘（盤）	舟＋皿	一盘菜／盘子／洗盘子
24	qīng	清	氵＋青（龶＋月）	清蒸鱼／清水／清茶
25	qǐng	请（請）	讠＋青（龶＋月）	请说／请坐／请教／请假
26	quán	全	人＋王	全家／全部／安全
27	ròu	肉	肉	烤肉／牛羊肉／肉包子
28	shāo	稍	禾＋肖（⺍＋月）	稍等
29	shuǐ	水	水	冰水／水果／喝水／自来水
30	suān	酸	酉＋夋	酸菜鱼／酸辣汤／酸醋
31	tián	甜	舌（千＋口）＋甘	甜酸苦辣／甜菜／甜点
32	tóu	头（頭）	头	半个钟头／头疼
33	tuī	推	扌＋隹	推车／推开／推倒

34	wǎn	碗	石+宛	一碗饭 / 一碗水
35	wèi	味	口+未	味道 / 色香味美 / 口味
36	wù	务（務）	夂+力	服务员 / 服务 / 务工
37	yā	鸭（鴨）	甲+鸟	烤鸭 / 鸭子 / 鸭毛
38	yú	鱼（魚）	鱼	清蒸鱼 / 鱼汤 / 三文鱼
39	zhàng	帐（帳）	巾+长	帐篷 / 蚊帐
40	zhēng	蒸	艹+丞+灬	清蒸鱼 / 蒸年糕 / 蒸饭 / 蒸包子
41	zuó	昨	日+乍	昨天 / 昨夜

Exercise 1

Copy the following single-component characters with correct stroke order in the spaces provided.

fēi	非	⺁ ⺁ ⺮ ⺡ ⺡ 非 非 非				
hù	户	丶 ⼀ 弖 户				
jiǔ	久	⼃ ⼅ 久				
kǎ	卡	丨 ⼂ 上 卡 卡				
mǎ	马	⼁ 马 马				
ròu	肉	丨 ⼏ 内 内 肉 肉				
shuǐ	水	⼃ ⺂ 水 水				
tóu	头	丶 ⼆ 三 头 头				
yú	鱼	⼃ ⺁ ⺈ 钅 ⾊ 鱼 鱼 鱼				

Exercise 2 📖 ✎

Read the following sentences and choose the correct characters to fill in the blanks.

1. 你们要不要喝点儿绿 _____（查　茶　茶）？

2. 我来一杯可乐，加 _____（冰　兵　并）。

3. 广东人喝茶喜欢用小 _____（壹　互　壶）。

4. 我们要了三碟 _____ 子，一盘春卷。（较　校　饺）

5. 我们点了很多菜，_____ 果还得打包带回家。（结　洁　拮）

6. 来来来，尝尝 (to taste) 这 _____ 清蒸肉。（盘　盆　盈）

7. 我在北京一家广东菜馆点甜 _____ 肉，他们说那叫"古老肉"。（酸　醋　醒）

8. 服务员，请给我来一杯冰 _____（水　氷　木）。

2. Common radicals (2)

(1) 氵（水）sāndiǎnshuǐ

The radical 氵 is derived from the pictographic character 🐟 (水 water), symbolizing a river. Thus, characters with this radical are related to water or liquid. The 氵 radical is usually put on the left side of a character, e.g. 洗 (xǐ, to wash); 澡 (zǎo, bath); 清 (qīng, clear); 没 (méi/mò, not have/to sink). When it is put on the bottom, it is written as 水, as in 泉 (quán, spring).

(2) 冫 liǎngdiǎnshuǐ

The radical 冫 is derived from a pictographic character symbolizing frozen water. Thus, characters with this radical are usually related to ice or coldness, e.g. 冰 (bīng, ice); 冷 (lěng, cold); 凉 (liáng, cool); 冬 (dōng, winter).

(3) 饣（食）shízìpáng

The radical 饣 is simplified from the pictographic character 🍱 (食 shí, food; to eat), thus characters with this radical are usually related to food, e.g. 饭 (fàn, cooked rice); 馆 (guǎn, place of accommodation); 饮 (yǐn, drink); 餐 (cān , meal).

(4) 鸟 niǎozìpáng

The radical 鸟 is derived from the pictographic character 🐦 (鸟 bird). Thus, characters with this radical originally related to a bird, e.g 鸡 (jī, chicken); 鸭 (yā, duck); 鹅 (é, goose); 鹏 (péng, roc).

Exercise 3 ✎

Fill in the chart below by writing down as many characters as you can.

Radical	Meaning of radical	Characters that you have learned containing this radical
氵		
冫		
饣		
鸟		

四、语言点 Language Points

1. The use of 来 (2)

In Lesson 5 we learned that 来 can indicate a motion towards the speaker and an intention to do something, like in "来来来，我来介绍一下吧。" In this lesson, we will learn another usage of the verb 来: to be used in place of a more specific verb, similar to the English verb "do". Here are some examples:

> (1) 服务员，请给我们来一壶绿茶，一杯冰水，一杯可乐！ (bring)
> Waiter, please bring us a pot of green tea, a glass of ice water, and a glass of coke!
>
> (2) 爸爸，我做的点心好吃吧？再来一个怎么样？ (eat)
> Dad, do you think the cookies I baked delicious? How about having another one?
>
> (3) 累了吧？要不要来一杯咖啡？ (drink)
> You are tired, aren't you? How about having a cup of coffee?
>
> (4) 您别动，我自己来。(do)
> Don't bother. I will do it myself.

2. The aspectual particle 着 (2)

In Lesson 11, we learned that the aspectual particle 着 can be attached to a verb to indicate a progressive action, like the verb suffix "–ing" in English. In this lesson we will learn that the aspectual particle 着 can be attached to the first verb to form an adverbial indicating the way the action of the second verb is done.

Subject + 1st Verb + 着 + (Object) + 2nd Verb + (Object)

(1) 一个服务员推着点心车过来。

A waiter came over pushing a cart loaded with dim sum.

(2) 我拿着菜单看了半天，最后点了一个甜酸肉。

Holding the menu, I examined it for a while and finally ordered sweet and sour pork.

(3) 他喜欢开着车打电话。他妈妈很不高兴。

He likes to make phone calls while driving. His mother is very unhappy about it.

3. A comparison of 再 and 又

Both 再 and 又 are adverbs meaning "again"; however their usages are different. 再 is used to indicate the future repetition of an action, like 再见 ("See you again"). While 又 is primarily used to indicate the repetition of an action that has already taken place or will certainly take place in the near future. See the following two sentences in this lesson:

(1) 下次我还要再来。

I will come again next time.

(2) 我很高兴，我又可以在周末中文学校和我的同学们在一起了。

I am very happy because I can hang out with my classmates again at the weekend Chinese school.

(3) "你怎么又迟到了？""对不起，以后我不再迟到了！"

"Why were you late again?" "Sorry, I won't be late again!"

(4) 万圣节又到了。今年的万圣节，我不再出去要糖了。

Halloween is coming again. I will not trick-or-treat this Halloween (as I did before).

4. The time and duration expression

There are two kinds of time expression in Chinese: time expression and duration expression. The time expression indicates the time when an action takes place while the duration expression shows the duration of an action or event. In Lesson 5 and other previous lessons, we have learned time expressions such as 早上, 晚上 and 五点三刻. They are always put before the main verb to serve as an adverbial. In this lesson, we will learn the duration expression which is always put after the main verb. For example:

(1) 结果，我们在外面等了<u>四十分钟</u>。

As a result, we waited outside for 40 minutes.

(2) 她在周末中文学校学习了<u>两年</u>中文。

She studied Chinese at the weekend Chinese school for two years.

The following chart shows more examples of time and duration expressions:

	Time Expressions	Duration Expressions
Year	2012 年，2020 年	两年，二十年
Month	一月，二月，十一月	一个月，两个月，十一个月
Date	一号（一日），二号（二日）	一天，两天
Day	星期一，星期二	一个星期，两个星期
Clock Hour	五点（钟），两点十五分	五个钟头，两个钟头十五分钟

5. The reduplicated nouns

In Chinese, some nouns can be reduplicated to convey the meaning "each and every".

在北京过年，家家户户都吃饺子。

In Beijing, every family eats dumplings on Chinese New Year's Eve.

Note that the reduplication pattern for one syllable nouns is A → AA, and for the disyllable nouns is AB → AABB. Here are more examples:

天→天天：他天天都很早起床。He gets up very early every day.

人→人人：人人都认识张老师。Everyone knows Mr. Zhang.

里外→里里外外：餐馆的里里外外都有不少人在等座位。
Many people were waiting for seats both inside and outside the restaurant.

前后→前前后后：屋子的前前后后都找不到她。
No one could find her either in front of or behind the house.

6. A review of measure words in Chinese

There are two kinds of measure words in Chinese: measure words for nouns and measure words for verbs. Here is a list of measure words we have learned so far.

Measure Words for Nouns	
杯：一杯咖啡 a cup of coffee	节：两节课 two periods of class
本：两本书 two books	块：一块面包 a piece of bread
道：三道菜 three dishes	口：五口人 five family members
碟：一碟蛋卷 a small plate of egg rolls	盘：一盘饺子 a plate of dumplings
顿：一顿饭 a meal	双：一双筷子 a pair of chopsticks
个：一个学生 a student	条：两条领带 / 短裤 two ties/shorts
家：一家饭馆 a restaurant	碗：一碗饭 a bowl of cooked rice
件：三件衬衫 three shirts	位：一位老师 a teacher

Note that a noun may have different measure words carrying different meanings:
一碗饭 a bowl of cooked rice; 一碟饭 a small plate of cooked rice; 一顿饭 a meal.

Measure Words for Verbs	
次：打了三次电话 made three phone calls	下：看一下 take a look

Exercise 1 👂 ✍

Listen to three short dialogs and answer the questions in Chinese characters. Pay attention to the time and duration expressions.

Dialog 1 Question: 小明什么时候回中国看父母？他要在中国住多久？	Answer:
Dialog 2 Question: "我"什么时候去看电影的？电影有多长？	Answer:
Dialog 3 Question: 小华上周末中文学校多长时间了？"我"什么时候也要去上中文学校？	Answer:

Exercise 2 ✍

Translate the following sentences into English paying attention to the use of the particle 着.

1. 约翰喜欢开着车打电话，他的女朋友很不高兴。

2. 林红笑着打开了男朋友寄来的圣诞礼物。

_____

3. 妈妈不喜欢她儿子看着手机跟她说话。

_____

4. 李文的小弟弟不认识汉字，他拿着中文菜单看了半天也不知道点什么菜。

_____

Exercise 3 📖 ✍

Read the following sentences and fill in the blanks with 再 or 又.

1. 老师，我没听懂这个问题，您能给我 _____ 讲一遍吗？

2. 小王昨天没来上课，今天怎么 _____ 没来？

3. 这是你三天的药，你吃完了药 _____ 来看一次。

4. 你怎么 _____ 来了？我不是告诉过你不用来吗？

5. 上个月我帮你找了一个辅导学中文，现在你怎么 _____ 要找一个辅导？

6. 爸爸妈妈，我在这儿一切都好。明年我会 _____ 回家看你们的。

7. 大卫，这个星期你已经迟到两次了，可别 _____ 迟到了。

8. 我以前去过北京，今年秋天我 _____ 去了一次，明年我还想 _____ 去。

Exercise 4 ✍

Follow the example and rewrite the following sentences using the reduplicated nouns.

Example:

他每天都要喝两杯咖啡。→　他天天都要喝两杯咖啡。

1. 在他的家，每个人都喜欢露营。

_____ 。

2. 过圣诞节的时候，每家都会买一棵圣诞树。

_____ 。

3. 我每年都回老家看我的爸爸、妈妈和弟弟。

_____ 。

4. 中国北方过年的时候，每一家每一户都会吃饺子。

_____ 。

5. 我和爸爸每天都练习打太极拳。

_____ 。

Exercise 5 ✍

Translate the following dialogs into English and pay attention to the different meanings of the verb 来.

Dialog 1

A：请问，你们三位想喝点什么？

B：请给我们<u>来两杯绿茶，一杯咖啡</u>。

_____

_____

Dialog 2

A：小华，你们家的饺子真好吃啊！

B：你喜欢吃就<u>再来一碗</u>吧。

_____

_____

Dialog 3

A：约翰，把那个大南瓜给我，我想做一个南瓜灯。

B：你忙，<u>还是我来吧</u>。

_____

_____

Dialog 4：

A：请问，<u>两位要来点什么</u>？

B：<u>来一个甜酸肉</u>，两碗米饭，<u>再来一盘春卷</u>。

A：要不要汤？

B：那就<u>再来一碗汤</u>吧。

_____

_____

_____

_____

Exercise 6

Fill in each blank with the measure words listed below. Some measure words may be used more than once.

双 家 碗 条 个 节 杯 次 块 位 盘 口 件 本

1. 你到家以后给我发 ＿＿＿＿ 短信吧。

2. 请问，哪 ＿＿＿＿ 老师教你们中文？

3. 我家有四 ＿＿＿＿ 人，爸爸、妈妈、弟弟和我。你家呢？

4. 每天我的早餐是一 ＿＿＿＿ 牛奶和一 ＿＿＿＿ 鸡蛋。

5. 我们每天上午八点到十一点上三 ＿＿＿＿ 课。

6. 小陈和小王去逛书店，他俩一共买了六 ＿＿＿＿ 书。

7. 你每个星期去几 ＿＿＿＿ 图书馆？

8. 你能帮我在小吃店买两 ＿＿＿＿ 面包和一 ＿＿＿＿ 咖啡吗？

9. 服务员，请给我们三 ＿＿＿＿ 筷子，三 ＿＿＿＿ 米饭，和一 ＿＿＿＿ 饺子。

10. 今天上午九点到十点，我给你打了三 ＿＿＿＿ 电话你都不在家。

11. 汤姆和我在中国城的一 ＿＿＿＿ 上海饭馆吃了晚饭。

12. 小明买了两 ＿＿＿＿ 领带，小文买了一 ＿＿＿＿ 西装上衣。

五、语言运用 Using the Language

Activity 1

Manli, Dawei and Xiaomei are having breakfast at a dim sum restaurant in Chinatown. Listen to their conversation and answer the questions orally in Chinese.

First, look at the following pictures of Chinese food and learn their names.

肠粉 chángfěn
rice flour roll

小笼蒸包 xiǎolóng zhēngbāo
steamed bun with fillings

烧卖 shāomài
steamed dumpling with the dough wrapping gathered at the top

Questions：

1. What are the prices for the small, medium and large dishes?

2. What does David say about dim sum in Beijing?

3. What are their favorite dim sum dishes, respectively?

Activity 2 📖 🗨

Read the following blog by a student who is learning Chinese in California and answer the questions below. Then number the photos in the proper order according to the text.

今天我和我的同学去了一趟旧金山的中国城。我们早上 7：45 从学校出发，10 点

多钟到了旧金山。我们先去了中文书店。我在那里买了一本写汉字的书，也买了一本画中国画儿的书，因为我女朋友想学学怎么画中国画儿。从书店出来后已经 11 点多了。我们找到一家饭馆吃广东点心。在饭馆里，服务员推着小车送来各种各样的点心。客人想吃什么就拿什么，吃完以后才付钱。我还买了几个包子带回来给我女朋友吃。我女朋友要上课，所以没跟我们去中国城。

Questions:
1. 今天他去哪儿了？
2. 他为什么买画中国画儿的书？
3. 饭馆里怎么样卖点心？
4. 他给女朋友买了什么？
5. 他女朋友为什么没和他一起去中国城？

Activity 3

You are Meihua. Your friend Hu Hong called you and left a message on the phone. Listen to the phone message, and then write an email to her. You want to ask her about the location of the place and make an appointment with her.

Activity 4

What do you say?

1. You want the waiter/waitress to bring you the things you want.
2. You want to tell the waiter you are not good at using something to eat with.
3. You are ready to pay after eating at the restaurant.
4. You are satisfied with the restaurant and want to come again.

Activity 5

Role Play

You and your three friends are in a Chinese restaurant. You want to order dim sum, as well as beer and coke. After eating, you want to pay with a credit card. Act it out in Chinese with your partner who will play the role of the waiter/waitress.

Sentences you may need to use:

服务员，给我们来……
你们有筷子吗？
你们收信用卡吗？

China is a vast country and there are many varieties of food. There is a common saying that food in the south is sweet, in the north, salty, in the east, spicy, and in the west, sour. However, a more accurate classification of Chinese cuisine is the so-called "Eight Styles of Chinese Cooking": Guangdong, Anhui, Fujian, Hunan, Jiangsu, Shandong, Sichuan and Zhejiang.

第十四课　情人节
Lesson Fourteen

情人节
Valentine's Day

一、导入 Lead-in

Exercise 1 📖 🗣️

Look at the pictures below and describe them in Chinese.

情人节送情人节卡片和鲜花。

巧克力也是情人节常见的礼物。

After learning this lesson, you will be able to:

1. Talk about customs and activities on Valentine's Day and Mother's Day.
2. Mail parcels in a post office or with a delivery service.
3. Recognize new characters in this lesson, and know the common radicals 礻, 衤, 忄 and 贝.
4. Use the descriptive complements, and expressions of 有一点儿 and 一下子 properly.

二、课文 Texts

课文（一）Text (1)

寄包裹

Xiaohua and her classmate Li Wen are on the phone.

小华：李文，不多说了。我现在得去一趟邮局。

李文：去邮局寄信吗？

小华：不是寄信，我是去寄包裹。下周是情人节，我要给我男朋友寄一张情人节卡片，还有一盒巧克力。

Tips: Valentine's Day related activities

李文：邮局寄包裹太慢了，为什么不用快递呢？

小华：快递邮费很贵吧？

李文：是有点儿贵，可是特别快。

小华：要不要买保险？

李文：不需要另外买保险，保险费已经包括在邮费里了。

小华：那还不错。

李文：你也可以试试网上的礼品公司。上次母亲节我给我妈妈送鲜花，早上订购，下午就送到了。他们还放了一张祝母亲节快乐的贺卡，贺卡上写着我的名字。

小华：那不行，我的情人节卡片必须有我的签名，别人不能替我写。

李文：那当然。你的情人节卡片上有那么多悄悄话，别人怎么能替你写呢！

飞跃——汉语初级教程学生用书 下册

简体版

寄包裹

繁体版

Xiaohua and her classmate Li Wen are on the phone.

小華：李文，不多説了。我現在得去一趟郵局。

李文：去郵局寄信嗎？

小華：不是寄信，我是去寄包裹。下周是情人節，我要
　　　給我男朋友寄一張情人節卡片，還有一盒巧克力。

李文：郵局寄包裹太慢了，爲什麼不用快遞呢？

小華：快遞郵費很貴吧？

李文：是有點兒貴，可是特別快。

小華：要不要買保險？

李文：不需要另外買保險，保險費已經包括在郵費裏了。

小華：那還不錯。

李文：你也可以試試網上的禮品公司。上次母親節我給
　　　我媽媽送鮮花，早上訂購，下午就送到了。他們
　　　還放了一張祝母親節快樂的賀卡，賀卡上寫着我
　　　的名字。

小華：那不行，我的情人節卡片必須有我的簽名，別人
　　　不能替我寫。

李文：那當然。你的情人節卡片上有那麼多悄悄話，別
　　　人怎麼能替你寫呢！

Kèwén (yī) *Text (1)*

Jì Bāoguǒ

拼音版

Xiaohua and her classmate Li Wen are on the phone.

Xiǎohuá: Lǐ Wén, bù duō shuō le. Wǒ xiànzài děi qù yí tàng yóujú.

Lǐ Wén: Qù yóujú jì xìn ma?

Xiǎohuá: Bú shì jì xìn, wǒ shì qù jì bāoguǒ. Xià zhōu shì Qíngrénjié, wǒ yào gěi wǒ nánpéngyou jì yì zhāng Qíngrénjié kǎpiàn, háiyǒu yì hé qiǎokèlì.

Lǐ Wén: Yóujú jì bāoguǒ tài màn le, wèi shénme búyòng kuàidì ne?

Xiǎohuá: Kuàidì yóufèi hěn guì ba?

Lǐ Wén: Shì yǒudiǎnr guì, kěshì tèbié kuài.

Xiǎohuá: Yào bu yào mǎi bǎoxiǎn?

Lǐ Wén: Bù xūyào lìngwài mǎi bǎoxiǎn, bǎoxiǎnfèi yǐjīng bāokuò zài yóufèi lǐ le.

Xiǎohuá: Nà hái búcuò.

Lǐ Wén: Nǐ yě kěyǐ shìshi wǎngshàng de lǐpǐn gōngsī. Shàng cì Mǔqīnjié wǒ gěi wǒ māma sòng xiānhuā, zǎoshang dìnggòu, xiàwǔ jiù sòngdào le. Tāmen hái fàngle yì zhāng zhù Mǔqīnjié kuàilè de hèkǎ, hèkǎ shang xiězhe wǒ de míngzì.

Xiǎohuá: Nà bù xíng, wǒ de Qíngrénjié kǎpiàn bìxū yǒu wǒ de qiānmíng, biéren bù néng tì wǒ xiě.

Lǐ Wén: Nà dāngrán. Nǐ de kǎpiàn shang yǒu nàme duō qiāoqiāo-huà, biéren zěnme néng tì nǐ xiě ne!

生词（一）New Words (1)

	简体（繁體）	拼音	词性	解释
1	趟（趟）	tàng	*m.*	(measure word for a trip) 去了一趟商店 / 你替我走一趟吧。
2	邮（郵）局	yóujú	*n.*	post office 到邮局寄信 / 邮局几点开门？
3	寄	jì	*v.*	mail, send 寄信 / 寄钱 / 寄包裹 / 给朋友寄信
4	信	xìn	*n.*	letter 信纸 / 信封 / 平信 / 挂号信 / 送信
5	包裹	bāoguǒ	*n.*	package 寄包裹 / 包裹单 / 挂号包裹
6	张（張）	zhāng	*m.*	(measure word for certain objects) 一张纸 / 一张床 / 一张桌子

简体（繁體）	拼音	词性	解释
7 卡	kǎ	*n.*	card 信用卡 / 公交卡 / 新年卡片
8 盒	hé	*m.*	box 一盒糖 / 一盒巧克力
9 巧克力	qiǎokèlì	*n.*	chocolate 巧克力糖 / 情人节送巧克力。
10 慢	màn	*adj.*	slow 他走路走得很慢。/ 你的车太慢了。
11 快递（遞）	kuàidì	*n.*	express delivery 请用快递寄给我。
12 邮费（郵費）	yóufèi	*n.*	postage 这个包裹邮费不贵。
13 保险（險）	bǎoxiǎn	*n.*	insurance 保险公司 / 房屋保险 / 汽车保险
14 需要	xūyào	*v.*	need 家里不需要的东西可以卖给别人。
15 另外	lìngwài	*conj.*	besides, moreover 我不喜欢中餐，另外我也不会用筷子。
17 包括	bāokuò	*v.*	include 房钱包括水电费。/ 所有的作业，包括写字练习，都得在星期一交上来。
18 礼（禮）品	lǐpǐn	*n.*	gift 礼品商店 / 送一个礼品
19 公司	gōngsī	*n.*	company 开公司 / 公司老板
20 母亲（親）	mǔqīn	*n.*	mother 我的母亲是老师。/ 黄河是中国人的母亲河。
21 鲜（鮮）花	xiānhuā	*n.*	fresh flowers 一把鲜花 / 院子里种着鲜花。
22 订购（訂購）	dìnggòu	*v.*	order 订购家具 / 订购礼物 / 上网订购商品
23 祝	zhù	*v.*	wish 祝你健康！/ 祝你新年快乐。
24 贺（賀）卡	hèkǎ	*n.*	greeting card 寄贺卡 / 新年贺卡
25 写（寫）	xiě	*v.*	write 写作业 / 写信 / 写书
26 必须（須）	bìxū	*a.v.*	must 我必须到你家去一下。/ 学生必须好好学习。
27 签（簽）名	qiānmíng	*n.*	signature 贺卡上有我的签名。/ 这本书上有作者的签名。
28 别人	biéren	*pron.*	other people 自己的事情自己做，不能让别人做。
29 替	tì	*prep.*	for; in someone's place 王老师病了，张老师替他上课。
30 悄悄话	qiāoqiāohuà	*n.*	whisper 说悄悄话

专有名词 Proper Noun			
情人节（節）	Qíngrénjié	*pn.*	Valentine's Day

Exercise 1 🎧 🗣

Listen to Text (1) and answer the questions orally in Chinese.

1. Why did Xiaohua go to the post office?

2. According to Li Wen, how should she mail it?

3. Why did Li Wen say online gift companies were good?

4. Why didn't Xiaohua shop online?

Exercise 2 📖 🗣

Read Text (1) and summarize the two ways of gifting for Valentine's Day orally in Chinese with details.

Exercise 3 📖 ✍

Read the following sentences and fill in the blanks with the words from the list below.

订购　　邮局　　方便　　保险　　礼品　　替

1. 昨天我去 ＿＿＿＿＿＿ 给我男朋友寄了一个情人节的包裹 。

2. 因为我的礼品不贵，所以我没有给包裹买 ＿＿＿＿＿＿ 。

3. 我还要给上海的一个朋友买 ＿＿＿＿＿＿ 。

4. 这个礼品我是在网上 ＿＿＿＿＿＿ 的。

5. 我上午付了钱以后，网上的公司下午就 ＿＿＿＿＿＿ 我把礼物送到我的朋友家，又快又 ＿＿＿＿＿＿ 。

Exercise 4

Match the following sentences in Column I with the appropriate responses in Column II.

Column I	Column II
（　）1. 我要去邮局。	a. 你可以用快递。
（　）2. 明天是我朋友的生日，我没时间给他寄礼物了。	b. 对不起，别人不能替你签名。
（　）3. 快递邮费还包括什么？	c. 去寄信吗？
（　）4. 这张卡我不签名行吗？	d. 什么都包了，还包括保险。

情人节快乐

简体版

John's email to his girlfriend Mary before Valentine's Day.

玛丽：

　　时间过得真快！你去中国学习已经一个多月了。你最近学习忙吗？身体怎么样？我很想念你。我从网上知道北京昨天下了一场大雪，气温一下子降到摄氏零下十度。你要多注意身体，不要着凉。

　　情人节就要到了。周末我和几个朋友逛商店，看到了你喜欢吃的那种巧克力糖，我就买了一盒给你寄去。我想你在北京不一定能买到这种巧克力。另外，我还给你寄了一张音乐光盘和情人卡。我没有去邮局，我用的是快递服务。我问工作人员包裹什么时候能到，她说用快递邮寄，三四天就能到北京。我想，在情人节前一天，你就可以收到我的包裹了。

　　祝
　　情人节快乐！

你的约翰

情人節快樂

繁体版

John's email to his girlfriend Mary before Valentine's Day.

瑪麗：

時間過得真快！你去中國學習已經一個多月了。你最近學習忙嗎？身體怎麼樣？我很想念你。我從網上知道北京昨天下了一場大雪，氣溫一下子降到攝氏零下十度。你要多注意身體，不要着涼。

情人節就要到了。周末我和幾個朋友逛商店，看到了你喜歡吃的那種巧克力糖，我就買了一盒給你寄去。我想你在北京不一定能買到這種巧克力。另外，我還給你寄了一張音樂光盤和情人卡。我沒有去郵局，我用的是快遞服務。我問工作人員包裹什麼時候能到，她說用快遞郵寄，三四天就能到北京。我想，在情人節前一天，你就可以收到我的包裹了。

祝

情人節快樂！

你的約翰

Kèwén (èr) *Text (2)*

Qíngrénjié Kuàilè

拼音版

John's email to his girlfriend Mary before Valentine's Day.

Mǎlì:

Shíjiān guò de zhēn kuài! Nǐ qù Zhōngguó xuéxí yǐjīng yí gè duō yuè le. Nǐ zuìjìn xuéxí máng ma? Shēntǐ zěnmeyàng? Wǒ hěn xiǎngniàn nǐ. Wǒ cóng wǎngshang zhīdào Běijīng zuótiān xiàle yì cháng dàxuě, qìwēn yíxiàzi jiàngdào shèshì líng xià shí dù. Nǐ yào duō zhùyì shēntǐ, búyào zháoliáng.

Qíngrénjié jiù yào dào le. Zhōumò wǒ hé jǐ gè péngyou guàng shāngdiàn, kàndàole nǐ xǐhuan chī de nà zhǒng qiǎokèlìtáng, wǒ jiù mǎile yì hé gěi nǐ jìqù. Wǒ xiǎng nǐ zài Běijīng bù yídìng néng mǎidào zhè zhǒng qiǎokèlì. Lìngwài, wǒ hái gěi nǐ jìle yì zhāng yīnyuè guāngpán hé qíngrénkǎ. Wǒ méiyǒu qù yóujú, wǒ yòng de shì kuàidì fúwù. Wǒ wèn gōngzuò rényuán bāoguǒ shénme shíhou néng dào, tā shuō yòng kuàidì yóujì, sān-sìtiān jiù néng dào Běijīng. Wǒ xiǎng, zài Qíngrénjié qián yì tiān, nǐ jiù kěyǐ shōudào wǒ de bāoguǒ le.

Zhù

Qíngrénjié kuàilè!

Nǐ de Yuēhàn

生词（二）New Words (2)

	简体（繁體）	拼音	词性	解释
1	过（過）	guò	v.	pass 时间过得真快！/ 日子过得很好。
2	身体（體）	shēntǐ	n.	body, health 身体好 / 检查身体
3	想念	xiǎngniàn	v.	miss 我很想念老朋友。/ 刚到美国的时候，我很想念中国的家人。
4	场（場）	cháng	m.	measure word for rain, snow, etc. 一场大雨 / 一场大雪
5	一下子	yíxiàzi	adv.	all of a sudden 这种礼物一下子就卖完了。/ 气温一下子降了下来。
6	降	jiàng	v.	fall, decline, land 气温降下来了。/ 飞机降到了地面。
7	注意	zhùyì	v.	pay attention to 出门时注意多穿衣服。/ 开车注意安全。
8	着凉（著涼）	zháoliáng	v.	catch a cold 我晚上睡觉时着凉了。
9	就要	jiù yào		be going to 我就要上学了。/ 万圣节就要到了。
10	种（種）	zhǒng	m.	kind, type 这种 / 那种 / 各种

	简体（繁體）	拼音	词性	解释
11	一定	yídìng	adv.	necessarily, surely 他一定很喜欢你。/ 他今天不一定会来。
12	音乐（樂）	yīnyuè	n.	music 听音乐 / 中国音乐 / 音乐学院
13	光盘（盤）	guāngpán	n.	compact disc 音乐光盘 / 电影光盘
14	服务（務）	fúwù	n.	service 服务员 / 服务生 / 这个旅馆的服务非常好。
15	人员（員）	rényuán	n.	personnel 工作人员 / 服务人员
16	邮（郵）寄	yóujì	v.	mail 邮寄平信是不是比挂号信便宜点儿？

Exercise 5 🎧 🗣✳

Listen to Text (2) and answer the questions orally in Chinese.

1. What is the weather like where Mary is now?

2. Why is John mailing chocolate to Mary?

3. How is he mailing the package?

4. When will Mary receive the package?

Exercise 6 📖

Read Text (2) and rearrange the following sentences according to the contents of the text.

1. 约翰用快递服务寄了包裹。

2. 逛街的时候，约翰看到一种新的巧克力。

3. 约翰买了巧克力放在包裹里。

4. 下个星期就是情人节了。

5. 他想玛丽买不到这种巧克力。

6. 约翰想给玛丽寄情人节礼物。

Exercise 7 📖 ✎

Read the following sentences and fill in the blanks with a word from Text (2).

1. 我们的学习很忙。一个星期很快就 _____ 去了。

2. 去了美国以后，他很 _____ 在国内的太太和孩子。

3. 这个城市气温变化很大。白天 60 多度，下午五六点就 _____ 到 50 度以下。

4. 虽然工作很忙，但是你也要 _____ 身体，别太累了。

5. 昨天晚上气温降了很多，不少人 _____ 了。

6. _____ 虽然贵一些，但是比普通邮寄快多了。

Exercise 8

Translate the following sentences orally into Chinese.

1. It has been three months since my girlfriend went to China.

2. It snowed last night and the temperature dropped below zero.

3. When I went window shopping with friends, I bought some chocolate.

4. I want to mail this package by express service.

三、汉字 Chinese Characters

1. New characters in this lesson

序号	拼音	简 / 繁	部件	构词
1	bǎo	保	亻 + 呆（口 + 木）	保险 / 保安 / 保证 / 保护
2	bì	必	必	必须 / 必要 / 必备
3	dì	递（遞）	弟（丷 + 弔）+ 辶	快递 / 邮递 / 邮递员
4	dìng	定	宀 + 疋	一定 / 决定 / 立定
5	dìng	订（訂）	讠 + 丁	订旅馆 / 订票 / 订餐
6	fèi	费（費）	弗 + 贝	邮费 / 花费 / 费用 / 浪费
7	gòu	购（購）	贝 + 勾（勹 + 厶）	订购 / 购物
8	guāng	光	⺌ + 兀	光盘 / 光线 / 光亮 / 灯光 / 月光
9	guǒ	裹	亠 + 果 + 衣	包裹
10	hé	盒	合 + 皿	一盒 / 盒子
11	hè	贺（賀）	加（力 + 口）+ 贝	贺卡 / 贺信 / 祝贺
12	jì	寄	宀 + 奇（大 + 可）	寄信 / 寄包裹 / 寄贺卡 / 邮寄
13	jú	局	尸 + 丁 + 口	邮局 / 公安局
14	kuò	括	扌 + 舌（千 + 口）	包括 / 括号
15	lìng	另	口 + 力	另外 / 另一半
16	màn	慢	忄 + 曼（曰 + 罒 + 又）	太慢了 / 慢走 / 慢慢讲
17	niàn	念	今 + 心	想念 / 纪念 / 念书
18	qiān	签（簽）	竹 + 金	签名 / 签字 / 签单

19	qiǎo	巧	工 + 丂	巧克力 / 巧手 / 灵巧
20	qīn	亲 (親)	亲	探亲 / 亲爱的 / 母亲 / 父亲
21	qíng	情	忄 + 青 (圭 + 月)	爱情 / 感情 / 情人 / 情人节
22	shēn	身	身	身体 / 身上 / 身外
23	sī	司	刁 + 一 + 口	公司 / 司法
24	tàng	趟 (趟)	走 + 尚	去一趟 / 走一趟
25	tǐ	体 (體)	亻 + 本	身体 / 体力 / 体会
26	tì	替	夫 + 夫 + 日	代替 / 替换
27	xiān	鲜 (鮮)	鱼 + 羊	鲜花 / 鲜鱼 / 鲜美 / 新鲜
28	xiǎn	险 (險)	阝 + 佥	保险 / 危险 / 险情
29	xiě	写 (寫)	冖 + 与	写作业 / 写字
30	xū	须 (須)	彡 + 页	必须 / 须知
31	yì	意	音 (立 + 日) + 心	注意 / 意见 / 主意 / 意外
32	yīn	音	立 + 日	音乐 / 音响 / 音调 / 高音 / 知音
33	yóu	邮 (郵)	由 + 阝	邮局 / 邮寄 / 邮包裹 / 电邮
34	yuè	乐 / 樂	乐	音乐 / 听音乐 / 音乐光盘
35	zháo	着 / 著	羊 + 目	着凉 / 点着 / 着火
36	zhǒng	种 (種)	禾 + 中	这种 / 那种 / 各种
37	zhù	注	氵 + 主	注意 / 注音 / 注定
38	zhù	祝	礻 + 兄	祝你健康 / 祝贺 / 祝好

Exercise 1 ✍

Copy the following single-component characters with correct stroke order in the spaces provided.

bì	必	丶 心 心 必 必		
shēn	身	丿 亻 鬥 自 自 身 身		
sī	司	𠃌 刁 刁 司 司		

Exercise 2

Read the following sentences and choose the correct characters to fill in the blanks.

1. 我要去邮局寄情人节卡片和包 _____。（裹　菓　果）

2. 情人节你给女朋友买 _____ 克力了吗？（巧　侨　窍）

3. 快递包裹不需要另外买保 _____。（险　检　先）

4. 我要给我的朋友寄一张 _____ 卡。（货　贺　喝）

5. 我给你买了一 _____ 广东点心。（盖　盒　盉）

6. 这个周末我们去听音 _____ 会，好吗？（乐　牙　月）

7. 快 _____ 公司的服务很好，可以上门来拿邮件。（递　第　弟）

8. 我想去 _____ 物中心买礼物。（构　购　拘）

2. Common radicals (3)

(1) 衤（衣）yībǔpáng

The radical 衤 is derived from the pictographic character 仌（衣 yī, clothes), symbolizing a piece of clothing. Thus, characters with this radical are usually related to clothes, e.g. 衫 (shān, upper garment); 裤 (kù, pants); 补 (bǔ, to mend, to repair). When it is put on the bottom of a character, it is written as 衣, e.g. 袋 (dài, pocket); 装 (zhuāng, dress up; to pack).

(2) 礻 shìbǔpáng

The radical 礻 is derived from the pictographic character 示 (示 shì, to indicate) denoting the gods giving indication from the sky. Thus, characters with this radical are related to spirit, god. This radical is written as 礻 when it is on the left side of a character and 示 at the bottom, e.g. 祝 (zù, to wish); 礼 (lǐ, ceremony); 神 (shén, god, spirit); 禁 (jìn, to prohibit).

(3) 贝 bèizìpáng

The radical 贝 is derived from the pictographic character 𧵫 (贝 bèi, shell), symbolizing a shell. Because shells were used as money in ancient time, characters with this radical are originally related to money, e.g. 贵 (guì, expensive); 货 (huò, goods); 费 (fèi, fee); 购 (gòu, to buy); 赢 (yíng, to win).

(4) 忄（心）xīn

The radical 忄 is derived from the pictographic character ♡（心 heart). The radical 忄 is usually placed on the left side of a character. When it is placed at the bottom, it is written as 心. Because the ancient people believed that the heart controls one's thinking, characters with this radical are usually related to thinking, feeling, and temperament, like 快 (kuài, happy); 想 (xiǎng, to think); 情 (qíng, feeling); 忙 (máng, busy); 懂 (dǒng, to understand); etc.

Exercise 3 ✎

Add components to the following components to form different characters.

1. 又 ___ ___ ___ ___ ___ ___ ___ ___
2. 工 ___ ___ ___ ___
3. 亡 ___ ___

四、语言点 Language Points

1. The adverb 有（一）点儿

Functioning as an adverb, 有（一）点儿 is often used before an adjective to indicate a slight degree of dissatisfaction. In 有一点儿, 一 is omissible.

> **Subject + 有（一）点儿 + Adjective**

Note that not all adjectives can be used in this structure. Adjectives with positive connotation are usually not paired with 有（一）点儿, for example, we cannot say 有（一）点儿好; but we can say 有（一）点儿坏. Here are more examples with the adverb 有（一）点儿：

> (1) 快递邮费是有点儿贵，可是特别快。
> Express mail is indeed a little bit expensive, but the delivery is fast.
> (2) 这些东西减价的时候，也还是有点儿贵。
> These things are still somewhat expensive even when they are sold at a discount.
> (3) 最近我工作有点儿忙，所以没来看你。
> Recently, I have been quite busy and therefore didn't come to see you.
> (4) 这次期末考试，我觉得有点儿难。
> I feel that this end-of-semester examination was a little bit difficult.

2. The aspectual particle 着 *(3)*

In previous lessons, we learned that 着 can be attached to a verb to indicate a progressive action or the way an action is done. In this lesson, we will learn that 着 can also be attached to a verb to indicate that a state or event continues. Note that the subject in this pattern is usually a place or a location.

> **Place / Location + Verb + 着 + Noun**

(1) 里面还放了一张祝母亲节快乐的贺卡，贺卡上写<u>着</u>我的名字。
A Happy Mother's Day greeting card was put inside with my name written on the card.

(2) 我们几个同学还凑钱给林华买了一个生日蛋糕，上面用中英文写<u>着</u>"生日快乐"。
We also chipped in to buy a birthday cake for Lin Hua, on which was written in Chinese and English "Happy Birthday".

(3) 他家开<u>着</u>门，可是里面没有一个人。
The door of his house was open, but nobody was inside.

(4) 她家的圣诞树下放<u>着</u>很多圣诞礼物。
Many Christmas gifts were put under the Christmas tree in her house.

3. The 是 ..., 可是 ... construction

In the 是…, 可是…construction, the first clause acknowledges a fact with 是; and the main clause states what the speaker really wants to say.

(1) 快递<u>是</u>有点儿贵，<u>可是</u>特别快。
Express mail is indeed a little bit expensive, but the delivery is fast.

(2) 中文<u>是</u>有点儿难，<u>可是</u>你一定能学好。
Chinese is indeed somewhat difficult, but I am sure you can learn it well.

(3) 我<u>是</u>很想去旅游，<u>可是</u>没有钱。
I indeed want to go traveling, but I have no money.

(4) 露营<u>是</u>很好玩儿，<u>可是</u>现在是冬天，不合适。
Camping is indeed fun. However, it is winter now which is not the right time.

4. The modal particle 吧 (2)

In Lesson 8, we learned that the modal particle 吧 can be used at the end of a sentence to indicate a suggestion or a request. In this lesson, we will learn that the modal particle 吧 can also indicate a query, in which the speaker has an idea in mind but needs a confirmation. In such cases, a question mark is usually added to the end of the sentence. Please compare the following two sentences:

你是中文系的学生<u>吗</u>?
Are you a student in the Chinese Department?

你是中文系的学生吧?

I presume you are a student in the Chinese Department, aren't you?

More examples of this usage of the modal particle 吧：

(1) 快递邮费很贵吧?

Express delivery is very expensive, I presume?

(2) 你那么忙，我想你很少去电影院看电影吧?

You are so busy. You seldom go to the cinema to see a movie, I think?

(3) 那么晚了，她大概不来了吧?

It is so late at night. She won't come, I think?

(4) 人人都知道这件事，你应该也知道吧?

Everybody knows about this matter. You also know about it, I presume?

5. The adverb 一下子

The adverb 一下子 means "suddenly". It is often used with the adverb 就 in a past event:

(1) 她很生气，一下子就把电话挂了。

She was very angry and hanged up abruptly.

(2) 气温一下子降到摄氏零下十度。

The temperature fell drastically to minus ten degrees Celsius.

(3) 老师说得很慢，我一下子就听懂了。

The teacher talked so slowly that I immediately understood what she was saying.

(4) 这个中餐馆的饺子很好吃，我一下子就吃了八个。

The dumplings at this Chinese restaurant were so delicious that I had eight in a row.

6. The descriptive complement (1)

Unlike the complement in a verb compound, like 完 and 好, a descriptive complement serves as a part of a sentence. A descriptive complement is a phrase used after a verb or an adjective to describe how an action is carried out or how a state exists. Here is the pattern and some examples:

Subject + Verb + 得 + Complement

(1) 我每天都<u>睡得晚</u>。Everyday I went to bed very late.

(2) 你的中文已经<u>说得很不错了</u>。You already speak Chinese very well.

(3) 时间<u>过得真快</u>！Time flies fast!

(4) 你的中文<u>说得好极了</u>。You speak Chinese extremely well.

Exercise 1 👂 ✍

Listen to three short dialogs and answer the questions in Chinese characters. Pay attention to the adverb 有一点儿 and the modal particle 吧.

New words: 红 hóng, red   饿 è, hungry

Dialog 1 Question: "我"为什么不想跟小明去看电影？	Answer:
Dialog 2 Question: 关于那双红运动鞋，大卫说了什么？	Answer:
Dialog 3 Question: 他俩为什么想找个饭馆吃饭？	Answer:

Exercise 2 ✍

Follow the example and complete the sentences with the 是 … 可是 … construction.

Example: 这个房子是有一点儿小，可是<u>很便宜</u>。(very cheap)

1. 这道菜是有一点儿贵，可是 _____。(good taste)

2. 坐飞机旅行是很舒服，可是 _____。(expensive)

3. 这个公园是有一点儿小，可是 _____。(beautiful)

4. 这件衬衫是不错，可是 _____。(a little bit small for you)

5. 这个房子是很大也很好看，可是 _____。(especially expensive)

6. 今天我是很忙，可是 _____。(very happy)

7. 今天是没有下雨，可是 _____。(very windy)

8. 上网买衣服是很方便，可是 _____。(can't try it on)

Exercise 3 ✍

Follow the example and answer the questions with a descriptive complement.

Example: 你上个周末过得怎么样？   <u>我上个周末过得很好 / 高兴。</u>

1. 你的汉字写得怎么样？ _____ 。

2. 你的舞跳得怎么样？ _____ 。

3. 约翰的中文现在说得怎么样？ _____ 。

4. 大卫的南瓜灯做得怎么样？ _____ 。

5. 圣诞节你们玩得怎么样？ _____ 。

6. 这家中餐馆的北京烤鸭做得怎么样？ _____ 。

Exercise 4 ✍

Translate the following dialogs into English paying attention to the adverb 一下子.

Dialog 1

A：时间过得真快啊！

B：是啊，一个星期一下子又过去了！

_____

_____

Dialog 2

A：昨天很暖和，可今天气温一下子就下降了十几度。

B：可不是吗！你得多穿点儿衣服。

_____

_____

Dialog 3

A：小李说得太快了，我一下子没听懂他在说什么。

B：我也没有听懂。下次我们可以请他说得慢一点儿。

_____

_____

Dialog 4

A：汤姆，我在网上替你找到了你想买的那本书。

B：我找了很长时间都没有找到，你怎么一下子就找到了呢？

_____

_____

Exercise 5 🗣

Use the aspectual particle 着 to describe the following pictures in Chinese.

五、语言运用 Using the Language

Activity 1 📖 🗣

Read the following sign and form, then answer the questions.

收寄地	北京市
寄达地	上海市
邮件种类	国内快递包裹

包裹总重量	2.5 千克
基本资费	16.00 元
挂号费	3.00 元
保价费	1.00 元 (保价金额 100.00 元)
合计金额	20.00 元 (人民币)

Questions:

1. What service does the sign advertise?

2. What is mailed, and from where to where?

3. How was it mailed?

Activity 2 🎧 🗣

A. Listen to the dialog and then decide whether the statements below are true or false.

1. The man wants to mail a package.	( )
2. The package can arrive within three days.	( )
3. You can put a letter in the express mail package.	( )
4. Insurance is not included in express mail postage.	( )
5. The man did not use express mail.	( )

B. Listen to the passage and select the correct answer to each question.

1. What am I studying in New York?

   a. Chinese   b. English

2. What is the temperature indoors?

   a. cold   b. warm

3. What does my girlfriend like?

   a. American music   b. chocolate

4. When will my girlfriend receive my stuff?

   a. tomorrow   b. soon after tomorrow

C. Listen to a conversation at a post office and answer the questions in Chinese.

1. What is the destination?

2. How was it mailed?

3. What was the total cost?

Activity 3 📖

Read the passage below and decide whether the statements are true or false.

怎样从美国往中国寄包裹

在美国的邮局往中国邮寄东西，可以寄普通 (ordinary) 包裹，也可以寄航空包裹 (airmail)。你可以到邮局寄，也可以先在网上看看邮费是多少。要是你要保险，得另外付钱。包裹都能寄到，所以要是你的包裹里的东西不是很贵，可以不买保险。

1. Only air mail is used for sending packages to China.	( )
2. You can find out the cost before you take the package to the post office.	( )
3. Buying insurance could be a waste of money because packages seldom get lost.	( )

Activity 4 📖

Read the statements followed by three responses. Choose the most logical response to the statement.

1. 我想去邮局寄个包裹。
   a. 你爸爸在邮局工作吗？
   b. 那多慢！为什么不用网上礼品公司？
   c. 情人节到了。很多人送礼物给朋友。

2. 昨天晚上降温了。
   a. 那你要多穿点儿衣服。
   b. 北京的冬天有三个月。
   c. 现在冬装卖得很快。

3. 快递的保险费贵吗？
   a. 邮费里边就包括了，不用再买。
   b. 买了保险的包裹到得快。
   c. 请你填这张保险单。

4. 情人节应该给朋友送什么礼物？
   a. 我男朋友说情人节是 2 月 14 号。
   b. 你觉得这种巧克力怎么样？
   c. 礼物贵不贵都可以。

Activity 5 📖 🗣✶

Read the photo description and sum up the main idea.

在中国寄包裹时，邮局会看看里边寄的是什么。邮局也会让你用邮局的盒子包你的包裹。如果你自己不想包，邮局的人可以给你包。这种服务是不要钱的，但是包包裹用的盒子是要收费的。过去寄包裹都用邮局，可是现在有很多快递公司。他们的服务又快又好。服务员还可以到你家来拿你的包裹，不用你自己去。

Activity 6 📖 🗣✶

Read the signs in the following photos and answer the questions.

Photo 1

订机票　找邮局
24 小时订票热线 11185

Questions:

1. Where can you find this sign?
2. What service does this sign advertise for?
3. How can you use this service?

Photo 2

邮政信箱
外埠　本埠
开筒时间
第一次：10:11
第二次：20:31
中国邮政
（埠 bù, place 筒 tǒng, barrel）

Questions:

1. What can you do here?
2. Do you have to do it in the morning?

飞跃——汉语初级教程学生用书　下册

Activity 7

Role Play

It is Valentine's Day. You want to mail a package of gifts to your friend. Go to the post office and talk with the postal clerk to find the fastest way to send the package. Ask about the postage, including insurance. Your partner will play the role of the postal clerk.

Sentences you may need to use:

请问，怎样寄包裹最快?
邮费包括保险吗?
多少天到?

第十五课 上网
Lesson Fifteen **Going Online**

飞跃——汉语初级教程学生用书 下册

一、导入 Lead-in

Exercise 1 📖 🗨

Look at the pictures below and describe the activities in Chinese.

我喜欢在谷歌网上查天气、订旅馆。

我常常上脸谱网站找我的同学和朋友。

After learning this lesson, you will be able to:

1. Talk about common websites and Internet-related activities.

2. Talk about the convenience and side effects of going online.

3. Recognize new characters in this lesson, and know the common radicals 日, 土, 页 and 月.

4. Use the 跟 … 一样 construction, the auxiliary verb 会, and the aspectual particle 过.

74

二、课文 Texts

课文（一）Text (1)

网上什么东西都有

简体版

　　Li Wen chatted with his mother about the Internet.

妈妈：小文啊，你为什么老待在网上啊？

李文：妈，我在找资料呢。现在网上什么东西都有！

妈妈：我知道，暴力和黄色的东西可不少！

李文：妈，您怎么就知道那些不好的东西？其实，网上好的东西多着呢！

妈妈：有什么好的东西？你说说看。

李文：先说网购吧，网上什么东西都可以买到，又方便，价钱又便宜。

妈妈：这我知道，咱们买过好几回了。

李文：网上还可以查地图，订旅馆，买飞机票。还能看到世界各地的新闻。

妈妈：是谷歌网吗？

李文：是的，雅虎、百度等网站都有这些服务。还有，在优酷网上可以听音乐，看电影。在脸谱网站还可以找到您中小学的同学。

妈妈：真的吗？那我得上网去试试。我还真想找找我的老同学！

網上甚麼東西都有

繁体版

　　Li Wen chatted with his mother about the Internet.

媽媽：小文啊，你爲什麼老待在網上啊？

李文：媽，我在找資料呢。現在網上什麼東西都有！

媽媽：我知道，暴力和黃色的東西可不少！

李文：媽，您怎麼就知道那些不好的東西？其實，網上好的東西多着呢！

媽媽：有什麼好的東西？你說說看。

李文：先說網購吧，網上什麼東西都可以買到，又方便，價錢又便宜。

媽媽：這我知道，咱們買過好幾回了。

李文：網上還可以查地圖，訂旅館，買飛機票。還能看到世界各地的新聞。

媽媽：是谷歌網嗎？

李文：是的，雅虎、百度等網站都有這些服務。還有，在優酷網上可以聽音樂，看電影。在臉譜網站還可以找到您中小學的同學。

媽媽：真的嗎？那我得上網去試試。我還真想找找我的老同學！

Kèwén (yī) *Text (1)*

Wǎngshang Shénme Dōngxi Dōu Yǒu

拼音版

Li Wen chats with his mother about the Internet.

Māma: Xiǎowén a, nǐ wèi shénme lǎo dāi zài wǎngshang a?

Lǐ Wén: Mā, wǒ zài zhǎo zīliào ne. Xiànzài wǎngshang shénme dōngxi dōu yǒu!

Māma: Wǒ zhīdao, bàolì hé huángsè de dōngxi kě bù shǎo!

Lǐ Wén: Mā, nín zěnme jiù zhīdao nàxiē bù hǎo de dōngxi? Qíshí, wǎngshang hǎo de dōngxi duō zhene!

Māma: Yǒu shénme hǎo de dōngxi? Nǐ shuōshuo kàn.

Lǐ Wén: Xiān shuō wǎnggòu ba, wǎngshang shénme dōngxi dōu

kěyǐ mǎidào, yòu fāngbiàn, jiàqian yòu piányi.

Māma: Zhè wǒ zhīdao, zánmen mǎiguo hǎo jǐ huí le.

Lǐ Wén: Wǎngshang hái kěyǐ chá dìtú, dìng lǚguǎn, mǎi fēijī piào. Hái néng kàndào shìjiè gè dì de xīnwén.

Māma: Shì Gǔgēwǎng ma?

Lǐ Wén: Shì de, Yǎhǔ, Bǎidù děng wǎngzhàn dōu yǒu zhèxiē fúwù. Háiyǒu, zài Yōukùwǎng shang kěyǐ tīng yīnyuè, kàn diànyǐng. Zài Liǎnpǔ wǎngzhàn hái kěyǐ zhǎodào nín zhōng-xiǎoxué de tóngxué.

Māma: Zhēn de ma? Nà wǒ děi shàngwǎng qù shìshi. Wǒ hái zhēn xiǎng zhǎozhao wǒ de lǎotóngxué!

生词（一）New Words (1)

	简体（繁體）	拼音	词性	解释
1	老	lǎo	*adv.*	always 你怎么一天到晚老上网？
2	上	shang	*n.*	on, upon 车上／飞机上／日历上有中文吗？／书上的这个字你会写吗？
3	资（資）料	zīliào	*n.*	material, data 资料室／找资料
4	暴力	bàolì	*n.*	violence 暴力电影／使用暴力／家庭暴力
5	黄色	huángsè	*adj.*	pornographic 黄色电影／黄色文学／黄色光盘
6	就	jiù	*adv.*	only 我就有五块钱，不能去饭馆。
7	网购（網購）	wǎnggòu		online shopping 你喜欢网购吗？
8	咱（们）	zán(men)	*pron.*	we (including both the speaker and listeners) 咱家／咱们俩／咱们一起去吧。
9	好	hǎo	*adv.*	quite 好几个人／好几本书／好多人／好久不见／天气好热
10	回	huí	*m.*	(measure word for an action) 我去过一回北京。／一回生，二回熟。／他家我已经去过好几回了。
11	查	chá	*v.*	check, search 查资料／查地图／查电话号码

简体（繁體）		拼音	词性	解释
12	地图（圖）	dìtú	n.	map 中国地图 / 世界地图
13	订（訂）	dìng	v.	reserve, order 订旅馆 / 订票 / 订餐
14	旅馆（館）	lǚguǎn	n.	hotel 住旅馆 / 订旅馆 / 汽车旅馆
15	飞机（飛機）	fēijī	n.	airplane 坐飞机 / 上飞机 / 下飞机
16	票	piào	n.	ticket 车票 / 电影票 / 戏票
17	世界	shìjiè	n.	world 全世界 / 世界各国
18	各地	gè dì		all parts of (a country, world); various regions 全国各地 / 世界各地
19	新闻（聞）	xīnwén	n.	news 听新闻 / 报告新闻 / 新闻联播
20	网（網）站	wǎngzhàn	n.	website 上购物网站买衣服。
21	中小学（學）	zhōng-xiǎoxué	n.	primary and middle school 中小学生 / 中小学同学
专有名词 Proper Nouns				
1	谷歌	Gǔgē	pn.	Google
2	雅虎	Yǎhǔ	pn.	Yahoo
3	百度	Bǎidù	pn.	Baidu
4	优（優）酷	Yōukù	pn.	Youku (a Chinese video sharing site)
5	脸谱（臉譜）	Liǎnpǔ	pn.	Facebook

Exercise 1 🎧 🗣

Listen to Text (1) and answer the questions orally in Chinese.

1. What is Li Wen doing?

2. What does Li Wen's mother know about the Internet?

3. Please make a list of the things one can do online, according to Li Wen.

Exercise 2 📖 ✍

Read Text (1) and fill in the chart in Chinese. You may supply the information according to your knowledge other than that learned in Text (1).

你想……	你去……网站
查地图	

买机票	
看新闻	
听音乐	
看电影	

Exercise 3

Match the following sentences in Column I with the appropriate responses in Column II.

Column I	Column II
(　) 1. 你在上网呢?	a. 谁看啦? 这是功夫电影!
(　) 2. 别看黄色的东西!	b. 上"脸谱"看看。
(　) 3. 我想知道怎么订机票和旅馆。	c. 对。我查点东西。
(　) 4. 我怎么找老同学?	d. 在网上都能订到。

Exercise 4 ✎

Fill in the blanks with the given words.

待　　翻译　　订　　网上　　优酷网　　地图

　　李国文喜欢上网。一天到晚他总是 ＿＿＿＿＿ 在网上。他说网上什么都有。他可以在 ＿＿＿＿＿ 找资料,也可以买东西。他去别的地方,都是在网上 ＿＿＿＿＿ 飞机票和旅馆。他开车出去的时候,也用谷歌 ＿＿＿＿＿＿。他有一个外国朋友,他给这个朋友写电子邮件的时候,用谷歌 ＿＿＿＿＿＿。他还在脸谱网上交了很多朋友。有的时候学习累了,就到 ＿＿＿＿＿＿ 去听音乐、看电影。他说,有了互联网,他一个月都可以不出门。

课文(二)Text (2)

网　瘾

简体版

From Li Wen's diary

　　今天是个不好的日子。我的数学考试不及格,妈妈知道了非常生气。她说我患上了网瘾,整天在电脑上玩游戏,和朋友聊天,很晚了还不睡觉,所以成绩不好。妈妈夸奖姐姐,说姐姐听话,从来不玩电子游戏,也很少上网,所以学习成绩很好。

其实我知道姐姐没少上网，她有空就上脸谱网站，她还有自己的网页。姐姐经常上购物的网站，看看有什么漂亮的衣服和鞋子。可是姐姐总是在做完功课以后才上网，而且从来不玩电子游戏。这跟我很不一样。我以后也要向姐姐学习，做完功课以后才上网，晚上十一点以前要上床睡觉。我想，我的学习成绩会慢慢好起来的。

網　癮

繁体版

From Li Wen's diary

今天是個不好的日子。我的數學考試不及格，媽媽知道了非常生氣。她說我患上了網癮，整天在電腦上玩游戲，和朋友聊天，很晚了還不睡覺，所以成績不好。媽媽誇獎姐姐，說姐姐聽話，從來不玩電子游戲，也很少上網，所以學習成績很好。

其實我知道姐姐沒少上網，她有空就上臉譜網站，她還有自己的網頁。姐姐經常上購物的網站，看看有什麼漂亮的衣服和鞋子。可是姐姐總是在做完功課以後才上網，而且從來不玩電子游戲。這跟我很不一樣。我以後也要向姐姐學習，做完功課以後才上網，晚上十一點以前要上床睡覺。我想，我的學習成績會慢慢好起來的。

Kèwén (èr) *Text (2)*

Wǎngyǐn

拼音版

From Li Wen's diary

Jīntiān shì ge bù hǎo de rìzi. Wǒ de shùxué kǎoshì bù jígé, māma zhīdàole fēicháng shēngqì. Tā shuō wǒ huànshàngle wǎngyǐn, zhěngtiān zài diànnǎoshang wán yóuxì, hé péngyou liáotiān, hěn wǎn le hái bú shuìjiào, suóyǐ chéngjì bù hǎo. Māma kuājiǎng jiějie, shuō jiějie tīnghuà, cónglái bù wán diànzǐ yóuxì, yě hěn shǎo shàngwǎng, suóyǐ xuéxí chéngjì hěn hǎo.

　　Qíshí wǒ zhīdào jiějie méi shǎo shàngwǎng, tā yǒukōng jiù shàng Liǎnpǔ wǎngzhàn, tā hái yǒu zìjǐ de wǎngyè. Jiějie jīngcháng shàng gòuwù de wǎngzhàn, kànkan yǒu shénme piāoliang de yīfu hé xiézi. Kěshì jiějie zǒngshì zài zuòwán gōngkè yǐhòu cái shàngwǎng, érqiě cónglái bù wán diànzǐ yóuxì. Zhè gēn wǒ hěn bù yíyàng. Wǒ yǐhòu yě yào xiàng jiějie xuéxí, zuòwán gōngkè yǐhòu cái shàngwǎng, wǎnshang shíyī diǎn yǐqián yào shàngchuáng shuìjiào. Wǒ xiǎng, wǒ de xuéxí chéngjì huì mànman hǎo qǐlái de.

生词（二）New Words (2)

	简体（繁體）	拼音	词性	解释
1	日子	rìzi	n.	day, date 今天是什么日子？/现在的日子好过多了。
2	数学（數學）	shùxué	n.	mathematics 数学家 / 数学老师 / 学数学
3	及格	jígé	v.	pass a test 我考试及格后，爸爸给我买了一个笔记本电脑。
4	生气（氣）	shēngqì	v.	be angry 她生气了。/ 你跟他生什么气？
5	患	huàn	v.	contract (a disease) 患病 / 患者 / 患了心脏病 / 患了网瘾
6	网瘾（網瘾）	wǎngyǐn	n.	Internet addiction 他患上网瘾了。
7	整天	zhěngtiān	n.	all day long 他整天不回家。/ 我忙了一整天，很累。
8	电脑（電腦）	diànnǎo	n.	computer 买电脑 / 用电脑 / 电脑软件
9	成绩（績）	chéngjì	n.	grades 学习成绩 / 提高成绩 / 成绩有进步。

简体（繁體）	拼音	词性	解释
10 夸奖（誇獎）	kuājiǎng	v./n.	praise 老师夸奖学生学习好。/ 孩子们得到了夸奖。
11 听话（聽話）	tīnghuà	adj.	obedient 他是一个听话的孩子。/ 听话，把药吃了。
12 从来（從來）	cónglái	adv.	always; at all times 我从来都不喜欢看电视。/ 他从来都是在网上看电影的。
13 网页（網頁）	wǎngyè	n.	web page 我做的网页非常有用。/ 你会设计网页吗？
14 经（經）常	jīngcháng	adv.	often 他经常在图书馆学习。/ 这里冬天经常下雨。
15 购（購）物	gòuwù	v.	go shopping 购物中心 / 星期天我去购物。
16 漂亮	piàoliang	adj.	pretty, beautiful 漂亮女孩 / 那个学生写的汉字很漂亮。
17 总（總）是	zǒngshì	adv.	always 放学后我们总是先复习课文，然后再去玩儿。
18 功课（課）	gōngkè	n.	homework 你每天几点钟做功课？
19 而且	érqiě	conj.	in addition 以后我要好好学习，而且还要帮助同学。
20 向	xiàng	prep.	from 我要向成绩好的学生学习。
21 上床	shàngchuáng	v.	go to bed 每天晚上我 11 点才上床睡觉。
22 起来（來）	qǐlái	v.	(after a verb or adjective) indicate the beginning and continuation of an action 他的病好起来了。/ 天气暖起来了。/ 房间里亮起来了。/ 我们的学习忙起来了。

Exercise 5 🎧 🗣

Listen to Text (2) and answer the questions orally in Chinese.

1. Why was Li Wen's mother angry?

2. What did his mother say about him?

3. How is his sister different from him, according to his mother?

4. What are the differences between Li Wen and his sister regarding Internet usage?

Exercise 6 📖

Read Text (2) and choose the correct answer for the following statements.

1. 李文妈妈很生气，因为李文 _____。
　　a. 花很多钱买电子游戏
　　b. 上网让他的学习成绩不好
　　c. 没有告诉妈妈姐姐总是上脸谱网

2. 李文的成绩会好起来，如果 _____。
　　a. 他能好好用自己的时间
　　b. 他妈妈让他多用电脑
　　c. 他姐姐放学后帮他学习

3. 李文的姐姐 _____。
　　a. 做功课以前上一会儿网
　　b. 喜欢在网上购物和交朋友
　　c. 没有帮助李文学习

Exercise 7 ✍️🗣️

Fill in the blanks with the words given and then translate the sentences into English.

　　　　　　　网瘾　　上网　　及格　　功课　　成绩　　网页

1. 我的中文考试 _____ 了。

2. 我觉得小王患了 _____，他整天在电脑上玩儿游戏。

3. 姐姐从来不玩儿电子游戏，她只 _____ 买东西。

4. 我在脸谱上有很多朋友。我还有自己的 _____。

5. 我们做完 _____ 以后再上网好不好？

6. 他的学习 _____ 怎么也好不起来。

Exercise 8

Translate the following sentences into Chinese characters on your computer.

1. I failed my math test today and my mother was very angry.

2. After becoming addicted to the Internet, he spends every evening online chatting with people.

3. I like Facebook, and I go to the website whenever I have time.

4. You should play computer games only on Saturdays. Your study grades are bad!

5. Do you like shopping online? Some pretty clothing can only be bought on the Internet.

6. If you spend less time online and more time on your studies, your grades will improve.

三、汉字 Chinese Characters

1. New characters in this lesson

序号	拼音	简/繁	部件	构词
1	bào	暴	日＋共＋水	暴力／暴风雨
2	chá	查	木＋旦	查资料／查找／查身体／查验
3	chéng	成	成	成绩／成果／成功／成立
4	dì	地	土＋也	地图／地铁／地方／地上
5	fēi	飞（飛）	飞	飞机／飞跃／起飞／高飞
6	gē	歌	哥＋欠	唱歌／写歌／歌唱家
7	gé	格	木＋各（夂＋口）	不及格／合格
8	gǔ	谷	八＋人＋口	谷歌／谷子／谷米
9	hǔ	虎	虍＋几	雅虎／老虎／虎山
10	huàn	患	串＋心	患病／患者
11	huáng	黄（黃）	共＋由＋八	黄色／黄土地／黄种人
12	jí	及	及	及格／及时／来不及
13	jì	绩（績）	纟＋责（主＋贝）	成绩／业绩／功绩
14	jiǎng	奖（奬）	丬＋夕＋大	夸奖／奖状
15	jiè	界	田＋介	世界／界线／分界
16	kòng	空	穴＋工	有空儿／没空儿
17	kù	酷	酉＋告（丷＋口）	优酷网／酷热／冷酷
18	kuā	夸（誇）	大＋亏	夸奖／夸口／夸大
19	liǎn	脸（臉）	月＋佥	洗脸／脸谱／圆脸
20	liàng	亮	亠＋口＋冖＋几	漂亮／天亮／灯亮
21	liào	料	米＋斗	资料／材料／衣料／饮料
22	nǎo	脑（腦）	月＋亠＋凶	电脑／大脑／动脑筋
23	piào	票	覀＋示	车票／电影票／戏票
24	piào	漂	氵＋票（覀＋示）	漂亮
25	pǔ	谱（譜）	讠＋普（並＋日）	脸谱／谱写／歌谱

26	qiě	且	且	而且 / 并且
27	shì	世	世	世界 / 在世 / 去世
28	shù	数（數）	娄（米＋女）＋攵	数学 / 数字
29	wén	闻（聞）	门＋耳	新闻 / 新闻联播 / 耳闻
30	xiàng	向	向	向……学习 / 向前
31	yǎ	雅	牙＋隹	雅虎 / 文雅
32	yè	页（頁）	页	网页 / 书页
33	yǐn	瘾（癮）	疒＋隐（阝＋急）	网瘾 / 烟瘾 / 赌瘾
34	yōu	优（優）	亻＋尤	优酷网 / 优秀 / 优良 / 优等
35	zán	咱	口＋自	咱家 / 咱们俩
36	zhàn	站	立＋占	网站 / 车站 / 站台 / 站立
37	zī	资（資）	次（冫＋欠）＋贝	资料室 / 工资 / 资历 / 资本
38	zǒng	总（總）	丷＋口＋心	总是 / 总结 / 总统

Exercise 1 ✎

Copy the following single-component characters with correct stroke order in the spaces provided.

fēi	飞	乙 飞 飞		
gǔ	谷	丶 八 夂 公 公 谷 谷		
huáng	黄	一 十 艹 艹 芢 苦 苗 苗 黄 黄		
jí	及	丿 乃 及		
qiě	且	丨 冂 月 月 且		
shì	世	一 十 卋 世 世		

xiàng	向	ノ 亻 冇 向 向 向		
yè	页	一 丆 丆 页 页 页		

Exercise 2 📖 ✍

Read the following sentences and choose the correct characters to fill in the blanks.

1. 小孩子不应该在网上看 _____ 力的东西。(爆 报 暴)

2. 你喜欢到购物中心买东西还是喜欢在电 _____ 上买？(恼 脑 垴)

3. 我把我的脸谱地 _____ 给你，你可以看到我的照片。(趾 址 芷)

4. 我现在不看电视，我的新 _____ (间 问 闻) 都是网上看来的。

5. 你怎么老在网上，是不是得了网 _____ ？(瘾 癌 病)

6. 我的汉语成 _____ 不太好。妈妈给我找了一个辅导。(渍 记 绩)

7. 我姐姐做完作业才上网，妈妈 _____ 奖她是好孩子。(挎 夸 垮)

8. 你会做网 _____ 吗？(页 贡 员)

2. Common radicals (4)

(1) 日 rìzìpáng

The radical 日 is derived from the pictographic character ⊖ (日), symbolizing the sun. Thus, characters with it are usually related to the sun or time, e.g. 明 (míng, bright; tomorrow); 昨 (zuó, yesterday); 早 (zǎo, early); 晚 (wǎn, late); 时 (shí, time). This radical often appears on the left or at the top of a character.

(2) 月 yuèròupáng

The radical 月 is actually a combination of two different characters: 月 (yuè, moon) and 肉 (ròu, flesh). The radical 月 is derived from the pictographic character 𝄏 symbolizing the moon in crescent. Only a few characters contain the moon radical, e.g. 期 (qī, period of time); 明 (míng, bright; tomorrow). The radical 肉 is derived from the pictographic character 𝄐 symbolizing a piece of meat. Thus the characters with this radical are mostly related to flesh or meat, e.g. 脑 (nǎo, brain); 脸 (liǎn, face); 肚 (dù, stomach).

(3) 页 yèzìpáng

The radical 页 is derived from the pictographic character 𝄞, resembling a head. Characters with 页 are mostly related to the head, e.g. 题 (tí, topic, the head of an article); 领 (lǐng, collar, the head of a garment); 顶 (dǐng, top).

(4) 土 tǔzìpáng

The radical 土 is derived from the pictographic character 𡊁 (土 tǔ, earth), indicating a plant growing from the earth. Characters with 土 are usually related to the earth, land, or soil, e.g. 地 (dì, land, ground); 块 (kuài, lump, piece); 坐 (zuò, to sit); 城 (chéng, city); 场 (chǎng, open field).

Exercise 3

Add different radicals to the following phonetic elements to form different characters.

1. 青 ____   ____   ____   ____
2. 己 ____   ____

四、语言点 Language Points

1. The adverb 可 indicating emphasis

可 is usually used as a conjunction to indicate a turn in meaning, similar to "but, however" in English. In this lesson, we will learn the usage of 可 as an adverb indicating emphasis. Here are some examples:

> (1) 我知道，网上暴力和黄色的东西可不少！
> I know there is a lot of violence and porn on the Internet!
> (2) 我们的老师可好了，谁都喜欢她。
> Our teacher is so nice that everyone likes her.
> (3) 快起床，可别迟到了！
> Get up! Don't be late!
> (4) 这件事，我可真不知道！
> I know nothing about this at all!

2. The modal particle 着呢

The modal particle 着呢 is mostly used after an adjective or a descriptive phrase to indicate a high degree. Note that both syllables are pronounced in the neutral tone.

> (1) 其实，网上好的东西多着呢！
> Actually, there is a lot of good stuff on the Internet.

(2) 我说广东点心好吃着呢！

I would say that Cantonese dim sum is very delicious.

(3) 没想到，这个外国人的普通话说得好着呢！

It never occurred to me that this foreigner speaks Mandarin so well.

(4) 外头是有点冷，可餐馆里头热着呢。

It is indeed somewhat cold outside, but inside the restaurant, it is very hot.

3. The auxiliary verb 会 (1)

The auxiliary verb 会 can be used to indicate the possibility, meaning "be likely to" or "be sure to".

(1) 我会在图书馆复习到九点半左右。

I would review my lessons in the library until about 9:30.

(2) 我想，以后我的学习成绩会慢慢好起来的。

I think my grades will improve over time.

(3) 明天不会下雨吧？

It is not going to rain tomorrow, is it?

(4) 要是明天下雨，你还会去野餐吗？

Are you still going to the picnic if it rains tomorrow?

4. The aspectual particle 过

The aspectual particle 过 is used right after a verb to indicate one's past experience, meaning "once have or had done it before". If the verb has an object or a quantity complement, the object and the complement go after 过.

Subject ＋ Verb ＋ 过 ＋ (Object/Quantity Complement)

(1) 这我知道，咱们买过好几回了。

I know what this is, we have bought things online several times.

(2) 你吃过中餐吗？

Have you ever tried Chinese food?

(3) 我去过北京三次了。

I have been to Beijing three times.

(4) 这本书我看过好几次了。

I have read this book several times.

The negative form of 过 is to put 没（有）before the verb and keep the particle 过. Make sure to drop the 了 at the end of the sentence.

> **Subject + 没（有）+ Verb + 过 + (Object/Quantity Complement)**

(5) 我没吃过中国餐。
I have never tried Chinese food.
(6) 我虽然去过中国三次，可是从来没去过上海。
Although I went to China three times, I have never been to Shanghai.
(7) 上大学以前，我从来没（有）学过中文。
I had never studied Chinese before entering university.
(8) 我就去过中国一次，没去过三次。
I have been to China only once, not three times.

5. The 跟 … 一样 construction

The 跟 … 一样 construction is used to indicate that two items are the same. The items being compared can be a noun, a pronoun, or a phrase. Some words in the second item may be dropped to avoid redundancy.

> **Item A + 跟 + Item B + 一样**

(1) 我弟弟的年龄跟你一样。
My younger brother is the same age as you.
(2) 我们学校用的课本跟你们学校的一样。
My school uses the same textbooks as your school does.
(3) 这个美国学生的中文名字听起来跟中国人一样。
This American student's Chinese name sounds the same as a Chinese person's name.

The negative form of this comparison is to add 不 right before 一样:

> **Item A + 跟 + Item B + 不 + 一样**

(4) 姐姐总是在做完功课以后才上网，而且从来不玩电子游戏，这跟我很不一样。

My elder sister always finishes her homework before going online and she never plays games. This is very different from me.

(5) 我跟你个子不一样高。

I am not of the same height as you.

(6) 在美国学中文跟在中国学不一样。

Learning Chinese in the U.S. is different from learning it in China.

6. The adverb 才 (3)

In Lesson 9 we learned that the adverb 才 can be used before number-measure words or time expressions, meaning "only". In this lesson, we will learn that the adverb 才 can also be used to indicate that only under certain conditions will an action occur. This condition can be another action (examples 1-3) or a certain circumstance (example 4). 只有 can be used to emphasize the absolute necessity of this condition.

(1) 姐姐总是在做完功课以后才上网。

My elder sister goes online only after finishing her homework.

(2) 我以后也要向姐姐学习，做完功课以后才上网。

I should learn from my elder sister and go online only after finishing homework.

(3) 你要常常练习说中文，才能学好中文。

Only if you practice speaking Chinese often will you learn the language well.

(4) 约翰告诉玛丽，这种巧克力只有在美国才能买到。

John told Mary that this type of chocolate could only be bought in the U.S.

Exercise 1 🔊 ✍

Listen to three short dialogs and answer the questions in Chinese characters. Pay attention to the adverb 可.

New word: 觉得, juéde, to think, to believe.

Dialog 1 Question: 为什么玛丽说要上网？	Answer:
Dialog 2 Question: 学生觉得王老师怎么样？	Answer:
Dialog 3 Question: 大卫觉得纽约怎么样？	Answer:

Exercise 2

Follow the example and rewrite the underlined parts with the adverb 可 for emphasis.

Example: 外面风<u>很大</u>，你不要出去。→外面风可大了，你不要出去。

1. 放学以后，<u>别忘了给我打电话</u>。

_____。

2. <u>那个南瓜很大</u>，我们要用它做一个南瓜灯。

_____。

3. 我们的学校在山上，<u>很漂亮</u>。

_____。

4. <u>我很喜欢这双鞋</u>，是我父母送给我的生日礼物。

_____。

5. <u>我们班有不少从中国来的学生</u>，我跟他们是好朋友。

_____。

6. <u>他妈妈做的饺子太好吃了</u>，我一下子就吃了二十个。

_____。

Exercise 3

Translate the following dialogs into Chinese and type the characters on your computer. Use the aspectual particle 过 to indicate past experience.

Dialog 1

A: Mary, have you ever been to New York City?

B: No, I haven't. Xiaohong, have you ever been there?

A: I haven't either. Let's visit New York City during vacation, how about that?

B: Good idea! You and I, and my boyfriend will go there together.

_____

_____

_____

_____

Dialog 2

A: Xiaohua, what do you want to drink? Black tea or green tea?

B: Green tea. I have never had black tea.

A: Actually, black tea is good for winter. Do you want to have a cup of it?

B: OK, give me a cup of black tea then.

_____

_____

_____

_____

Dialog 3

A: Xiao Wang, did you buy anything from that store?

B: Yes, of course. I have bought things from that store three or four times.

A: What have you bought there?

B: I've bought books, plates, and masks for Halloween.

_____

_____

_____

_____

Dialog 4

A: Xiao Jiang, have you ever been to Shanghai?

B: Yes, I've been there many times.

A: How could you have been there many times?

B: Because my grandparents live there and I visit them once a year.

_____

_____

_____

_____

Exercise 4 ✎

Follow the example and answer the questions with 跟 … 一样 / 不一样.

Example: 这盒巧克力跟那盒巧克力一样吗？

这盒巧克力跟那盒巧克力<u>一样 / 不一样</u>。

1. 你点的菜跟他点的菜一样吗?

_____。

2. 这儿的天气跟你老家的天气一样吗?

_____。

3. 这句话跟那句话的意思一样吗?

_____。

4. 你的衣服跟你姐姐的衣服一样吗?

_____。

5. 这本书的价钱跟那本书一样吗?

_____。

6. 他爷爷跟他奶奶的年纪一样吗?

_____。

Exercise 5

Translate the following dialogs into Chinese using 会.

Dialog 1

A: It looks like there's going to be heavy rain tonight.

B: Will the rain stop tomorrow morning?

_____

_____

Dialog 2

A: Will Lin Hua invite us to her birthday party next week?

B: I think she will.

_____

_____

Dialog 3

A: When will you go to Beijing to study Chinese?

B: I'll go to Beijing to study Chinese next summer.

_____

_____

Dialog 4

A: The dishes have been ordered. Why hasn't Xiaoming come? Is it possible that he will not come?

B: He likes roast duck very much. He will certainly come. Let's wait for him for a little while longer.

_____

_____

Exercise 6 ✍️

Complete the following dialogs by using 才 or 着呢. Use the English in the parentheses as a guide.

Dialog 1

A：丽莎，我们在这儿已经逛了两个多小时了，回去吧。

B：_____！现在才四点半，再逛半个小时吧。(It's still early!)

Dialog 2

A：小文，你们家每个周末都去中餐馆吃饭吗?

B：不是。_____。(My family just eats at the Chinese restaurant once a month.)

Dialog 3

A：比尔，你的作业做好了吗?

B：没有，_____！我还得做大约一个小时。(There is still a lot.)

Dialog 4

A：汤姆，你的汉字写得真好，你是怎么学的?

B：_____。(You won't be able to write beautiful Chinese characters unless you practice a lot.)

五、语言运用 Using the Language

Activity 1 🎧 🗣️

Listen to the following phone conversation between Li Ming and Zhang Li and answer the questions orally in Chinese.

_1._ What are Li Ming's evening plans?

_2._ What does Zhang Li invite Li Ming to do?

_3._ Who is Wang? What problem does he have?

_4._ What have Wang's parents done? Were they successful?

Activity 2 📖

Read the following blog written by a Chinese student and answer the questions below. Type your answers in characters.

　　我这个人有网瘾，不管多忙我都要上网。我每天一放学就上网进我的脸谱页面，看看谁写了新的东西，然后用很多时间在脸谱上写东西。

　　我为什么这么爱上网呢？因为在网上我可以找到很多朋友。虽然网上的朋友都没有见过，可是我知道很多人都是好人。我喜欢网上的朋友们，所以常常在网上跟他们聊天，一天不聊都不行。

　　可是这两天我的电脑不给力，有点慢。这个周末我得请人替我看一下。下个星期我还得跟朋友聊天呢！

Questions:

1. Why does he say he is addicted to the Internet?

2. Why does he love the Internet?

3. What is his weekend plan?

Activity 3 📖 🗣

Look at the following pictures and read the descriptions, then answer the questions in Chinese.

Picture 1

　　我家住的地方离市中心比较远，买东西不方便。网购公司在我家附近放了网上购物箱。我们在网上买了东西以后，商店会把买的东西送过来，放到这个箱里。有了这个网购箱以后，我们的生活方便多了，不出家门，家里常用的和常吃的东西都能买到。

Questions:

1. What is this box for?

2. How does it change our lives?

Picture 2

　　王小朋在美国学习。他的爸爸以前想他的时候就给他打电话。后来有人告诉王小朋，中国的 Qzone 网站很方便。在那里不但可以写东西，还能上传照片。王小朋就用 Qzone，他让爸爸也用。这样，王小朋在美国照的照片，他爸爸很快就能看到。他爸爸也把在中国照的照片放上去，小朋也能很快看到。现在他们天天上网，都得了网瘾了。

Questions:

1. How did Wang Xiaopeng's father communicate with him before?

2. How do they connect with each other now? What can they see now?

3. How does his father benefit from this connection?

4. What do they do everyday?

Activity 4

You will hear four statements followed by three responses. Choose the most logical response to the statement.

1. a. 今天我考试不及格。

   b. 是的，我 11 点以前就上床睡觉。

   c. 没有啊，我每天只玩一个小时游戏。

2. a. 网上可以订飞机票，很方便。

   b. 她从来不玩电子游戏。

   c. 我知道姐姐常常上网，不好好学习。

3. a. 电子游戏很贵。你儿子不应该买。

   b. 你有空就上网吗?

   c. 我儿子每天不到 12 点半不睡觉。

4. a. 对，我以后要向小明学习。

   b. 好，脸谱网站是一个很有用的网站。

   c. 是，我在那里有很多朋友呢。

Activity 5

What do you say?

1. You want to question why a person always does something.

2. You want to tell your friend not to do the same thing all the time.

3. You want to know why your friend knows nothing but doing one certain thing.

4. You want to say you have watched the movie many times and you are fed up with it.

5. You want to report someone's habitual behavior online, which is chatting with friends.

   (use the 一 … 就 …pattern).

Activity 6

Role Play

Your friend has become addicted to the Internet and his school work has been affected. Ask about why his studies are so poor now. Tell him to change his daily habits so that he can balance his time between the Internet and school work.

Sentences you may need to use:

你的学习成绩怎么这么不好?
你最好不要老是上网。
你应该学会怎么利用时间。
你应该做完功课以后再上网。

第十六课 生病
Lesson Sixteen **Getting Sick**

一、导入 Lead-in

Exercise 1 📖 🗣

Look at the pictures below and talk about them in Chinese.

我们家的小狗贝贝。

药店里有很多感冒药。

我家附近有一家宠物医院。

After learning this lesson, you will be able to:

1. Tell and ask about symptoms of sickness and give advice.

2. Talk about one's pet and pet-related activities.

3. Recognize new characters in this lesson, and know the common radicals 宀, 穴, 疒 and 犭.

4. Use the affirmative-negative question and expressions of 起来 and 好久不见.

飞跃——汉语初级教程学生用书 下册

二、课文 Texts

课文（一）Text (1)

请病假

简体版

    Xiaohua, a high school student, was woken up by her mother in the morning.

妈妈：小华，小华！七点了！还不起床，要迟到了！

小华：妈妈，我很不舒服。我不想上学了！

妈妈：啊，你不舒服？是不是昨天晚上上网睡得太晚了？

小华：妈，不是的！我昨天晚上就开始头疼、咳嗽，现在觉得更难受了。

妈妈：发烧吗？   **Tips:** common symptoms of a cold

小华：好像有点儿发烧。

妈妈：我想你可能感冒了。我得给咱们的家庭医生打个电话，替你约个时间去看病。

小华：妈妈，我不想看医生。家里有感冒药吗？我吃点儿药就行了。

妈妈：这不行，有病要及时看大夫。今天不要上学了，请大夫检查一下。

小华：妈妈，那你得给我请假。

妈妈：我先给你的学校打个电话请假。你看完病以后，再给你的老师写个电子邮件吧。

請病假

繁体版

    Xiaohua, a high school student, was woken up by her mother in the morning.

媽媽：小華，小華！七點了！還不起床，要遲到了！

小華：媽媽，我很不舒服。我不想上學了！

媽媽：啊，你不舒服？是不是昨天晚上上網睡得太晚了？

小華：媽，不是的！我昨天晚上就開始頭疼、咳嗽，現在覺得更難受了。

媽媽：發燒嗎？

小華：好像有點兒發燒。

媽媽：我想你可能感冒了。我得給咱們的家庭醫生打個電話，替你約個時間去看病。

小華：媽媽，我不想看醫生。家裏有感冒藥嗎？我吃點兒藥就行了。

媽媽：這不行，有病要及時看大夫。今天不要上學了，請大夫檢查一下。

小華：媽媽，那你得給我請假。

媽媽：我先給你的學校打個電話請假。你看完病以後，再給你的老師寫個電子郵件吧。

Kèwén (yī) *Text (1)*

Qǐng Bìngjià

Xiaohua, a high school student, was woken up by her mother in the morning.

Māma: Xiǎohuá, Xiǎohuá! Qī diǎn le! Hái bù qǐchuáng, yào chídào le!

Xiǎohuá: Māma, wǒ hěn bù shūfu. Wǒ bù xiǎng shàngxué le!

Māma: Á, nǐ bù shūfu? Shì bu shì zuótiān wǎnshang shàngwǎng shuì de tài wǎn le?

Xiǎohuá: Mā, bú shì de! Wǒ zuótiān wǎnshang jiù kāishǐ tóu téng, késou, xiànzài juéde gèng nánshòu le.

Māma:	Fāshāo ma?	
Xiǎohuá:	Hǎoxiàng yǒudiǎnr fāshāo.	
Māma:	Wǒ xiǎng nǐ kěnéng gǎnmào le. Wǒ děi gěi zánmen de jiātíng yīshēng dǎ ge diànhuà, tì nǐ yuē ge shíjiān qù kànbìng.	
Xiǎohuá:	Māma, wǒ bù xiǎng kàn yīshēng. Jiā li yǒu gǎnmàoyào ma? Wǒ chīdiǎnr yào jiù xíng le.	
Māma:	Zhè bù xíng, yǒu bìng yào jíshí kàn dàifu. Jīntiān búyào shàngxué le, qǐng dàifu jiǎnchá yíxià.	
Xiǎohuá:	Māma, nà nǐ děi gěi wǒ qǐngjià.	
Māma:	Wǒ xiān gěi nǐ de xuéxiào dǎ ge diànhuà qǐngjià. Nǐ kànwán bìng yǐhòu, zài gěi nǐ de lǎoshī xiě ge diànzǐ yóujiàn ba.	

生词（一）New Words (1)

	简体（繁體）	拼音	词性	解释
1	舒服	shūfu	*adj.*	comfortable; feeling well 这件衣服穿起来很舒服。/ 睡了一觉后，我觉得舒服一点儿了。
2	头（頭）	tóu	*n.*	head 头发 / 我感冒以后，头疼得很厉害。
3	疼	téng	*adj.*	aching 头疼 / 腿疼 / 嗓子疼
4	咳嗽	késòu	*v.*	cough 咳嗽药 / 他咳嗽了一夜。
5	难（難）受	nánshòu	*adj.*	difficult to bear; uncomfortable 吃了饭以后，我肚子很难受。/ 我头疼得很难受。
6	发烧（發燒）	fāshāo	*v.*	have a fever 发高烧 / 发低烧
7	可能	kěnéng	*adv.*	maybe; it is possible that 他可能病了。/ 他可能不在家。
8	感冒	gǎnmào	*v.*	catch a cold 他夜里没有睡好，感冒了。/ 吃点儿感冒药吧。

简体（繁體）	拼音	词性	解释
9 家庭	jiātíng	n.	family, household 他的家是一个老师家庭，爸爸妈妈都是老师，他自己也是。
10 约（約）	yuē	v.	make an appointment 晚上我约了小王看电影。/ 我跟大夫约好了今天下午去看病。
11 看病	kànbìng	v.	visit a doctor 今天我不上学，因为我要去看病。
12 药（藥）	yào	n.	medicine 吃药 / 买药 / 药方 / 药片 / 药水
13 及时（時）	jíshí	adv.	in time; timely 有病要及时看。/ 有问题要及时解决。
14 大夫	dàifu	n.	doctor 看大夫 / 大夫给我看了病。
15 检（檢）查	jiǎnchá	v.	examine, check 医生给我检查了身体。/ 我的电脑坏了，请你给我检查检查。
16 请（請）假	qǐngjià	v.	ask for leave 请长假 / 明天我请假。

Exercise 1 🦻

Listen to Text (1) and choose the correct answer to the following questions.

1. Why does Xiaohua's mother wake her up?

a. Xiaohua's mother is sick and wants Xiaohua to call the doctor.

b. Xiaohua's mother is afraid Xiaohua will be late for school.

c. Xiaohua's mother heard Xiaohua coughing.

2. Why does Xiaohua feel uncomfortable?

a. She has a stomachache.

b. She has a fever and headache.

c. She is sneezing a lot.

3. What does Xiaohua's mom want to do?

a. She wants to call the doctor to make an appointment.

b. She wants to call the teacher to ask for leave.

c. She wants to email the school to ask for leave.

4. What does Xiaohua think?

a. She thinks she needs an injection.

b. She thinks she needs to take some Chinese herbal medicine.

c. She thinks seeing the doctor is not necessary.

Exercise 2 📖

Read Text (1) and decide whether the following statements are true or false.

1. 小华起床以后觉得不舒服。	(	)
2. 小华家里人有病的时候都看同一个医生。	(	)
3. 小华不喜欢看医生。	(	)
4. 小华的妈妈觉得小华说得对。	(	)
5. 妈妈觉得小华不能去上学，小华也这样想。	(	)

Exercise 3 ✎

Fill in the blanks with the given words.

吃点儿药　　迟到　　聊天　　发烧　　舒服　　请了假

国华最近患上了网瘾,常常到脸谱网站跟网友 _____ 聊到半夜一两点钟。今天,他起床起晚了。妈妈要他快点儿起床，因为他要 _____ 了。国华说他不 _____，头疼。妈妈一看，国华 _____ 发到 38 度，就说要给家庭医生打电话。国华说他不想看医生。他想休息休息，_____ 就行了。妈妈说有病一定要看大夫。国华就让妈妈给学校打了一个电话，给他 _____。国华起床以后，给老师写了个电子邮件，告诉老师他今天不能上学了。

Exercise 4 ✎

Translate the following sentences into Chinese.

1. Hurry! Don't be late for class!

_____

2. I have a headache and a fever.

_____

3. I coughed the whole night and could not sleep.

_____

4. Have you called the family doctor?

_____

5. I do not like taking medicine. I will just rest.

_____

6. Xiaoming asked for leave because he caught a cold.

_____

给小狗看病

飞跃——汉语初级教程学生用书 下册

简体版

Lin Hua sent an email to David about her pet's sickness.

大卫：

Tips: a common way to start a letter in Chinese

你好！好久不见。最近学习很忙吧？

今天有一件急事要向你请教。我们家的小狗贝贝本来一直挺好的，我每天放学后就带它出去散步、大小便，每星期给它洗一次澡，它的身体很健康。可是不知道为什么，贝贝今天突然病了，而且看起来病得挺厉害的。它不吃东西，鼻子很烫，还咳嗽。妈妈说不要紧，贝贝可能是感冒了，赶快带它去看医生。可是，我不知道狗是不是跟人一样也会感冒。我也不知道应该带它去哪家宠物医院看病。还有，我们没有给贝贝买医疗保险，给它看病是不是很贵啊？

请你赶快给我出个主意。我等着你的回信。谢谢！

祝好！

Tips: a common way to end a letter in Chinese

林华

給小狗看病

繁体版

Lin Hua sent an email to David about her pet's sickness.

大衛：

你好！好久不見。最近學習很忙吧？

今天有一件急事要向你請教。我們家的小狗貝貝本來一直挺好的，我每天放學後就帶它出去散步、大小便，每星期給它洗一次澡，它的身體很健康。可是不知道爲什麼，貝貝今天突然病了，而且看起來病得挺厲害的。它不吃東西，鼻子很燙，還咳嗽。媽媽説不要緊，貝貝可能是感冒了，趕快帶它去看醫生。可是，我不知道狗是不是跟人一樣也會感冒。我也不知道應該帶它去哪家寵物醫院看病。還有，我們沒有給貝貝買醫療保險，給它看病是不是很貴啊？

請你趕快給我出個主意。我等着你的回信。謝謝！

祝好！

林華

Kèwén (èr) *Text (2)*

Gěi Xiǎogǒu Kànbìng

拼音版

Lin Hua sent an email to David about her pet's sickness.

Dàwèi:

Nǐ hǎo! Hǎo jiǔ bú jiàn. Zuìjìn xuéxí hěn máng ba?

Jīntiān yǒu yí jiàn jíshì yào xiàng nǐ qǐngjiào. Wǒmen jiā de xiǎogǒu Bèibei běnlái yìzhí tǐng hǎo de, wǒ měi tiān fàngxué hòu jiù dài tā chūqu sànbù, dà-xiǎobiàn měi xīngqī gěi tā xǐ yí cì zǎo, tā de shēntǐ hěn jiànkāng. Kěshì bù zhīdào wèi shénme, Bèibei jīntiān tūrán bìng le, érqiě kàn qǐlái bìng de tǐng lìhai de. Tā bù chī dōngxi, bízi hěn tàng, hái késou. Māma shuō bú yàojǐn, Bèibei kěnéng shì gǎnmào le, gǎnkuài dài tā qù kàn yīshēng. Kěshì, wǒ bù zhīdào gǒu shì bu shì gēn rén yíyàng yě huì gǎnmào. Wǒ yě bù zhīdào yīnggāi dài tā qù nǎ jiā chǒngwù yīyuàn kànbìng. Háiyǒu, wǒmen méiyǒu gěi Bèibei mǎi yīliáo bǎoxiǎn, gěi tā kànbìng shì bu shì hěn

guì a?

　　Qǐng nǐ gǎnkuài gěi wǒ chū ge zhǔyi. Wǒ děngzhe nǐ de huíxìn.

Xièxie!

　　Zhù hǎo!

Lín Huá

生词（二）New Words (2)

	简体（繁體）	拼音	词性	解释
1	好久	hǎojiǔ	adj.	for a long time 好久不见了。/ 他好久没给我打电话了。
2	急	jí	adj.	urgent 这件事很急。/ 我有点儿急事要办。
3	请（請）教	qǐngjiào	v.	seek advice 我有事要请教你。/ 我们应该向老师请教。
4	狗	gǒu	n.	dog 我家养了一只狗。/ 我家的狗狗很听话。
5	它	tā	pron.	it 我家小狗病了，给它吃饭它不吃。
6	散步	sànbù	v.	take a walk 吃完饭我常常散步。/ 你喜欢带着狗散步吗？
7	健康	jiànkāng	adj.	healthy 爸爸妈妈身体很健康。/ 祝你身体健康。
8	突然	tūrán	adv.	suddenly 他一直好好的，怎么突然就病了？
9	病	bìng	v./n.	fall ill/illness 病得很厉害 / 去医院看病 / 他病了。
10	看起来（来）	kàn qǐlái		seem 看起来他病得很厉害。/ 看起来我要迟到了。
11	厉（厲）害	lìhài	adj.	severe 病得很厉害
12	鼻子	bízi	n.	nose 感冒的时候，鼻子不通。
13	烫（燙）	tàng	adj.	burning hot 刚出锅的饺子很烫，要小心吃。/ 他发烧发得脑门很烫。
14	不要紧（緊）	bú yàojǐn		it doesn't matter 不要紧，吃点儿药就好了。

	简体（繁體）	拼音	词性	解释
15	赶（趕）快	gǎnkuài	adv.	at once; quickly 请你赶快来。/ 要迟到了，我们赶快走吧。
16	跟……一样（樣）	gēn … yíyàng		same as 狗跟人一样，也会生病。/ 我跟你不一样。
17	应该（應該）	yīnggāi	a.v.	should 病了就应该看大夫。/ 我们不应该迟到。
18	宠（寵）物	chǒngwù	n.	pet 养宠物 / 宠物商店 / 宠物医院
19	医（醫）院	yīyuàn	n.	hospital 北京有很多大医院。/ 医院里病人很多。
20	医疗（醫療）	yīliáo	n.	medical service 医疗服务 / 医疗保险 / 医疗队
21	主意	zhǔyi	n.	idea 好主意 / 你有什么主意？ / 这下他没了主意。
22	回信	huíxìn	n./v.	a letter in reply/reply a letter 等你的回信 / 收到他的信后，我一直没给他回信。
	专有名词 Proper Noun			
	贝贝（貝貝）	Bèibei	pn.	name of the dog in the text

Exercise 5 👂 🗣

Listen to Text (2) and answer the questions orally in Chinese.

1. What does Lin Hua do everyday with her dog?

2. What happened to the dog today?

3. What did Lin Hua's mother think about the situation?

4. Why did Lin Hua write to David?

Exercise 6 📖 ✍

Read Text (2) and answer the following questions in Chinese characters.

1. Does Lin Hua often see David? How do you know?

_____

2. What is the general health condition of Lin's pet dog?

_____

3. What symptoms does Lin's dog have today?

_____

4. What doesn't Lin Hua know?

_____

Activity 7

Read the following dialog and answer the questions orally in Chinese.

大卫：喂，林华吗？我收到你的邮件了。你的小狗现在怎么样啦？

林华：大卫，你好。我的小狗还是不吃东西。

大卫：我想你妈说得对，你的小狗可能是感冒了。

林华：那我要不要带它去看病呀？

大卫：我有个朋友在宠物医院工作。你去他那里看吧。

林华：我可没有给贝贝买保险。

大卫：没关系。我朋友能帮你忙。花不了多少钱。

林华：你跟我一起去好吗？

大卫：好的。放学以后我就去你家。

Questions:

1. How was Beibei when David called?

2. What did David think about the dog?

3. What was Lin Hua worried about?

4. What did David assure Lin Hua of?

Exercise 8

Translate the following sentences into English.

1. 吃了晚饭后我就觉得发烧和头疼。

_____

2. 妈妈送我到医院看病，大夫说我得了感冒。

_____

3. 今天我在医院看病，花了半天时间。

_____

4. 你感冒了，不要去上学了，在家里休息两天。

_____

5. 你给老师打电话替我请假了吗？

_____

三、汉字 Chinese Characters

1. New characters in this lesson

序号	拼音	简 / 繁	部件	构词
1	bèi	贝（貝）	贝	贝贝 / 宝贝
2	bí	鼻	自 + 田 + 丌	鼻子 / 鼻涕
3	bìng	病	疒 + 丙	老师病了 / 生病
4	chǒng	宠（寵）	宀 + 龙	宠物 / 宠爱
5	gāi	该（該）	讠 + 亥	应该 / 不该
6	gǎn	感	咸 + 心	感恩节 / 感情 / 感谢 / 感动
7	gǎn	赶（趕）	走 + 干	赶快 / 赶紧
8	hài	害	宀 + 丰 + 口	厉害 / 害怕
9	jí	急	刍 + 彐 + 心	急事 / 着急
10	jiǎn	检（檢）	木 + 佥	检查 / 检验 / 体检
11	jiàn	健	亻 + 建（聿 + 廴）	健康 / 健美
12	jiào	教	孝（耂 + 子）+ 攵	请教 / 教练
13	jǐn	紧（緊）	𦥑 + 幺 + 小	不要紧 / 紧张
14	kāng	康	广 + 隶	健康
15	ké	咳	口 + 亥	咳嗽 / 咳嗽药
16	lì	厉（厲）	厂 + 万	厉害
17	liáo	疗（療）	疒 + 了	医疗 / 治疗
18	mào	冒	冃 + 目	感冒 / 感冒药 / 冒火 / 冒烟
19	sàn	散	肯（龷 + 月）+ 攵	散步 / 散开
20	shāo	烧（燒）	火 + 尧（戈 + 兀）	发烧 / 火烧 / 烧饭
21	tā	它	宀 + 匕	小狗它病了
22	tàng	烫（燙）	汤（氵 + 𠃓）+ 火	很烫 / 烫伤
23	shòu	受	爫 + 冖 + 又	难受
24	shū	舒	舍（人 + 干 + 口）+ 予	舒服 / 舒心
25	sou	嗽	口 + 束 + 欠	咳嗽 / 咳嗽药

26	téng	疼	疒+冬	头疼 / 腿疼 / 心疼 / 疼爱
27	tíng	庭	广+廷（壬+廴）	家庭 / 庭院
28	tū	突	穴+犬	突然 / 突出
29	yào	药（藥）	艹+约（纟+勺）	吃药 / 买药 / 药方
30	yīng	应（應）	应	应该 / 应有 / 应得
31	zhēn	针（針）	钅+十	打针 / 针线
32	zhǔ	主	丶+王	主意 / 主人

Exercise 1 ✎

Copy the following single-component characters with correct stroke order in the spaces provided.

bèi	贝	丨 冂 贝 贝		
zhǔ	主	丶 亠 宀 主 主		

Exercise 2 📖 ✎

Read the following sentences and choose the correct characters to fill in the blanks.

1. 我家的小 _____ 从昨天起就拉肚子了。(句　狗　够)

2. 他感冒以后，一直 _____ 嗽。(刻　咳　该)

3. 你好像 _____ 得挺厉害，还是去医院看看吧。(病　屏　并)

4. 医院里有自己的 _____ 房吗？(约　药　要)

5. 我的小狗病了，我很着 _____ 。(急　及　极)

6. 为了学习好，我们一定要有 _____ 康的身体。(健　建　键)

7. 我们的公寓不可以有 _____ 物。(庞　宠　笼)

8. 我的小狗昨天 _____ 然发烧了。(突　哭　茶)

2. Common radicals (5)

(1) 宀 bǎogàitóu

The radical 宀 is derived from the pictographic character 冂 (宀) indicating a house, thus characters with it are usually related to house and family, e.g. 家 (jiā, family, house); 室 (shì, room); 宿 (sù, to lodge); 寄 (jì, to mail); 寓 (yù, to reside; residence); 客 (kè, guest).

(2) 宀 xuézìtóu

The radical 穴 (xué), is a character itself, meaning "cave". Thus, characters with this radical are usually related to caves, holes, e.g. 空 (kōng, empty); 穿 (chuān, to wear); 窄 (zhǎi, narrow); 窗 (chuāng, window); 突 (tū, suddenly).

(3) 疒 bìngzìpáng

The original form of 疒 symbolizes a sick man lying in bed. Thus, characters with the 疒 radical are always related to sickness, e.g. 病 (bìng, sickness); 痛 (tòng, pain); 瘾 (yǐn, addiction); 癌 (ái, cancer).

(4) 犭 quǎnzìpáng

The radical 犭 is derived from the pictographic character 犬, symbolizing a dog. Thus characters with this radical are usually related to dogs or animals. This radical is always put on the left side, e.g. 狗 (gǒu, dog); 猫 (māo, cat); 猪 (zhū, pig); 狂 (kuáng, crazy, mad as an animal). When it is put at the bottom, it is written as 犬 quǎn, e.g. 哭 (kū, to cry).

Exercise 3 ✍

Fill in the chart below by writing down as many characters as you can.

Radical	Meaning of the radical	Characters that you have learned containing this radical
宀		
穴		
疒		
犭		

四、语言点 Language Points

1. The idiomatic expression 好久不见

The idiomatic expression 好久不见 has an exact meaning, "long time no see", in English. It is widely used for greetings orally or in writing among Chinese people. Here are some examples:

> (1) 你好！好久不见，最近学习很忙吧？
> Hi, long time no see. You must have been busy with your studies, huh?

111

(2) 小王，好久不见了，你身体怎么样？

Xiao Wang, long time no see. How is your health?

(3) 张老师，好久不见，您最近工作忙吗？

Mr. Zhang, long time no see. Have you been busy with work recently?

(4) 好久不见！家里人都挺好啊？

Long time no see. How is your family?

2. The adverb 更

The adverb 更 is used right before an adjective to indicate a higher degree in a comparison, which usually involves two parties indicated in the context. It is equal to "more" in English. For example:

(1) 我昨天晚上就开始头疼、咳嗽，现在觉得更难受了。

 I started to have a headache and cough last night, and now I feel even worse.

(2) "我喜欢在网上买，又便宜，又方便，不过得花点儿时间上网。"

"我想，去商店买得花更多的时间。"

"I like to shop online. It is both inexpensive and convenient, and you only need to spend a little time looking for what you want."

"I think shopping in a store costs more time."

3. The verb 起来

The original meaning of the verb 起来 is "get up". The verb 起来 can also be used as a complement of a verb or an adjective in a sentence. In lesson 15, we learned that 起来 can be used after a verb or an adjective as a complement meaning "begin and keep on".

(1) 我要向姐姐学习，做完功课以后才上网。我想，我的学习成绩会慢慢好起来的。

I will learn from my sister and go online only after finishing my homework. I think my grades will gradually improve.

(2) 下了三天雨，今天天气好起来了。

It rained for three days, but it is starting to get clear today.

(3) 听完她的话，我们都大笑起来了。

Hearing her words, we all started laughing.

起来 can be used after a verb to indicate estimation or an opinion, like 看起来, 听起来, 说起来, 做起来. For example:

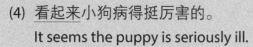

(4) 看起来小狗病得挺厉害的。

It seems the puppy is seriously ill.

(5) 你这个主意听起来不错。

Your idea sounds good.

(6) 这件事说起来容易，做起来难。

As for this, it is easier said than done.

4. The affirmative-negative question (2)

We learned the affirmative-negative questions in the previous lessons:

(1) 你是不是学生？

Are you a student or not?

(2) 不便宜啊！可不可以打个折？

It is expensive! Can you give me a discount or not?

(3) "考试难不难？""我觉得不太难。"

"Was the test hard?" "I don't think it was hard."

(4) 你不舒服？是不是晚上上网睡得太晚？

You don't feel well? Is it because you stayed online all night and went to bed too late?

In this lesson, we will learn that an affirmative-negative question can be transformed into an object clause of a verb. Here are some examples:

(5) 我不知道狗是不是跟人一样也会感冒。

I do not know if dogs catch cold like humans do.

(6) 我想知道你是不是学生。

I want to know if you are a student or not.

(7) 她没说可不可以打个折。

She did not say if she could give us a discount or not.

(8) 请你告诉我考试难不难。

Please tell me if the test was difficult or not.

(9) 妈妈问林华是不是昨天晚上上网睡得太晚。

Mother asked Lin Hua if she stayed online too late last night.

5. The adverb 就 (2)

The adverb 就 can also be used to indicate that two actions or events are closely linked together, happening one after another. To stress the closeness of the two actions, 一 may be used with the first verbal expression to form a 一 … 就 … construction. We will learn more about this pattern in later lessons.

> (1) 其实我知道姐姐没少上网，她有空就上脸谱 网站。
>   Actually, I know that my elder sister goes online a lot. She logs on to Facebook whenever she has time.
> (2) 我们家的小狗贝贝本来一直挺好的，我每天放学后就带它出去散步。
>   Beibei, our family puppy, was always in good shape. I walk her every day after school.
> (3) 妈妈说，有病就得及时看大夫。
>   Mom says you need to see the doctor in time when getting sick.
> (4) 请等我一下，我一做完功课就跟你走。
>   Please wait for me a bit. I will go with you as soon as I finish my homework.

Exercise 1 👂 ✍

Listen to three short dialogs and answer the questions in Chinese characters. Pay attention to the use of the adverb 更 and the idiomatic expression 好久不见.

Dialog 1 Question: 为什么张老师的工作更忙了？	Answer:
Dialog 2 Question: 为什么乐乐做的中国菜更好吃了？	Answer:
Dialog 3 Question: 小雨为什么喜欢上网买东西？	Answer:

Exercise 2 ✍

Follow the example and complete each of the sentences with an affirmative-negative clause as an object.

Example: 他是英国人吗？ → 我不知道他是不是英国人。

1. 明天会下雨吗？

我不知道 _____。

2. 你是小华的姐姐吗？

我想知道 _____。

3. 这条裤子可以打折吗？

我不知道 _____。

4. 小红是从北京来美国的吗？

请告诉我 _____。

5. 他们俩去过纽约吗？

   我不知道 _____ 。

6. 李老师下午有课吗？

   请告诉我 _____ 。

7. 王太太的工作很忙吗？

   我想知道 _____ 。

8. 他把他的手机号码给了你吗？

   我想知道 _____ 。

9. 你的小狗还咳嗽吗？

   我不知道 _____ 。

10. 大夫要你在家里休息吗？

    请告诉我 _____ 。

Exercise 3 ✍

Follow the example and write complete sentences using the adverb 就 to indicate two actions or events that closely follow one another.

Example: 买水果 / 参加野餐 → 我买了水果就去参加野餐了。

1. 下了课 / 去食堂吃饭

   _____

2. 考完试 / 去电影院看电影

   _____

3. 找到工作 / 买了一部新车

   _____

4. 收到来信 / 打电话给你

   _____

Exercise 4 📖 ✍

Read the following sentences and fill in the blanks with the proper complement phrases. Some phrases may be used more than once.

看起来   听起来   说起来   做起来   冷起来   好起来

1. 大卫 _____ 有一点儿不高兴，你知道为什么吗？

2. 最近天气 _____ 了。爸爸妈妈，你们要多注意身体。

3. 这件蓝色的衬衫 _____ 很不错，请问多少钱一件？

4. _____ 我们也认识三年了，可是没有在一起吃过饭。

5. 吃了三天药以后她的病慢慢地 _____ 了。

6. _____ 天要下雨了，你不要出去了。

7. 看到姐姐在做作业，李文也拿出作业 _____ 了。

8. 我跟王老师聊了一会儿。 _____ 他很喜欢当老师。

Exercise 5

Translate the following sentences into Chinese using the words in the parentheses.

1. Students started to stand up when the teacher walked into the classroom. (站起来)

_____

2. I do not know if shopping online takes less time. (是不是)

_____

3. Haven't seen you for a long time. How are you? (好久不见)

_____

4. Do you know if it's going to rain this weekend? (会不会)

_____

5. I will call you as soon as I finish my homework. (就)

_____

6. David is not here today. I don't know whether he is sick or not. (是不是)

_____

7. It looks it's going to snow. Please wear more clothes. (看起来)

_____

8. Xiaohong is pretty, but her elder sister is even prettier. (更好看)

_____

9. "What do you think of this idea?" "It sounds just fine." (听起来)

_____

10. Can you tell me if a dog catches cold like a human does? (是不是)

_____

飞跃——汉语初级教程学生用书 下册

五、语言运用 Using the Language

Activity 1

Read the following medicine labels and tell what illness each is for and how it should be taken.

New words: 粒 lì, tablet   克 kè, gram   毫升 háoshēng, milliliter

1.

感冒清熱膠囊

口服，一次 3 粒，一日 2 次。

2.

复方桑菊感冒冲剂

开水冲服，一次 20 克，一日 2~3 次。

3.

清肺止咳糖浆

口服，一次 10 毫升，一日 3 次。

Activity 2

Listen to a patient describing his sickness and sum it up in English.

_____

_____

_____

Activity 3

What do you say?

1. You caught a cold and your symptoms are a headache and diarrhea.

2. The medicine your doctor prescribed for you did not relieve your headache.

3. You want to make an appointment with your family doctor because your daughter has a cold with severe symptoms.

4. You did not sleep well last night because today you have a vocabulary test.

5. Tell your patient that his sickness is only a common cold and he just needs a little medicine.

6. Tell your mother that the doctor wants you to have a good rest and drink a lot of water.

Activity 4 📖 🗣

Read the following diary written by a Chinese student and answer the questions in Chinese.

我爸爸妈妈最近很忙，所以我住到了奶奶家。前几天，我有点儿头疼。可是我学习很忙，就没有去看病。第二天下午，我的头越来越疼。我自己吃了一包感冒药，但是没有用。奶奶看我这样，就给我量了体温。一看，都快 39 度了。奶奶马上给爸爸打电话，叫他带我去看病。爸爸带我到了急诊部，带着我去打针，忙了一晚上。

Questions:

1. Why didn't the student go to see a doctor in the first place?

2. What did he do to relieve his headache? Did it work?

3. Why did his grandma call his father?

4. What did his father do?

Activity 5 📖 🗣

Read the following sentences and answer the questions briefly in Chinese.

1. 一个小孩得了感冒。

What is the problem with the kid?

2. 不好的吃饭习惯也是头疼发病的原因。

What might happen if you have bad eating habits?

3. 最近我没吃什么不好的东西，可是却一直拉肚子。

What puzzles this person?

4. 清晨起床前量血压比较好。

What is considered good?

Activity 6

Role Play

Your friend calls you because you did not meet him/her to go to school together. Tell your friend that you are sick. Describe your symptoms and tell him/her how long you have been sick. Your friend tries to get you to see a doctor, but you do not want to.

Sentences you may need to use:

我病了。

我头疼 / 发烧 / 呕吐 / 拉肚子。

我头疼 / 发烧 / 呕吐已经……天了。

没关系，我吃点儿药就行了。

我不喜欢看医生。

Activity 7

The following pictures represent a story of a girl getting sick. Tell this story to your partner and then type it out. Your story should have a beginning, middle and an end.

第十七课 过生日
Lesson Seventeen　Celebrating Birthday

一、导入 Lead-in

Exercise 1 📖 💬

Look at the pictures below and describe them in Chinese.

我们点着了生日蛋糕上的蜡烛。

祝你生日快乐!

红烧肉是我的拿手菜。

我只会做西红柿炒鸡蛋。

After learning this lesson, you will be able to:

1. Talk about one's birthday party including food and drink, and activities.

2. Give and accept an invitation to a party.

3. Recognize new characters in this lesson, and know the common radicals 力, 刂, 艹 and 竹.

4. Use the expressions of 一点儿, 有一点儿, 能 and 会 correctly.

二、课文 Texts

课文（一）Text (1)

请吃饭

简体版

Lin Hua invites her friend Peter to her birthday party over the phone.

Tips: how to answer a phone call

彼得：喂，哪位？

林华：是彼得吗？我是林华。

Tips: how to ask about the purpose of a call

彼得：林华，你好！找我有事吗？

林华：这个星期天是我的生日。我想请你和几位同学来我这儿聚一聚，吃顿便饭。

Tips: how to invite a friend for dinner at home

彼得：那太麻烦你了。

林华：一点儿也不麻烦。我和我的室友打算请你们吃我们的拿手菜！

彼得：好啊，谢谢！我们几点钟吃饭呢？

林华：你们四点钟来吧。咱们先聊聊天，六点左右吃饭，怎么样？

彼得：行。那我也带一个菜吧，我可以做一个红烧肉。

林华：好啊！我们也尝尝你做的菜。

Tips: offering to bring some drink

彼得：我再带点儿可乐和啤酒吧。

林华：不用了，饮料已经有了。你们喜欢喝葡萄酒吗？

彼得：喜欢啊！

林华：太好了，我刚买了两瓶加州出的红葡萄酒。那我们就星期天见吧。

彼得：好，星期天见！

第十七课 过生日

121

請吃飯

Lin Hua invites her friend Peter to her birthday party over the phone.

彼得：喂，哪位？

林華：是彼得嗎？我是林華。

彼得：林華，你好！找我有事嗎？

林華：這個星期天是我的生日。我想請你和幾位同學來我這兒聚一聚，吃頓便飯。

彼得：那太麻煩你了。

林華：一點兒也不麻煩。我和我的室友打算請你們吃我們的拿手菜！

彼得：好啊，謝謝！我們幾點鐘吃飯呢？

林華：你們四點鐘來吧。咱們先聊聊天，六點左右吃飯，怎麼樣？

彼得：行。那我也帶一個菜吧，我可以做一個紅燒肉。

林華：好啊！我們也嘗嘗你做的菜。

彼得：我再帶點兒可樂和啤酒吧。

林華：不用了，飲料已經有了。你們喜歡喝葡萄酒嗎？

彼得：喜歡啊！

林華：太好了，我剛買了兩瓶加州出的紅葡萄酒。那我們就星期天見吧。

彼得：好，星期天見！

Kèwén (yī) *Text (1)*

Qǐng Chīfàn

拼音版

Lin Hua invites her friend Peter to her birthday party over the phone.

Bǐdé: Wèi, nǎ wèi?

Lín Huá: Shì Bǐdé ma? Wǒ shì Lín Huá.

Bǐdé: Lín Huá, nǐ hǎo! Zhǎo wǒ yǒu shì ma?

Lín Huá: Zhège Xīngqītiān shì wǒ de shēngrì. Wǒ xiǎng qǐng nǐ hé jǐ wèi tóngxué lái wǒ zhèr jù yi jù, chī dùn biànfàn.

Bǐdé: Nà tài máfan nǐ le.

Lín Huá: Yìdiǎnr yě bù máfan. Wǒ hé wǒ de shìyǒu dǎsuàn qǐng nǐmen chī wǒmen de náshǒucài!

Bǐdé: Hǎo a, xièxie! Wǒmen jǐ diǎnzhōng chīfàn ne?

Lín Huá: Nǐmen sì diǎnzhōng lái ba. Zánmen xiān liáoliáotiān, liù diǎn zuǒyòu chīfàn, zěnmeyàng?

Bǐdé: Xíng. Nà wǒ yě dài yí gè cài ba, wǒ kěyǐ zuò yí gè hóng- shāoròu.

Lín Huá: Hǎo a! Wǒmen yě chángchang nǐ zuò de cài.

Bǐdé: Wǒ zài dàidiǎnr kělè hé píjiǔ ba.

Lín huá: Búyòng le, yǐnliào yǐjīng yǒu le. Nǐmen xǐhuan hē pútao- jiǔ ma?

Bǐdé: Xǐhuan a!

Lín Huá: Tài hǎole, wǒ gāng mǎile liǎng píng Jiāzhōu chū de hóng- pútaojiǔ. Nà wǒmen jiù Xīngqītiān jiàn ba.

Bǐdé: Hǎo, Xīngqītiān jiàn!

生词（一）New Words (1)

	简体（繁體）	拼音	词性	解释
1	生日	shēngrì	n.	birthday 生日晚会 / 生日蛋糕 / 生日礼物 / 祝你生日快乐！
2	便饭	biànfàn	n.	simple meal 明晚请来我家吃便饭。
3	麻烦（煩）	máfan	v.	bother, trouble 我不想麻烦你。/ 太麻烦你了，不好意思。
4	打算	dǎsuàn	v./n.	plan 我打算周末去看电影。/ 你的生日有什么打算？ 聚会吗？
5	拿手菜	náshǒucài	n.	specialty (dish) 让我给你做两个拿手菜。/ 这个饭馆的拿手菜是麻婆豆腐。
6	红烧（紅燒）肉	hóngshāoròu	n.	pork braised in brown sauce 我每次回家都让妈妈给我做红烧肉。
7	尝（嚐）	cháng	v.	taste 尝一尝 / 请你尝尝这个菜好吃不好吃。
8	啤酒	píjiǔ	n.	beer 青岛啤酒 / 北京啤酒 / 喝啤酒 / 啤酒节
9	饮（飲）料	yǐnliào	n.	drink, beverage 可乐，茶，果汁都是饮料。
10	葡萄酒	pútaojiǔ	n.	wine 红葡萄酒 / 白葡萄酒 / 加州出产葡萄酒。
11	刚（剛）	gāng	adv.	just, barely 他刚离开，你还能赶上他。/ 我刚看了十分钟电视你就让我做作业！
12	瓶	píng	m.	bottle 一瓶酒 / 一瓶水 / 一瓶可乐
专有名词 Proper Noun				
	加州	Jiāzhōu	pn.	California (U.S.) 加州在美国的西部。

Exercise 1 🎧 💬✱

Listen to text (1) and answer the questions orally in Chinese.

1. Why did Lin Hua call Peter?

2. What did Lin Hua and her roommate prepare?

3. What did Peter offer?

4. What part of his offer was accepted and what part was declined?

5. What did Lin Hua just buy?

Exercise 2 📖

Read Text (1) and put the following sentences in the right order according to the contents of Text (1).

1. 彼得带了一个红烧肉。

2. 彼得和同学们四点钟来到林华的家。

3. 她请了彼得和几个同学到她家吃饭。

4. 林华已经准备了饮料，所以彼得没有带饮料。

5. 上星期天是林华的生日。

6. 他们在一起聊天吃饭，还喝了两瓶葡萄酒。

Exercise 3 🖎

Complete the following dialog according to the context.

A：小王，明天是我的生日。我请你吃饭。

B：_____，_____？

A：就在我家。我还有另外一个朋友也来。

B：_____？

A：不用带。我们家什么都有。

B：_____。

A：那也好。我知道红烧肉是你的拿手菜。

B：_____？

A：我那个朋友是我中学的同学。

B：_____？

男：你六点来吧。我们先聊天，然后吃饭。

Exercise 4

Translate the following sentences into Chinese characters and type them out.

1. I want to invite some friends for a gathering on my birthday.

2. Lin Hua invited her friends to eat a simple homemade meal at her place.

3. Do you know what this restaurant's best dish is?

4. After chatting for a while, they began to eat.

5. I will bring some coke and beer.

6. California has very good wine.

生日聚会

Peter goes to Lin Hua's birthday party. He writes about the party in his journal afterwards.

今天是林华的生日，我和几个同学参加了她的生日聚会。林华住在学校附近一个两室一厅的公寓里。她的室友叫王红，是从北京来的，她也参加了我们的聚会。我们每个人都带了自己做的菜。王红做了宫保鸡丁和北京泡菜，林华做了四川麻婆豆腐和酸辣汤，比尔做了西红柿炒鸡蛋。我本来不太会做中国菜，今天也学着做了一个红烧肉。我们几个同学还凑钱给林华买了一个生日蛋糕，上面用中英文写着"生日快乐"。

吃完饭以后，我们点着了蛋糕上的蜡烛，一起唱生日歌。林华许了个愿，吹灭蜡烛。我们问林华许了什么愿，她不肯说。王红笑着说："你们别问了。她是希望毕业后，能很快找到一个男朋友。"

生日聚會

Peter goes to Lin Hua's birthday party. He writes about the party in his journal afterwards.

今天是林華的生日，我和幾個同學參加了她的生日聚會。林華住在學校附近一個兩室一廳的公寓裏。她的室友叫王紅，是從北京來的，她也參加了我們的聚會。我們每個人都帶了自己做的菜。王紅做了宮保鷄丁和北京泡菜，林華做了四川麻婆豆腐和酸辣湯，比爾做了西紅柿炒鷄蛋。我本來不太會做中國菜，今天也學着做了一個紅燒肉。我們幾個同學還湊錢給林華買了一個生日蛋糕，上面用中英文寫着"生日快樂"。

吃完飯以後，我們點着了蛋糕上的蠟燭，一起唱生日歌。林華許了個願，吹滅蠟燭。我們問林華許了什麼願，她不肯説。王紅笑着説："你們別問了。她是希望畢業後，能很快找到一個男朋友。"

Kèwén (èr) *Text (2)*

Shēngrì Jùhuì

拼音版

Peter goes to Lin Hua's birthday party. He writes about the party in his journal afterwards.

Jīntiān shì Lín Huá de shēngrì, wǒ hé jǐ gè tóngxué cānjiāle tā de shēngrì jùhuì. Lín Huá zhù zài xuéxiào fùjìn yí gè liǎng shì yì tīng de gōngyù li. Tā de shìyǒu jiào Wáng Hóng, shì cóng Běijīng lái de, tā yě cānjiāle wǒmen de jùhuì. Wǒmen měi gè rén dōu dàile zìjǐ zuò de cài. Wáng Hóng zuòle gōngbǎojīdīng hé Běijīng pàocài, Lín Huá zuòle Sìchuān mápódòufu hé suānlàtāng, Bǐ'ěr zuòle xīhóngshì-chǎojīdàn. Wǒ běnlái bú tài huì zuò Zhōngguócài, jīntiān yě xuézhe zuòle yí gè hóngshāoròu. Wǒmen jǐ gè tóngxué hái còu qián gěi Lín Huá mǎile yí gè shēngrì dàngāo, shàngmian yòng Zhōng-Yīngwén xiězhe "shēngrì kuàilè".

Chīwán fàn yǐhòu, wǒmen diǎnzháole dàngāo shang de làzhú, yìqǐ chàng shēngrìgē. Lín Huá xǔle ge yuàn, chuīmiè làzhú. Wǒmen wèn Lín Huá xǔle shénme yuàn, tā bù kěn shuō. Wáng Hóng xiàozhe shuō: "Nǐmen bié wèn le. Tā shì xīwàng bìyè hòu, néng hěn kuài zhǎodào yí gè nánpéngyou."

生词（二）New Words (2)

	简体（繁體）	拼音	词性	解释
1	参（參）加	cānjiā	v.	participate 参加活动 / 参加一个小组
2	聚会（會）	jùhuì	n.	party 同学聚会 / 搞一个聚会
3	住	zhù	v.	live, stay 你住在哪里？/ 我住在朋友家。
4	室	shì	n.	room 教室 / 卧室 / 活动室 / 阅览室
5	厅（廳）	tīng	n.	living room 两室一厅的公寓
6	公寓	gōngyù	n.	apartment 公寓楼 / 住公寓 / 租一个公寓
7	宫保鸡（雞）丁	gōngbǎojīdīng	n.	Kung Pao chicken 我只会做宫保鸡丁。
8	泡菜	pàocài	n.	pickled vegetables 韩国泡菜很好吃。/ 你会做泡菜吗？/ 中国各地都有自己的泡菜。
9	麻婆豆腐	mápódòufu	n.	Mapo tofu 麻婆豆腐都是辣的吗？
10	酸辣汤（湯）	suānlàtāng	n.	sour and spicy soup 中国饭馆里一般有酸辣汤。
11	西红（紅）柿	xīhóngshì	n.	tomato 西红柿可以生吃。/ 西红柿营养很丰富。
12	炒	chǎo	v.	stir-fry 炒菜 / 炒饭 / 炒鸡蛋
13	凑	còu	v.	put together; amass 凑钱 / 凑份子 / 小王结婚的时候，办公室的人都凑了钱给他买礼物。
14	蛋糕	dàngāo	n.	cake 生日蛋糕 / 烤蛋糕
15	上面	shàngmian	n.	on top of 床上面 / 桌子上面放了一个大蛋糕。
16	点着（點著）	diǎnzháo	v.	light; set fire to 把蜡烛点着 / 你别把房子点着了。
17	蜡烛（蠟燭）	làzhú	n.	candle 点蜡烛 / 蜡烛的光 / 一根蜡烛
18	唱	chàng	v.	sing 唱歌 / 我们都唱了起来。
19	歌	gē	n.	song 歌曲 / 民歌 / 歌星 / 歌手
20	许（許）	xǔ	v.	make a wish 他吹蜡烛的时候，许了一个愿。
21	愿（願）	yuàn	n.	hope, wish 愿望 / 心愿 / 你有什么愿望？
22	吹	chuī	v.	blow 风把门吹开了。/ 他先许了一个愿，然后吹灭了蜡烛。

飞跃——汉语初级教程学生用书　下册

简体（繁體）	拼音	词性	解释
23 灭（滅）	miè	*v.*	extinguish; put out 灭火 / 别忘了把火灭了。
24 肯	kěn	*a.v.*	willing to 他不肯来。/ 你肯不肯帮我们？
25 希望	xīwàng	*v.*	wish for; hope 希望你参加我的生日聚会。
26 毕业（畢業）	bìyè	*v.*	graduate 毕业生 / 他是北大毕业的。
专有名词 Proper Noun			
四川	Sìchuān	*pn.*	Sichuan Province

Exercise 5

Listen to Text (2) and choose the right answer to the following questions.

1. What did Peter bring to the party?
   a. Mapo tofu.
   b. Braised pork.
   c. Kung Pao chicken.

2. What did they buy for Lin Hua?
   a. A birthday card.
   b. A birthday cake.
   c. A non-food gift.

3. What did Lin Hua do after dinner?
   a. She played music for them to dance to.
   b. She sang a song for her friends.
   c. She made a wish and blew out the candles.

4. What was Lin Hua's wish?
   a. Finding a good job.
   b. Finding a boyfriend.
   c. It is unknown.

Exercise 6

Read Text (2) and decide whether the following statements are true or false.

1. 林华和朋友们在彼得的公寓有一个聚会。	(	)
2. 林华住的地方离学校很近。	(	)
3. 她们的菜里有两个地方菜 (local dish)。	(	)
4. 王红送给林华一个生日蛋糕。	(	)

5. 林华觉得生日聚会上的许愿会变成真的。	（　　）
6. 林华现在是大学三年级的学生。	（　　）

Exercise 7 ✍

Fill in the blanks with the given words.

凑钱　　毕业　　宫保　　蛋糕　　豆腐　　烧肉　　公寓

张小星 ＿＿＿＿＿＿ 那天，我们 ＿＿＿＿＿＿ 给他买了一个大 ＿＿＿＿＿＿。在他的两室一厅的 ＿＿＿＿＿＿ 里，我们庆祝他毕业。他的室友也参加了。我们每个人都做了一个菜。我做的是红 ＿＿＿＿＿＿。李民带了一个麻婆 ＿＿＿＿＿＿。张小星的室友做了一个 ＿＿＿＿＿＿ 鸡丁。我们买的蛋糕上写着"祝你找到好工作"。

Exercise 8 👂

Listen to a conversation and decide whether the following statements are true or false.

1. The dialog takes place in a restaurant.	（　　）
2. It is a birthday dinner.	（　　）
3. They had braised pork, but not chicken.	（　　）
4. They also bought a cake from the restaurant.	（　　）

三、汉字 Chinese Characters

1. New characters in this lesson

序号	拼音	简 / 繁	部件	构词
1	bì	毕（畢）	比（ᄂ+匕）+ 十	毕业 / 毕竟 / 完毕
2	cān	参（參）	ム + 大 + 彡	参加 / 参军
3	cháng	尝（嘗）	⿱ + 冖 + 云	尝尝 / 品尝 / 尝味道
4	chàng	唱	口 + 昌（日 + 日）	唱歌 / 唱戏 / 唱机
5	chǎo	炒	火 + 少	炒菜 / 炒饭 / 炒年糕
6	chuān	川	川	四川 / 川菜 / 山川
7	chuī	吹	口 + 欠	吹蜡烛 / 吹气球 / 吹灯 / 吹牛

8	còu	凑	冫+奏（夫+天）	凑钱 / 凑合 / 凑份子
9	dīng	丁	丁	宫保鸡丁 / 布丁
10	dòu	豆	豆	豆腐 / 黄豆 / 红豆 / 豆芽
11	fán	烦（煩）	火+页	麻烦 / 烦人 / 烦恼
12	fǔ	腐	广+付（亻+寸）+肉	豆腐 / 腐化 / 腐烂 / 腐败
13	gāng	刚（剛）	冈+刂	刚刚 / 刚开始 / 刚才 / 刚好
14	gōng	宫	宀+口+口	宫保鸡丁 / 故宫
15	jiǔ	酒	氵+酉	葡萄酒 / 红酒 / 白酒 / 喝酒
16	jù	聚	取（耳+又）+乑	聚会 / 聚集 / 聚合
17	kěn	肯	止+月	不肯说 / 不肯来
18	là	辣	辛+束	酸辣汤 / 辣椒
19	là	蜡（蠟）	虫+昔(艹+日)	蜡烛 / 蜡笔 / 打蜡
20	má	麻	广+林（木+木）	麻烦 / 麻花 / 麻子
21	miè	灭（滅）	一+火	吹灭 / 灭火 / 熄灭 / 消灭
22	pào	泡	氵+包（勹+巳）	泡菜 / 泡水 / 泡澡
23	pí	啤	口+卑	啤酒 / 啤酒肚
24	píng	瓶	并+瓦	两瓶酒 / 瓶子 / 瓶装水
25	pú	葡	艹+匍（勹+甫）	葡萄酒 / 葡萄架
26	shì	柿	木+市	西红柿 / 柿子
27	suàn	算	竹+目+廾	打算 / 算术 / 算题
28	táo	萄	艹+匋（勹+缶）	葡萄 / 葡萄酒
29	tīng	厅（廳）	厂+丁	两室一厅 / 客厅 / 饭厅
30	wàng	望	亡+月+王	希望 / 看望 / 愿望
31	xī	希	乂+布	希望
32	xǔ	许（許）	讠+午	许愿 / 许可 / 不许
33	yù	寓	宀+禺	公寓 / 寓所
34	yuàn	愿（願）	原（厂+白+小）+心	愿望 / 自愿 / 志愿者
35	zhōu	州	州	加州 / 美洲 / 非洲 / 亚洲
36	zhú	烛（燭）	火+虫	蜡烛 / 烛光 / 烛火

| 37 | zhù | 住 | 亻 + 主 | 住在北京 / 住下 |

Exercise 1 ✎

Copy the following single-component characters with the correct stroke order in the spaces provided.

chuān	川	丿 川 川		
dīng	丁	一 丁		
dòu	豆	一 亠 亓 豆 豆 豆 豆		
zhōu	州	丶 丿 少 州 州 州		

Exercise 2 📖 ✎

Read the following sentences and choose the correct characters to fill in the blanks.

1. 今天是小王生日。她来到教室的时候，我们给她 _____ 了生日歌。（倡　唱　喝）
2. 我们几个人 _____ 钱给小王买了一个生日蛋糕。（楼　凑　奏）
3. 这个饭馆的麻婆豆 _____ 很好吃。（腐　府　服）
4. 这个长周末，我们到林华家 _____ 一下吧！（句　娶　聚）
5. 吃完饭一 _____ ，才知道花了三百多块钱。（蒜　算　笁）
6. 你带两 _____ 啤酒来就可以了。（瓶　苹　屏）
7. 中国烟台的葡 _____ 酒很有名。（桃　套　萄）
8. 我们 _____ 唱完生日歌，她就吹灭了蜡烛。（纲　钢　刚）

2. Common radicals (6)

(1) 刂 lìdāopáng

The radical 刂 is derived from the pictographic character 刀 (刀, dāo, knife). Thus, characters with it are originally related to knife. The radical is usually written as 刂 when standing on the right side and as 刀 when at the bottom, e.g. 别 (bié, pin on; don't); 刻 (kè, to cut, to carve); 刚 (gāng, strong, just); 剪 (jiǎn, scissors; to cut).

(2) 力 lì

The radical 力 is also a character meaning strength, thus characters with this radical are usually related to strength or power, e. g. 动 (dòng, to move); 助 (zhù, to help); 加 (jiā, to add); 努 (nǔ, exert efforts).

(3) ⺾ cǎozìtóu
The radical ⺾ is derived from the pictographic character Ψ Ψ, like grass. Thus, characters with the ⺾ radical are related to grass or plants, e.g. 草 (cǎo, grass); 花 (huā, flower); 菜 (cài, vegetable); 茶 (chá, tea).

(4) ⺮ (竹)zhúzìtóu
This radical is derived from the pictographic character ⺮ (竹 zhú, bamboo), symbolizing bamboo leaves. Thus, characters with this radical are mostly related to bamboo. The radical is always put on the top of a character, e.g. 笔 (bǐ, pen); 筷 (kuài, chopsticks); 篮 (lán, basket); 算 (suàn, to calculate).

Exercise 3 ✑

How many characters can you form with the following character components?

讠	亻	父	口	囗	氵	鸟	忄	贝	日	土
月	宀	力	刂	⺾	青	也	又	巴	十	元

四、语言点 Language Points

1. The use of 一点儿

Functioning as a compound of number-measure word, 一点儿 refers to a small amount "a little; a bit". Sometimes, 一 is dropped. It is often used after a verb or an adjective. When it is used after an adjective, it implies a comparison.

> **Verb / Adjective + 一点儿**

> (1) 我再带 (一) 点儿可乐和啤酒吧。
> Let me bring some coke and beer.

(2) 那天我没去，这件事我只知道<u>一点儿</u>。

I did not go there that day. I know only a little bit about this matter.

(3) 我试了试那件灰色的大衣，好像<u>小了（一）点儿</u>。

I tried the gray coat. It seems a little bit small.

(4) 约翰和大卫都在学中文，约翰的中文学得<u>好一点儿</u>。

Both John and David are learning Chinese. John's Chinese is a bit better.

一点儿 can be used with 也不 or 都不 to indicate a complete negation, meaning "not even a bit; not at all". 一 cannot be dropped in this usage.

Subject ＋ 一点儿 ＋ 也不 / 都不 ＋ Adjective / Verb

(5) "那太麻烦你了。""<u>一点儿也不</u>麻烦。"

"It will be too much trouble for you." "Not at all."

(6) 这件事我<u>一点儿都不</u>知道。

I know nothing about this matter.

(7) 他送给我的圣诞礼物，我<u>一点儿也不</u>喜欢。

I did not like the Christmas gift he gave me at all.

(8) 她昨天真的病了，她说的<u>一点儿都不</u>错。

She was indeed sick yesterday. She did not lie at all.

2. The comparison between 一点儿 and 有（一）点儿

We learned the usage of 有（一）点儿 in Lesson 14. 一点儿 and 有（一）点儿 appear similar; however, they are quite different. The nominal 一点儿 refers to a small amount while 有（一）点儿 functions as an adverb meaning "slightly". Usually, 一点儿 is put after an adjective or a verb while 有（一）点儿 is used before an adjective or a verb.

有（一）点儿 + Adjective /Verb	Adjective / Verb + 一点儿
有（一）点儿大　a bit too big	大一点儿　a bit bigger
有（一）点儿慢　a bit too slow	慢一点儿　a bit slower
有（一）点儿不舒服　a bit uncomfortable	知道一点儿　know a bit
有（一）点儿不喜欢　dislike a bit	有一点儿钱　have a bit money

(1) "这件大衣是不是<u>大了一点儿</u>？""没错，是<u>有点儿大</u>。"

"Is this overcoat a little too big?" "Yes, it is indeed a little too big."

(2) 咱们走慢一点儿吧，我<u>有点儿</u>累了！

Let's walk a little slower. I feel slightly tired.

(3) 昨天她<u>有点儿</u>不舒服，今天<u>好一点儿</u>了。

Yesterday she felt a little sick. Today she felt a little better.

(4) "我觉得今天有点儿冷。""是的，今天（比昨天）冷<u>一点儿</u>。"

"I feel a little cold today." "Yes, today is a bit colder (than yesterday)."

3. The emphatic use of 是

We learned various usages of the linking verb 是 in the previous lessons. In this lesson, we will learn the emphatic use of 是, which indicates a strong affirmation, meaning "indeed". The following are the pattern and examples:

> ## Subject + 是 + Verb / Adjective

(1) 她<u>是</u>希望毕业后，能很快找到一个男朋友。

What she hoped for is to find a boyfriend soon after graduation.

(2) 那天我<u>是</u>病了，不能到学校上课。

I was really sick that day and could not come to class.

(3) 这件西服<u>是</u>便宜，你在哪儿都找不到这样便宜的西服了。

This Western suit is indeed inexpensive. Nowhere else can you find such a bargain.

(4) 她<u>是</u>走了，再也不回来了！

She really has left and will never return.

Note: The above sentences are still grammatically correct without the emphatic 是.

4. The auxiliary verb 会 (2)

In Lesson 15, we learned 会 indicating possibility with the following example:

> 我想，我的学习成绩<u>会</u>慢慢好起来的。
> I think that my grades will improve gradually.

In this lesson, we will learn another usage of the auxiliary 会 to indicate one's ability, meaning "can".

(1) 我本来不太**会**做中国菜，今天也做了一个红烧肉。

I am not very good at cooking Chinese food, but today I prepared braised pork.

(2) 他**会**说好几种外语，中文、日文、法文他都**会**说。

He can speak several foreign languages. He can speak Chinese, Japanese and French.

(3) 现在，我**会**写三百多个汉字了。

Now I can write more than 300 Chinese characters.

(4) 玛丽去中国餐馆吃了几次饭，现在**会**用筷子了。

After eating in Chinese restaurants several times, Mary can now use chopsticks.

5. *The comparison between 能 and 会*

Both 能 and 会 can be translated into "can", but they are different in usage.

会 indicates an ability acquired through learning, while 能 does not. The following sentences show the differences:

(1) 我**会**开车，可是今天喝了酒，不**能**开了。

I know how to drive, but I cannot drive today because I have had some liquor.

(2) 她**会**做好几个中国菜，可是今天她有事不**能**来参加我们的聚会。

She can cook several Chinese dishes, but today she cannot come to our party due to other obligations.

(3) 我们都**会**游泳，可是今天太冷，不**能**游了。

We all can swim but today it is too cold for us to swim.

Exercise 1 👂

Listen to four short dialogs and choose the right answer to each question. Pay attention to the different meanings of the two phrases 一点儿 and 有一点儿 .

Dialog 1

What does Bill think of the Chinese tests?

a. The listening test is a bit too difficult.

b. The reading test is a bit too difficult.

c. Both tests are too difficult.

Dialog 2

Does Mark know how to order fresh flowers at the gift store online?

a. Yes, he knows a lot about it.

b. He only knows a little bit about it.

c. He knows everything about it.

Dialog 3

1. What was Xiaohua's comment on the Beijing roast duck ordered by her father?

    a. It's very delicious and reasonably priced.

    b. It's very delicious but a little bit too expensive.

    c. It's not very delicious but not expensive either.

2. What was the father's comment?

    a. It's really a very expensive dish.

    b. The price doesn't matter as long as the food is delicious.

    c. The price is not expensive at all.

Dialog 4

1. What is Mary's opinion about the blue jacket?

    a. good price

    b. a little bit too small

    c. good color but a little bit too big

2. What does Mary say about the black jacket?

    a. good color

    b. a little bit too small

    c. good color and price

Exercise 2

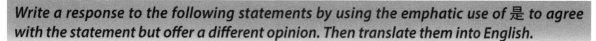

Write a response to the following statements by using the emphatic use of 是 ***to agree with the statement but offer a different opinion. Then translate them into English.***

Example: 这种巧克力很好吃。（不能多吃）

           这种巧克力是很好吃，可是也不能多吃。

           This kind of chocolate is indeed very delicious; however, one shouldn't eat too much.

1. 这道菜很好吃。（贵）

_____。

_____.

2. 他的中文说得很快。（不清楚）

_____ 。

_____ .

3. 上网买东西很方便。（逛商店）

_____ 。

_____ .

4. 我老家的夏天很热，常常是摄氏三十多度。（晚上凉快）

_____ 。

_____ .

Exercise 3 📖 ✎

Read the following sentences and fill in the blanks with the auxiliary verbs 会 and 能 .

1. 我的眼睛很好，_____ 看见很远的人。

2. 我妈妈很喜欢做饭，她 _____ 做不同国家的饭。

3. 你最近学习那么忙，还 _____ 来参加我的生日聚会吗？

4. 现在雨太大，我不 _____ 开车去你家。

5. 我 _____ 说中文，可是我不认识汉字。

6. 你 _____ 帮我找一件中号的灰色西装上衣吗？

7. 我知道你是学语言的，你 _____ 说多少种语言？

8. 我不 _____ 做中国菜，可是我喜欢吃中国菜。

Exercise 4

Translate the following dialogs into Chinese using the words in the parentheses. Type the Chinese characters on your computer.

Dialog 1

A: Can you join us to watch a movie tonight?

B: Sorry, I can't. We are going to have a quiz tomorrow and I have to review my lessons.（能）

Dialog 2

A: This pair of shoes is really good and I'd like to buy them.

B: It is indeed a good pair, but it is a bit too expensive.（是）

Dialog 3

A: Can you make a birthday cake?

B: No, I can't. My girlfriend can, she can make very delicious cakes.（会）

Dialog 4

A: Xiao Wen, are you free this long weekend? Let's have a picnic in the park.

B: Sorry, I can't go with you. I feel a little bit sick. (有一点儿)

Dialog 5

A: This cell phone is a little bit too expensive. Can I get it for a little bit cheaper?

B: How about a 20 percent discount?　(有一点儿, 一点儿)

Dialog 6

A: Do you like drinking beer?

B: No, I don't like beer at all. I like drinking coke. (一点儿也)

五、语言运用 Using the Language

Activity 1

Read the following texts and discuss what they are about.

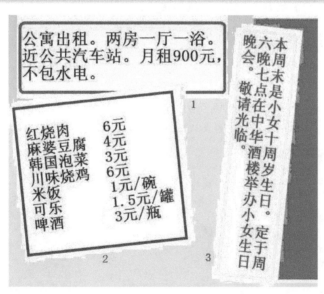

Activity 2

Read the following diary of Lin Hua and answer the questions orally in Chinese.

　　今天是我十八岁的生日。早晨起来，妈妈祝我生日快乐，爸爸说晚上在家里为我过生日。妈妈计划着晚上做什么好吃的，爸爸给我买好了生日礼物。晚上有很多朋友和我一起庆祝。他们都送了礼物给我。切蛋糕的时候，大家为我唱生日歌。吹蜡烛前，我为自己许下一个愿，希望我一年以后，能成为一个大学生。

Questions:

1. What is so special about today?

2. Where was the party held?

3. What did the father do?

4. What did her friends do in the evening?

5. What was her birthday wish?

Activity 3

You are Sun Yun. Your friend called you and left a message on your phone. Listen to the message and fill in the chart in pinyin and/or characters.

Caller	
The person mentioned in the phone call	
What the mentioned person wants to do	
The caller's plan	
Location of the caller's plan	
Reason for the location	
Things available at the location	
Information about the adjacent location	

Activity 4

Write as much as you can in Chinese on your computer about each of the following pictures using the words from the texts and the words given. Then talk with your partner in Chinese about what you wrote.

1

爷爷，奶奶，孙女，饭馆，蛋糕，吹，许愿

2

星期六，林华的生日，同学，生日聚会，凑钱，做了很多菜，带果汁，糖果

Activity 5 🎧 ✍

Xiao Li, Lin Hua, David and Miss Jiang are eating at a restaurant. Learn the names for the following dishes and then listen to their conversation. Write the price of each dish under the corresponding picture.

1. 冬瓜汤 dōngguātāng—winter melon soup

2. 炒肉片 chǎoròupiàn—stir-fried sliced meat

3. 烤鸡 kǎojī—roast chicken

4. 清蒸鱼 qīngzhēngyú—steamed fish

Activity 6 🗣

What do you say?

1. You want to tell the date of someone's birthday.

2. You want to suggest a party for someone.

3. You ask your friend what wish he/she made when blowing out the birthday candles.

4. You want to raise money for buying someone a birthday gift.

Activity 7 🗣

Role Play

Tomorrow is Wang Lin's birthday. You call Lin Hua to plan a birthday party as a surprise for Wang Lin. Discuss with Lin Hua the time, location, food and drink, flowers, and the birthday cake. Your partner will play the role of Lin Hua.

Sentences you may need to use:

我们给王林庆祝生日怎么样？

我们在……（时间、地点）给王林过生日。

我们会给王林买生日蛋糕。

你想我们要买什么吃的和喝的？

祝王林生日快乐。

王林吹蜡烛的时候可要许一个好愿。

Cultural Tip

The Chinese custom of birthday celebrations varies with location. In northern China, people used to eat "longevity noodles". The noodle is supposed to be a single long piece and should not break while being picked up with chopsticks. Steamed buns in the shape of peaches are also a form of traditional birthday food.

Nowadays, young people celebrate their birthdays in the Western way, with a cake, candles, and a dinner party.

第十八课
Lesson Eighteen
看电影
Watching Movies

一、导入 Lead-in

Exercise 1 📖 🗣

Look at the pictures below and describe them in Chinese.

这是我们城里的电影院。

我喜欢看卡通片。

丽莎的太极拳打得很不错。

李小龙的功夫片在网上就能看到。

After learning this lesson, you will be able to:

1. Talk about watching movies both in a theater and online.

2. Talk about famous movies and movie stars related to Chinese kung fu.

3. Recognize new characters in this lesson, and know the common radicals 女, 王, 木 and 禾.

4. Use 一 … 就, 如果 … 就 structures, the idiomatic expression 不怎么样, and the particle 得.

二、课文 Texts

课文（一）*Text (1)*

上网看电影

Lin Hua and Peter are talking about watching movies online.

林华：彼得，很久没去电影院看电影了吧！

彼得：是的。最近电影院放的那些电影都不怎么样。

林华：那你有没有去录像带
店租电影看呢？

Tips: a comment on current movies

彼得：没有。去录像带店租电影，又贵又不方便。

林华：那你就不看电影了吗？

彼得：当然不是！我常常直接上网看电影。

林华：在网上看电影不花钱吗？

彼得：电影网站很多是不收费的。但是，如果你想看新
的电影，那也得付点儿钱。

林华：虽然网上可以看免费电影，但我还是喜欢跟朋友
一起坐在真正的电影院里，一边吃爆米花，一边
看电影。

彼得：我知道！还可以一边看电影，一边聊天。

飞跃——汉语初级教程学生用书　下册

简体版

上網看電影

Lin Hua and Peter are talking about watching movies online.

林華：彼得，很久沒去電影院看電影了吧！

彼得：是的。最近電影院放的那些電影都不怎麼樣。

林華：那你有沒有去錄像帶店租電影看呢？

彼得：沒有。去錄像帶店租電影，又貴又不方便。

林華：那你就不看電影了嗎？

彼得：當然不是！我常常直接上網看電影。

林華：在網上看電影不花錢嗎？

彼得：電影網站很多是不收費的。但是，如果你想看新
　　　的電影，那也得付點兒錢。

林華：雖然網上可以看免費電影，但我還是喜歡跟朋友
　　　一起坐在真正的電影院裏，一邊吃爆米花，一邊
　　　看電影。

彼得：我知道！還可以一邊看電影，一邊聊天。

Kèwén (yī) Text (1)

Shàngwǎng Kàn Diànyǐng

Lin Hua and Peter are talking about watching movies online.

Lín Huá: Bǐdé, hěn jiǔ méi qù diànyǐngyuàn kàn diànyǐng le ba!

Bǐdé: Shìde. Zuìjìn diànyǐngyuàn fàng de nàxiē diànyǐng dōu bù
　　　zěnmeyàng.

Lín Huá: Nà nǐ yǒu méiyǒu qù lùxiàngdàidiàn zū diànyǐng kàn ne?

Bǐdé: Méiyǒu. Qù lùxiàngdàidiàn zū diànyǐng, yòu guì yòu bù
　　　fāngbiàn.

Lín Huá: Nà nǐ jiù bú kàn diànyǐng le ma?

Bǐdé: Dāngrán bú shì! Wǒ chángcháng zhíjiē shàngwǎng kàn diànyǐng.

Lín Huá: Zài wǎngshang kàn diànyǐng bù huāqián ma?

Bǐdé: Diànyǐng wǎngzhàn hěn duō shì bù shōufèi de. Dànshì, rúguǒ nǐ xiǎng kàn xīn de diànyǐng, nà yě děi fùdiǎnr qián.

Lín Huá: Suīrán wǎngshang kěyǐ kàn miǎnfèi diànyǐng, dàn wǒ háishi xǐhuan gēn péngyou yìqǐ zuò zài zhēnzhèng de diànyǐngyuàn li, yìbiān chī bàomǐhuā, yìbiān kàn diànyǐng.

Bǐdé: Wǒ zhīdao! Hái kěyǐ yìbiān kàn diànyǐng, yìbiān liáotiān.

生词（一）New Words (1)

	简体（繁體）	拼音	词性	解释
1	电（電）影院	diànyǐngyuàn	n.	cinema; movie theater 我在电影院门口等你。
2	录（錄）像带（帶）	lùxiàngdài	n.	video cassette 现在很少人用录像带了，都用光盘了。
3	租	zū	v.	rent 租书 / 租电影 / 租光盘 / 租公寓
4	直接	zhíjiē	adv.	directly 放学后我直接回家。/ 请你直接告诉我，你来不来？
5	收费（費）	shōufèi	v.	charge a fee 有些公园是不收费的。/ 请到收费处交钱。
6	如果	rúguǒ	conj.	if; in case 如果我们三点放学，就去逛街。
7	坐	zuò	v.	sit, take 坐车 / 坐地铁 / 坐飞机 / 坐在电影院看电影
8	真正	zhēnzhèng	adj.	genuine, real 我还是喜欢真正的电影院。/ 真正的古玩很贵。
9	爆米花	bàomǐhuā	n.	popcorn 不少人看电影的时候喜欢吃爆米花。

Exercise 1 🎧

Listen to Text (1) and decide whether the following statements are true or false.		
1. Peter does not have time to go to the movie theater.	(	)
2. Peter is unwilling to rent movies from movie stores.	(	)
3. One does not pay to watch online movies.	(	)

4. Lin Hua likes watching movies in the theater.	( )
5. Peter does not like Lin Hua's idea about where to watch movies.	( )

Exercise 2 📖 🗣

Read Text (2) and answer the following questions orally in Chinese.

1. 彼得最近常常去电影院吗？为什么？

2. 林华常常在哪儿看电影？

3. 网上什么样的电影免费？

4. 林华看电影的时候喜欢做什么？

Exercise 3 ✍

Fill in the blanks with Chinese characters according to the English given, and then translate the sentences into English.

1. 那家电影院放的电影 _____(not so good)。

_____

2. 到 _____(video rental) 租电影是不是很贵？

_____

3. 用快递寄东西又快又 _____(convenient)。

_____

4. 你不用问我怎么去那里，你 _____(go online directly) 查地图就行了。

_____

5. "请问，我在哪儿 _____(pay)？""到前边那个 _____(cashier) 付就可以了。"

_____

6. "你爱吃 _____(popcorn) 吗？""我只在电影院吃。"

_____

Exercise 4 👂 📖

You will hear three statements followed by four responses. Choose the most logical response to the statement.

1. a. 学校的电影院是去年才有的。

　　b. 看来我们得去租一个电影看了。

　　c. 中国电影很有意思。

　　d. 我在电影院碰见小王了。

2. a. 我不想用爸爸的钱看电影。

b. 今天你去电影院了吗?

c. 同学们很喜欢在电影院里聊天。

d. 有啊，只有新的电影才要钱。

3. a. 电影院门口有卖爆米花的。

b. 我们带一个红烧肉吧。

c. 北京泡菜很好吃。

d. 林华说那部电影不怎么样。

课文（二）*Text (2)*

电影迷

Lisa is a movie fan.

丽莎非常喜欢看电影。她一有空儿就去看电影。城里哪个电影院放新的电影，网上哪个网站有免费的电影，哪个电影明星最近演了什么电影，她都知道得很清楚。她什么电影都爱看，卡通片、故事片、功夫片、喜剧片，她都喜欢。大家都说丽莎是个电影迷。

丽莎看过好些中国电影，《花木兰》《少林寺》等电影她都看过。她特别喜欢李小龙的中国功夫片，看过了以后，她迷上了中国武术。她觉得，学习中国武术不但可以锻炼身体，还可以了解和学习很多中国文化。她在中国城的一家武术学校学习了两年，现在她的太极拳打得很不错，汉语也说得很流利。

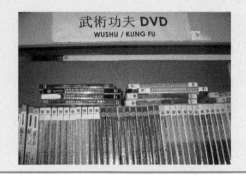

電影迷

繁体版

Lisa is a movie fan.

麗莎非常喜歡看電影。她一有空兒就去看電影。城裏哪個電影院放新的電影，網上哪個網站有免費的電影，哪個電影明星最近演了什麼電影，她都知道得很清楚。她什麼電影都愛看，卡通片、故事片、功夫片、喜劇片，她都喜歡。大家都說麗莎是個電影迷。

麗莎看過好些中國電影，《花木蘭》《少林寺》等電影她都看過。她特別喜歡李小龍的中國功夫片，看過了以後，她迷上了中國武術。她覺得，學習中國武術不但可以鍛煉身體，還可以了解和學習很多中國文化。她在中國城的一家武術學校學習了兩年，現在她的太極拳打得很不錯，漢語也說得很流利。

Kèwén (èr) *Text (2)*

Diànyǐngmí

拼音版

Lisa is a movie fan.

Lìshā fēicháng xǐhuan kàn diànyǐng. Tā yì yǒu kòngr jiù qù kàn diànyǐng. Chéng li nǎge diànyǐngyuàn fàng xīn de diànyǐng, wǎngshang nǎge wǎngzhàn yǒu miǎnfèi de diànyǐng, nǎge diànyǐng míngxīng zuìjìn yǎnle shénme diànyǐng, tā dōu zhīdao de hěn qīngchu. Tā shénme diànyǐng dōu ài kàn, kǎtōng piàn, gùshipiàn, gōngfupiàn, xǐjùpiàn, tā dōu xǐhuan. Dàjiā dōu shuō Lìshā shì ge diànyǐngmí.

Lìshā kànguo hǎoxiē Zhōngguó diànyǐng, "Huā Mùlán", "Shàolín Sì" děng diànyǐng tā dōu kànguo. Tā tèbié xǐhuan Lǐ Xiǎolóng de Zhōngguó gōngfupiàn. Kànguòle yǐhòu, tā míshàngle

Zhōngguó wǔshù. Tā juéde, xuéxí Zhōngguó wǔshù búdàn kěyǐ duànliàn shēntǐ, hái kěyǐ liǎojiě hé xuéxí hěn duō Zhōngguó wénhuà. Tā zài Zhōngguóchéng de yì jiā wǔshù xuéxiào xuéxíle liǎng nián, xiànzài tā de tàijíquán dǎ de hěn búcuò, Hànyǔ yě shuō de hěn liúlì.

生词（二）New Words (2)

	简体（繁體）	拼音	词性	解释
1	空儿（兒）	kòngr	n.	spare time; free time 你有空儿吗？
2	免费（費）	miǎnfèi	v.	free of charge 这家图书馆常常有免费的旧书可以拿走。
3	明星	míngxīng	n.	star, celebrity 电影明星／大明星
4	演	yǎn	v.	perform 演出／演员／演电影
5	清楚	qīngchu	adj.	clear 这个字不清楚。／你看得清楚吗？
6	爱（愛）	ài	v.	love, like 她什么电影都爱看。
7	卡通	kǎtōng	n.	cartoon 日本的卡通片很好看。
8	片	piàn	n.	movie 武打片／故事片／纪录片
9	故事	gùshi	n.	fiction, story 讲故事／说故事／编故事
10	喜剧（劇）	xǐjù	n.	comedy《第十二夜》是喜剧。
11	迷	mí	n./v.	fan/become very interested in 电影迷／球迷／戏迷／她迷上了中国武术。
12	好些	hǎoxiē	adj.	a lot of 他收藏了好些古钱币。
13	武术（術）	wǔshù	n.	Chinese martial arts 中国武术／武术家／武术学校／练武术
14	锻炼（鍛煉）	duànliàn	v.	do physical exercise 锻炼身体／锻炼意志／我喜欢早上锻炼。
15	了（瞭）解	liǎojiě	v.	understand; learn something about 他对功夫很了解。／我想向你了解一下小王的学习。
16	拳	quán	n.	fist; a set of movements of fist fighting 太极拳／长拳

	简体（繁體）	拼音	词性	解释
17	流利	liúlì	*adj.*	fluent 他说中文说得很流利。/ 他能说一口流利的汉语。
	专有名词 Proper Nouns			
1	花木兰（蘭）	Huā Mùlán	*pn.*	Hua Mulan, legendary woman warrior; protagonist of the Chinese fiction movie Hua Mulan; protagonist of the Hollywood cartoon Mulan
2	少林寺	Shàolín Sì	*pn.*	The Shaolin Temple; a Chinese fiction movie
3	李小龙（龍）	Lǐ Xiǎolóng	*pn.*	Bruce Lee

Exercise 5 🦻 🗣

Listen to Text (2) and answer the questions orally in Chinese.

1. How does Lisa like movies? Give an example.

2. Are the kinds of movies she likes limited?

3. What has Lisa learned from movies? Give an example.

4. Where did she practice for two years? What is the result of her practice?

Exercise 6 📖 🗣

Read Text (2) and answer the questions orally in Chinese.

1. 什么东西玛丽知道得很清楚？

2. 玛丽喜欢看什么电影？

3. 李小龙是什么人？

4. 玛丽觉得练习中国功夫有什么好处？

Exercise 7 ✍

Fill in the blanks with the given words.

流利　　中文　　打　　练习　　文化　　功夫

约翰是个电影迷。他在中国一所大学学 _____ 的时候，喜欢看中国 _____ 片。他说看功夫片不但可以 _____ 听中文，还可以学习中国 _____。在学校里，他选修了武术课，学会了 _____ 少林拳。现在他的汉语说得很 _____，拳也打得不错。

Exercise 8

Translate the following sentences into Chinese characters.

1. My elder brother is a movie fan. Whenever there is a new movie he always goes to see it.

_____

2. I do not like kung fu movies. I like fiction and cartoon movies.

_____

3. Many people started learning Chinese kung fu after watching Bruce Lee's movies.

_____

4. Practicing taichi not only builds up one's body, but also helps one learn about Chinese culture.

_____

三、汉字 Chinese Characters

1. New characters in this lesson

序号	拼音	简 / 繁	部件	构词
1	ài	爱（愛）	⺥＋冖＋友	爱好 / 亲爱的 / 爱情
2	bào	爆	火＋暴（日＋共＋氺）	爆米花 / 爆炸
3	chǔ	楚	林（木＋木）＋疋	清楚 / 清清楚楚
4	duàn	锻（鍛）	钅＋段（𠃊＋殳）	锻炼
5	fù	付	亻＋寸	付钱 / 付款 / 付帐单
6	gù	故	古＋攵	故事 / 故乡 / 故人 / 故意
7	jiě	解	角＋刀＋牛	了解 / 解开 / 解放
8	jù	剧（劇）	居（尸＋古）＋刂	电视剧 / 喜剧 / 话剧
9	lán	兰（蘭）	⺌＋三	花木兰 / 兰花 / 玉兰树
10	lì	利	禾＋刂	流利 / 顺利 / 胜利
11	liàn	炼（煉）	火＋东	锻炼
12	liǎo	了 / 瞭	了	了解 / 明了 / 一目了然
13	liú	流	氵＋㐬（云＋儿）	流利 / 流泪 / 流感
14	lóng	龙（龍）	龙	李小龙 / 中国龙 / 龙虎斗

15	lù	录（錄）	彐+氺	录像带 / 录影 / 录音机 / 纪录
16	mí	迷	米+辶	功夫迷 / 篮球迷 / 歌迷
17	mǐ	米	米	玉米 / 大米 / 米饭
18	miǎn	免	免	免费 / 免票 / 免谈
19	mù	木	木	花木兰 / 木头 / 木材 / 树木
20	piàn	片	片	片场 / 电影片 / 纪录片
21	shù	术（術）	术	武术 / 学术 / 算术
22	sì	寺	土+寸	少林寺 / 寺院
23	tōng	通	甬（マ+用）+辶	卡通片 / 通过 / 通信
24	wǔ	武	止+弋	武术 / 武术学校 / 武功
25	yǎn	演	氵+寅	演员 / 演习
26	zū	租	禾+且	租电影 / 租房 / 出租
27	zuò	坐	人+人+土	坐车 / 坐地铁 / 坐下

Exercise 1 ✍

Copy the following single-component characters with correct stroke order in the spaces provided.

lóng	龙	一 ナ 尢 龙 龙	
mǐ	米	丶 丷 ⺍ 半 米 米	
mù	木	一 十 才 木	
piān	片	丿 丿' 尸 片	
shù	术	一 十 才 木 术	

Exercise 2 📖 ✍

Read the following sentences and choose the correct characters to fill in the blanks.

1. 每天下午下课后，我到操场 _____ 炼一个小时。（段　煅　锻）

2. 她喜欢看中国大陆的电视 _____。（剧　句　居）

3. 玛丽的汉语说得很流 _____。（利　莉　例）

4. 玛丽开始学中文以后，就 _____ 上了中国饮食文化。（谜　迷　眯）

5. 你想 _____ 什么样的影片？（租　组　祖）

6. 玛丽说她最爱看的电影是 _____ 事片。（姑　故　古）

7. 我喜欢 _____ 在电影院里，一边看电影，一边吃爆米花。（座　昨　坐）

8. 你去河南旅游的时候，一定要去看看少林 _____。（待　侍　寺）

2. Common radicals (7)

(1) 王 wánzìpáng

The radical 王 was derived from the character 玉 (yù), meaning jade. It is always used as a radical on the left-hand side of a character. Characters with this radical are originally related to jade, e.g. 玩 (wán, to play); 球 (qiú, ball); 现 (xiàn, present, current); 珠 (zhū, pearl).

(2) 木 mùzìpáng

The radical 木 is also a character, which is derived from the pictographic character 朿, indicating a tree. Thus, characters with this radical are originally related to wood or plants, e.g. 林 (lín, forest); 校 (xiào, school); 机 (jī, machine); 楼 (lóu, building); 杯 (bēi, cup); 桌 (zhuō, table).

(3) 禾 hémùpáng

The radical 禾 is also a character. It is derived from the pictographic character 禾 (禾 hé), a simplified picture of ripe rice. Thus, characters with this radical are originally related to grain or crops, e.g. 种 (zhòng, to plant); 租 (zū, to rent); 和 (hé, mild; and); 秋 (qiū, fall, autumn); 季 (jì, season).

(4) 夂 fǎnwénpáng

The radical 夂 is derived from a pictographic character showing a hand holding a stick, indicating the meaning of "control". Thus, characters with this radical are originally related to "control". This radical is always on the right side of a character, e.g. 放 (fàng, set free); 收 (shōu, to collect); 教 (jiāo, to teach); 改 (gǎi, to correct); 政 (zhèng, politics).

Exercise 3

Fill in the chart below by writing down as many characters as you can.

Radical	Meaning of the radical	Characters that you have learned containing this radical
攵		
王		
木		
禾		

四、语言点 Language Points

1. The idiomatic expression 不怎么样

The idiomatic expression 不怎么样 means "not very good; relatively bad".

> (1) 最近电影院放的那些电影都<u>不怎么样</u>。
> The movies shown recently at the theater are not so good.
>
> (2) "小王，你的中文学得怎么样了？" "<u>不怎么样</u>，昨天考试才得了 70 分。"
> "Xiao Wang, how is your Chinese going?" "Not so good. I only got a 70 on my test yesterday."
>
> (3) 我去过那个餐馆几次，觉得<u>不怎么样</u>。
> I have been to that restaurant several times and I don't think it is very good.
>
> (4) 人人都说她的新衣服很好看，我觉得<u>不怎么样</u>。
> Everyone says her new dress is pretty, but I don't think so.

2. The 如果 … 就 structure

In Lesson 10, we learned the 要是 … 就 structure with the example sentence 要是下雨，就在家里睡觉好了。(If it rains, we'll sleep at home.) In this lesson, we will learn a similar structure 如果 … 就，in which 如果 can be replaced by 要是 without changing the meaning.

> 如果 / 要是 + First Clause, Subject + 就 / 会 + Verb + (Object)

In the 如果 / 要是 … (就) structure, 如果 / 要是 is used in the first clause introducing a supposition or a hypothesis; and 就 in the second clause telling the result. The subject of

155

the two clauses may or may not be the same.

Note that 就 is an adverb that must always be put after the subject. Sometimes, 就 can be replaced by or combined with 会.

(1) 如果你想看新的电影，那你就得付点儿钱。
    If you want to watch a new movie, you need to pay.
(2) 明天如果 / 要是下雨，我们就不去露营了。
    If it rains tomorrow, we will not go camping.
(3) 如果 / 要是你有很多钱，你会做什么?
    What would you do if you have a lot of money?
(4) 如果 / 要是我是你，那我就肯定不会去。
    If I were you, I would surely not go.

3. The structural particle 得

The principal function of the structural particle 得 is to link a complement, often a phrase, to a verb or an adjective.

Subject + Verb /Adjective + 得 + Complement

(1) 你来得正好。我忘了带手表，不知道时间，现在几点了?
    You came at the right moment. I forgot my watch at home and do not know what time it is now.
(2) 今天我和几个同学在公园野餐，玩儿得很高兴。
    Today my classmates and I had a good time having a picnic in the park.
(3) 你的中文已经说得很不错了。
    You already speak Chinese very well.
(4) 时间过得真快! 你去中国学习已经一个多月了。
    How time flies! It has been more than a month since you left for China to study.
(5) 啊，你不舒服? 是不是昨天晚上上网睡得太晚了?
    You don't feel well? Did you go to bed late because you stayed online?
(6) 贝贝今天突然病了，而且看起来病得挺厉害的。
    Beibei suddenly fell sick today and it seems he is seriously ill.
(7) 现在她的太极拳打得很不错，汉语也说得很好。
    Now she practices taichi very well and speaks Chinese very well, too.

4. The verb complement 上

The word 上 has various usages. In this lesson, we will learn 上 as a verb complement to indicate "begin and keep on".

> **Verb + 上 (on) → Verb Complement Compound**

患 + 上 → 患上 (contract a disease)
迷 + 上 → 迷上 (be addicted to)
爱 + 上 → 爱上 (fall in love with)
穿 + 上 → 穿上 (put on clothes)
写 + 上 → 写上 (write down something)

(1) 她说我患上了网瘾，整天在电脑上玩游戏，和朋友聊天，很晚了还不睡觉，所以成绩不好。
   She said I was addicted to the Internet because I play games on the computer and chat with friends all day long and stay up very late. She said that was why my grades were bad.

(2) 她特别喜欢李小龙的中国功夫片，看过了以后，她迷上了中国武术。
   She especially likes Bruce Lee's kung fu movies. She became a fan of Chinese kung fu after watching his movies.

(3) 在中国学了一年的中文以后，他爱上了一个中国女孩儿。
   He fell in love with a Chinese girl after learning Chinese in China for a year.

5. The 一 … 就 construction

The 一 … 就 construction indicates that one action occurs immediately after another, meaning "as soon as…".

> **Subject 1 + 一 + Verb 1, (Subject 2) + 就 + Verb 2**

In the 一 … 就 construction, subject 1 and subject 2 may or may not be the same. If there is only one subject, like in examples (1) and (2), the 一 … 就 construction will be simplified as a phrase put after the subject. If there are two subjects like in the following examples (3) and (4), there will be two clauses separated by a comma.

(1) 丽莎非常喜欢看电影。她一有空儿就去看电影。

Lisa likes watching movies very much. Whenever she has time she goes to see a movie.

(2) 我的弟弟一放学就上网玩儿电子游戏。

My younger brother goes online to play games as soon as he gets out of school.

(3) 老师一说我们就明白了。

As soon as the teacher explained it, we understood.

(4) 小狗一生病，林华就急了。

As soon as the puppy fell sick, Lin Hua became deeply worried.

Exercise 1 👂 ✍

Listen to three short dialogs and answer the questions in Chinese characters. Pay attention to the idiomatic expression 不怎么样.

Dialog 1 Question: 比尔他们昨天的野餐怎么样？	Answer:
Dialog 2 Question: 小红觉得江小姐上个月买的房子怎么样？	Answer:
Dialog 3 Question: 李文觉得他中文现在说得怎么样？	Answer:

Exercise 2 ✍

Translate the following sentences into Chinese characters using the 如果 ... 就 / 会 construction. You may type them out on your computer.

1. If I miss home, I will call my parents.

_____

2. If it won't rain tomorrow, we will go camping.

_____

3. If you can't cook, you may buy a dish from a Chinese restaurant.

_____

4. If you don't understand, you should ask the teacher.

_____

5. If I am not happy, I would go to the movie theater to see a movie.

_____

飞跃——汉语初级教程学生用书　下册

6. If I get a 100 on my exam, my parents will buy me a gift.

_____

Exercise 3

Complete the following sentences with the structural particle 得, based on the information given in the parentheses.

1. 他虽然学跳舞的时间不长，_____。(but he dances very well)

2. 虽然她只学了一年的中文，_____。(but she speaks Chinese very fluently)

3. _____很快就是母亲节了。(Time flies really fast)

4. 他三天没来上课了，_____。(it seems he is seriously ill)

5. 她是很有钱，_____。(but she has an unhappy life)

6. 彼得今天早上上课迟到了，_____。(went to bed too late last night because of staying online)

Exercise 4

Translate the following sentences into Chinese using 上 as a verb complement.

1. You look beautiful wearing this shirt.

_____

2. Mary became addicted to Chinese martial arts as soon as she arrived in China.

_____

3. Peter fell in love with skiing when he was in high school.

_____

4. This is your book. Please write your name on the first page.

_____

5. Can you close the door?

_____

Exercise 5

Follow the example and rewrite the sentences using the 一 ... 就 construction.

Example: 我每天回到家就上网查我的邮件。
        我每天一回到家就上网查我的邮件。

1. 我姐姐大学毕业以后就开始在银行工作。

_____。

2. 我每天放学回家以后带小狗出去散步。

_____。

3. 他到了北京以后给我打了一个电话。

_____。

4. 丽莎有时间就打太极拳。

_____。

5. 冬天到了他就和朋友们一起去滑雪。

_____。

6. 今天早上我起床后觉得很不舒服。

_____。

7. 他很爱音乐，有钱就去买音乐光盘。

_____。

8. 中国人听你说话会知道你学中文的时间不长。

_____。

Exercise 6

Complete the following sentences using proper structures.

1. 如果我有很多钱，_____。

2. 我们一下课，_____。

3. 虽然天很冷，_____。

4. 如果明天下大雨，_____。

5. 我一到十八岁，_____。

6. 虽然我们没有很多钱，_____。

7. 这部电影我看过了，_____。

8. 如果我的老师病了，_____。

五、语言运用 Using the Language

Activity 1 📖 ✎

Match the following news titles in Column I with the English in Column II.

Column I	Column II
( ) 1. 上海电影节今天开始。	a. New Movies During Spring Festival
( ) 2. 电影院今日上映美国大片《功夫熊猫》。	b. Cartoon Movies Dubbed in Local Dialects
( ) 3. 一录像带店出租黄色录像被关门。	c. Shanghai Movie Festival Kicks off
( ) 4. 网上电影出租受到网友欢迎。	d. The Shutting Down of a Video Rental Store
( ) 5. 四川出现四川话卡通片。	e. *Kung Fu Panda* Released
( ) 6. 春节期间将有百部春节故事片上演。	f. Jackie Chan Chats with Fans Online
( ) 7. 电影明星成龙跟网友聊天。	g. Online Movie Rentals

Activity 2 👂 ✎

You overheard a male and a female talking about movies. Fill in the gist of their conversation in the following chart.

Male	Female

Activity 3 ✎

You go to see a friend but he is not at home. Leave him a written note telling him that you have rented a nice Chinese movie and you want to watch it with him. Tell him to contact you as soon as possible through the contact number provided. Type the note out on your computer.

Activity 4 📖 💬

Read the photo descriptions and sum up the similarities and differences between Mr. Li and Mr. Zhang.

| 李老师是个电影迷。学校的图书馆里有几台电视机，这种电视机可以放电影光盘。李老师下班后，喜欢到图书馆去看电影光盘。她看的电影都是新出来的故事片，她很少看功夫片。有时候她也看自己租来的电影。 | 张老师工作很忙，可是他又特别爱看电影。怎样才能有时间看电影呢？张老师家的电脑可以上网。他喜欢在家里一边工作，一边在网上看电影。他什么电影都看，故事片、纪录片，新电影、老电影他都看。 |

Activity 5 💬

Give an oral interpretation of the following passage in Chinese.

Yesterday I went to the movie rental store to rent a movie. When I watched it at home, I found it was rather old. Still, I watched it with a friend. My friend said he liked old movies a lot. He said that he often watched old movies online, but he also said that if he were to watch a movie with his girlfriend, he would prefer the theater, because they could eat popcorn while watching the movie.

Activity 6 💬

Role Play

You want to invite a friend to a movie. Call your friend to ask about the movies he/she likes the best and suggest a movie at a certain time and place. Also suggest some post-movie activities.

Sentences you may need to use:

你喜欢什么电影？
这个周末电影院有一个新电影。
我们一起去看好吗？
看完电影我们可以去做……

Activity 7

What do you say?

1. Call the movie rental store to see if they stock Chinese kung fu movies.

2. You like new movies more than old movies.

3. You learned a lot about Chinese culture by watching Chinese movies. They helped you improve your listening, too.

4. You not only watch movies on Youtube, but also rent movies online. Renting movies online is both convenient and inexpensive.

5. Make an appointment with your friend to meet at the theater. There is a new release.

Activity 8

The following pictures represent a story of three friends going to a movie. You are one of the friends. Tell this story to your partner and then type it out on your computer. Your story should have a beginning, middle and an end.

Cultural Tip

Chinese martial arts, or kung fu, consists of many different styles. There is a common saying that the southern style features the use of punches, and the northern style features the use of kicking. Kung fu styles are also associated with the religions of Buddhism and Taoism. The former's typical representative is Shaolin kung fu and the latter's, Wudang Mountain kung fu. Perhaps the most well-known  Taoist kung fu style is taichi, now widely practiced as a popular form of exercise.

第十九课 问路
Lesson Nineteen
Asking Directions

一、导入 Lead-in

Exercise 1 📖 🗣

Look at the pictures below and describe them in Chinese.

这儿就是旧金山的中国城。

公共厕所就在那儿。

考驾照要通过笔试和路试两个考试。

爸妈送给我一辆新汽车。

After learning this lesson, you will be able to:

1. Ask and give directions to a certain place with common landmarks.
2. Narrate one's past experience in getting a driver's license.
3. Recognize new characters in this lesson, and know the common radicals 钅, 走, 马 and 车.
4. Use 对 … 来说 structure, expressions of 不好意思, 离 and 从, and the particle 地.

二、课文 Texts

课文（一）*Text (1)*

去中国城怎么走？

A tourist asks Li Wen how to get to Chinatown.

游客：请问，去中国城怎么走？ **Tips:** a common way to ask for directions

李文：中国城离这儿挺远的，您是坐车去还是开车去？

游客：我是从中国来的游客，我想坐车去。

李文：那您坐地铁去吧！坐三站地铁就到了。

游客：地铁站在哪儿？

李文：从这儿一直往前走，过了第一个十字路口，地铁站就在你的右手边。

游客：上了地铁以后，在哪一站下车呢？

李文：在市场大街站下车。下车后，您先出站，再向左拐，您会看见一些中国商店的牌子。 **Tips:** how to give directions 沿着那条大街一直往前走，过了两个红绿灯，就到中国城了。

游客：谢谢您！不好意思，我还想问一下，中国城有公共洗手间吗？ **Tips:** how to ask an awkward question

李文：有，我知道那儿有一个公共厕所。

游客：太谢谢您了！

李文：不客气。

去中國城怎么走?

繁体版

A tourist asks Li Wen how to get to Chinatown.

游客：請問，去中國城怎麼走?

李文：中國城離這兒挺遠的，您是坐車去還是開車去?

游客：我是從中國來的游客，我想坐車去。

李文：那您坐地鐵去吧！坐三站地鐵就到了。

游客：地鐵站在哪兒?

李文：從這兒一直往前走，過了第一個十字路口，地鐵站就在你的右手邊。

游客：上了地鐵以後，在哪一站下車呢?

李文：在市場大街站下車。下車後，您先出站，再向左拐，您會看見一些中國商店的牌子。沿着那條大街一直往前走，過了兩個紅綠燈，就到中國城了。

游客：謝謝您！不好意思，我還想問一下，中國城有公共洗手間嗎?

李文：有，我知道那兒有一個公共廁所。

游客：太謝謝您了！

李文：不客氣。

Qù Zhōngguóchéng Zěnme Zǒu?

拼音版

A tourist asks Li Wen how to get to Chinatown.

Yóukè: Qǐngwèn, qù Zhōngguóchéng zěnme zǒu?

Lǐ Wén: Zhōngguóchéng lí zhèr tǐng yuǎn de, nín shì zuòchē qù háishì kāichē qù?

Yóukè: Wǒ shì cóng Zhōngguó lái de yóukè, wǒ xiǎng zuòchē qù.

Lǐ Wén: Nà nín zuò dìtiě qù ba! Zuò sān zhàn dìtiě jiù dào le.

Yóukè: Dìtiězhàn zài nǎr?

Lǐ Wén: Cóng zhèr yìzhí wǎng qián zǒu, guòle dì-yī gè shízìlùkǒu, dìtiězhàn jiù zài nǐ de yòushǒu biān.

Yóukè: Shàngle dìtiě yǐhòu, zài nǎ yí zhàn xià chē ne?

Lǐ Wén: Zài shìchǎng-dàjiēzhàn xià chē, xià chē hòu, nín xiān chū zhàn, zài xiàng zuǒ guǎi, nín huì kànjiàn yìxiē Zhōngguó shāngdiàn de páizi. Yánzhe nà tiáo dàjiē yìzhí wǎng qián zǒu, guòle liǎng gè hónglǜdēng, jiù dào Zhōngguóchéng le.

Yóukè: Xièxie nín! Bù hǎo yìsi, wǒ hái xiǎng wèn yíxià, Zhōngguó-chéng yǒu gōnggòng xǐshǒujiān ma?

Lǐ Wén: Yǒu, wǒ zhīdào nàr yǒu yí gè gōnggòng cèsuǒ.

Yóukè: Tài xièxie nín le!

Lǐ Wén: Bú kèqi.

生词（一）New Words (1)

	简体（繁體）	拼音	词性	解释
1	游客	yóukè	*n.*	traveler, tourist 夏天海边有很多游客。/ 游客们都上车了。
2	走	zǒu	*v.*	walk, go 走到学校 / 走到图书馆 / 沿着大道走

	简体（繁體）	拼音	词性	解释
3	离（離）	lí	v.	away from 我家离学校不远。/ 现在离新年还有一个半月。
4	远（遠）	yuǎn	adj.	far 走远路 / 远方的城市
5	地铁（鐵）	dìtiě	n.	subway 地铁线路 / 北京地铁票 2 元一张。
6	往	wǎng	prep.	toward 往外走 / 往右走 / 往左拐
7	十字	shízì		cross-shaped 十字路口 / 十字架
8	路口	lùkǒu	n.	intersection 丁字路口 / 三岔路口 / 我在路口等你。
9	右手	yòushǒu	n.	right hand 大部分人用右手写字。/ 电影院在你的右手边。
10	边（邊）	biān	n.	side 路边 / 河边 / 湖边
11	市场（場）	shìchǎng	n.	market 超级市场 / 菜市场 / 农贸市场
12	大街	dàjiē	n.	street 一条大街 / 大街上人来人往。
13	出	chū	v.	come out 出站 / 出门 / 他出去了。
14	左	zuǒ	n.	left 左边 / 左手 / 往左拐
15	拐	guǎi	v.	turn 拐弯 / 拐过去 / 拐回来
16	看见（見）	kànjiàn	v.	see 我看了看，可是什么都没看见。
17	牌子	páizi	n.	sign 商店的牌子 / 汽车站的牌子 / 路边有个牌子。
18	沿	yán	prep.	along, following 沿着路走 / 沿着河边走
19	红绿灯（紅綠燈）	hónglǜdēng	n.	traffic lights 在下一个红绿灯往右拐。
20	不好意思	bù hǎo yìsi		excuse me; pardon me 不好意思，把你的名字写错了。
21	公共	gōnggòng	adj.	public 公共汽车 / 公共电话
22	洗手间（間）	xǐshǒujiān	n.	toilet, lavatory 厕所也叫洗手间。/ 车站里有洗手间。
23	厕（廁）所	cèsuǒ	n.	toilet, lavatory 公共厕所 / 上厕所
24	不客气（氣）	bú kèqi		not at all; don't mention it "谢谢。""不客气。"

Exercise 1 🎧 🗣

Listen to Text (1) and answer the questions orally in Chinese.

1. Where does the man want to go?

2. What does the woman suggest he should take?

3. Where is the place to take it?

4. How should the man get to this place after getting off?

Exercise 2 📖 ✍

Match the verbs in Column I with the words/phrases in Column II.

Column I	Column II
(　　) 1. 坐	a. 前走
(　　) 2. 往	b. 火车站
(　　) 3. 过	c. 地铁
(　　) 4. 出	d. 十字路口

Exercise 3 ✍

Translate the following sentences into Chinese.

1. Excuse me, may I ask where the Chinese bookstore is?

_____

2. The Chinese bookstore is in Chinatown. You need to take Bus Line 2.

_____

3. Walk three blocks from here and turn right at the cross section.

_____

4. The bookstore is on your left side.

_____

5. You will see a lot of hotels along that street.

_____

6. I need to use the public toilet. Where can I find one?

_____

Exercise 4 ✍ 🗣

Fill in the blanks with the words below. Then translate the sentences into English.

站　公共　走路　红绿灯　大街　问　商店　十字　左

1. 您是 _____ 去还是开车去？

2. 从这儿坐汽车，坐三 _____ 就到了。

3. 从这儿一直往前走，过了第一个 _____ 路口，书店就在你的 _____ 手边。

4. 在市场 _____，您会看见很多中国 _____ 的牌子。

5. 沿着那条大街一直往前走，过了两个 _____，就到中国城了。

6. 我想 _____ 一下，这里有 _____ 洗手间吗？

课文（二）Text (2)

学开车

简体版

In her diary, Jiang Xiaohua writes about her experience in getting a driver's license.

九月十二号　　　　　　星期五

今天是我十九岁生日，我很高兴，因为今天我通过了路试，终于拿到了驾驶执照！

在加州，考驾照要通过笔试和路试两个考试。笔试对我来说很容易，我考了一次就通过了。可是路试对我来说，真是太难了，我一开车，心里就很紧张。结果，三个星期前，我第一次考路试，考了一个不及格。

Tips: telling a past experience of failing a test

今天是我第二次考路试，考官是一位中年女士，说话很客气。我告诉她，今天是我十九岁生日，她笑着祝我生日快乐。不知道为什么，我今天一点儿都不紧张，转弯、倒车、停车，我都做得很好。结果，我顺利地通过了路试，拿到了驾照。

Tips: passing a test

今天晚上，爸爸妈妈给我买了生日蛋糕，还送给我一个最好的生日礼物：一辆新汽车！

學開車

In her diary, Jiang Xiaohua writes about her experience in getting a driver's license.

九月十二號　　　　　　　星期五

今天是我十九歲生日，我很高興，因爲今天我通過了路試，終于拿到了駕駛執照！

在加州，考駕照要通過筆試和路試兩個考試。筆試對我來説很容易，我考了一次就通過了。可是路試對我來説，眞是太難了，我一開車，心裏就很緊張。結果，三個星期前，我第一次考路試，考了一個不及格。

今天是我第二次考路試，考官是一位中年女士，説話很客氣。我告訴她，今天是我十九歲生日，她笑着祝我生日快樂。不知道爲什麼，我今天一點兒都不緊張，轉彎、倒車、停車，我都做得很好。結果，我順利地通過了路試，拿到了駕照。

今天晚上，爸爸媽媽給我買了生日蛋糕，還送給我一個最好的生日禮物：一輛新汽車！

Kèwén (èr) *Text (2)*

Xué Kāichē

In her diary, Jiang Xiaohua writes about her experience in getting a driver's license.

jiǔ yuè shí'èr hào　　　　　　Xīngqīwǔ

Jīntiān shì wǒ shíjiǔ suì shēngrì, wǒ hěn gāoxìng, yīnwèi

jīntiān wǒ tōngguòle lùshì, zhōngyú nádàole jiàshǐ zhízhào!

Zài Jiāzhōu, kǎo jiàzhào yào tōngguò bǐshì hé lùshì liǎng gè kǎoshì. Bǐshì duì wǒ lái shuō hěn róngyì, wǒ kǎole yí cì jiù tōngguò le. Kěshì lùshì duì wǒ lái shuō, zhēn shì tài nán le, wǒ yì kāichē, xīn li jiù hěn jǐnzhāng. Jiéguǒ, sān gè xīngqī qián, wǒ dì-yī cì kǎo lùshì, kǎole yí gè bù jígé.

Jīntiān shì wǒ dì-èr cì kǎo lùshì, kǎoguān shì yí wèi zhōngnián nǚshì, shuōhuà hěn kèqi. Wǒ gàosu tā, jīntiān shì wǒ shíjiǔ suì shēngrì, tā xiàozhe zhù wǒ shēngrì kuàilè. Bù zhīdào wèi shénme, wǒ jīntiān yìdiǎnr dōu bù jǐnzhāng, zhuǎnwān, dàochē, tíngchē, wǒ dōu zuò de hěn hǎo. Jiéguǒ, wǒ shùnlì de tōngguòle lùshì, nádàole jiàzhào.

Jīntiān wǎnshang, bàba māma gěi wǒ mǎile shēngrì dàngāo, hái sònggěi wǒ yí gè zuì hǎo de shēngrì lǐwù: yí liàng xīn qìchē!

生词（二）New Words (2)

	简体（繁體）	拼音	词性	解释
1	通过（過）	tōngguò	v.	pass 通过考试／通过面试
2	路试（試）	lùshì	n.	road test 考路试的时候我很紧张。
3	终于（終於）	zhōngyú	adv.	at last; eventually 考了三次以后我终于通过了。
4	驾驶（駕駛）	jiàshǐ	v.	drive 驾驶汽车／她是一个驾驶员。
5	执（執）照	zhízhào	n.	license 驾驶执照／营业执照／行医执照
6	驾（駕）照	jiàzhào	n.	driver's license 美国人的驾照也是身份证。
7	笔试（筆試）	bǐshì	n.	written test 应聘那家公司需要参加笔试和面试。
8	对（對）……来说（來說）	duì … lái shuō		as far as…is concerned 对我来说，能去中国学习是难得的机会。
9	容易	róngyì	adj.	easy 这次考试不容易。／那还不容易吗？
10	难（難）	nán	adj.	difficult 这次考试很难。／这没什么难的。

简体（繁體）	拼音	词性	解释
11 紧张（緊張）	jǐnzhāng	*adj.*	nervous 面试的时候不要紧张。/ 我一考试就紧张。
12 考官	kǎoguān	*n.*	examiner 考官很严厉，但是也很友好。
13 中年	zhōngnián	*n.*	middle-age 中年人 / 人到中年
14 女士	nǚshì	*n.*	lady, madam 女士们、先生们，你们好。/ 那位女士是谁？
15 转弯（轉彎）	zhuǎnwān	*v.*	turn 汽车转弯的时候应该减速。
16 倒车（車）	dàochē	*v.*	back up 我倒车的时候没倒好，碰了别人的车。/ 你的倒车灯不亮了。
17 停车（車）	tíngchē	*v.*	stop a car 我不会在路边侧方位停车。/ 司机，请停车！
18 顺（順）利	shùnlì	*adj.*	smooth 考试很顺利。/ 一切都很顺利。
19 辆（輛）	liàng	*m.*	(measure word for vehicles) 一辆自行车 / 三辆汽车
20 汽车（車）	qìchē	*n.*	automobile 汽车站 / 在加州没有汽车很不方便。

Exercise 5

Listen to Text (2) and take notes in the following chart about the information provided in the text. Compare your work with your partner's orally in Chinese.

Jiang Xiaohua, today	
Examiner, today	
Jiang Xiaohua, three weeks ago	
Jiang Xiaohua, about the written test, three weeks ago	

Jiang Xiaohua, about the road test, three weeks ago	

Exercise 6 📖

Read Text (2) and decide whether the following statements are true or false.

1. 我生日的前一天拿到了驾驶执照。	(	)
2. 我觉得第一次路考和笔试都不难。	(	)
3. 路考的时候，考官对我很好，所以我不紧张。	(	)
4. 我第二次路考有一些地方没做好。	(	)
5. 爸爸送给我他开过的车。	(	)

Exercise 7

Match the verb phrases in Column I with the words in Column II.

Column I	Column II
(　　) 1. 拿到了	a. 路试
(　　) 2. 向左转	b. 生日快乐
(　　) 3. 祝我	c. 驾照
(　　) 4. 通不过	d. 弯
(　　) 5. 停一下	e. 车

三、汉字 Chinese Characters

1. New characters in this lesson

序号	拼音	简 / 繁	部件	构词
1	bǐ	笔（筆）	竹 + 毛	笔试 / 毛笔 / 铅笔 / 笔记
2	cè	厕（廁）	厂 + 则（贝 + 刂）	厕所 / 女厕 / 男厕 / 入厕
3	dào	倒	亻 + 到（至 + 刂）	倒车 / 那倒是
4	guǎi	拐	扌 + 另	拐弯 / 拐棍 / 拐骗

5	guān	官	宀+吕	考官 / 当官 / 大官 / 官司
6	jià	驾（駕）	加（力+口）+马	驾驶 / 驾照 / 驾车 / 驾飞机
7	kè	客	宀+各（夂+口）	客气 / 客人 / 不客气
8	lí	离（離）	离+内	离开 / 离别 / 分离
9	liàng	辆（輛）	车+两	车辆 / 一辆汽车
10	lù	路	𧾷+各（夂+口）	走路 / 道路 / 铁路 / 公路
11	pái	牌	片+卑	路牌 / 名牌 / 招牌 / 牌子
12	qì	汽	氵+气	汽车 / 汽水 / 水汽
13	róng	容	宀+谷	容易 / 包容 / 容下
14	shǐ	驶（駛）	马+史	驾驶 / 驶过
15	shì	士	士	女士 / 护士 / 士兵
16	shùn	顺（順）	川+页	顺利 / 顺道 / 顺便
17	sī	思	田+心	意思 / 思想 / 思念
18	tiě	铁（鐵）	钅+失	地铁 / 铁路
19	tíng	停	亻+亭	停车 / 停止 / 停下
20	wān	弯（彎）	亦+弓	弯路 / 转弯 / 弯曲
21	wǎng	往	彳+主	往前 / 往后 / 往往 / 以往
22	yán	沿	氵+㕣（几+口）	沿着 / 沿河 / 沿路
23	yì	易	日+勿	容易 / 不易 / 易拉罐
24	yú	于（於）	于	于是 / 关于
25	yuǎn	远（遠）	元+辶	远路 / 远方 / 长远
26	zhào	照	日+召（刀+口）+灬	驾照 / 照片 / 照明 / 照亮
27	zhí	执（執）	扌+九	执照 / 执行
28	zhōng	终（終）	纟+冬	终于 / 终点 / 终止 / 始终
29	zhuǎn	转（轉）	车+专	转弯 / 转折 / 转身
30	zǒu	走	走	走到学校 / 走路

Exercise 1 ✎

Copy the following single-component characters with correct stroke order in the spaces provided.

shì	士	一 十 士
yú	于	一 二 于
zǒu	走	一 十 土 キ キ 走 走

Exercise 2 📖 ✎

Read the following sentences and choose the correct characters to fill in the blanks.

1. 我考 _____ 照的时候很紧张，倒车没有考好。（加　架　驾）

2. 有 _____ 人从远方来，不是很高兴的事吗？（课　克　客）

3. 请问，去北京站坐几号线地 _____ ？（铁　贴　轶）

4. 先生，不好意 _____ ，请问这里有公共厕所吗？（恩　寺　思）

5. 我 _____ 利通过了期末考试，可以好好休息一下了。（顺　师　圳）

6. 出了地铁车站以后，你往前 _____ 100 米，就看见中国书店了。（徒　走　陡）

7. 考官说我转 _____ 不太好，还要练习。（弯　湾　鸾）

8. 走路去太远了，你还是坐车吧。你看，来了一 _____ 。（两　辆　俩）

2. Common radicals (8)

(1) 钅 (金) jīnzìpáng

The radical 钅 is derived from the character 金 (jīn), meaning gold or metal. Thus, characters with this radical are usually related to money or metal. When this radical is on the left side of a character, it is written as 钅, e.g. 钱 (qián, money); 银 (yín, silver, money); 针 (zhēn, needle); 钟 (zhōng, clock); 铁 (tiě, iron). When this radical is on the bottom of a character, it is written as 金, e.g. 鉴 (jiàn, ancient bronze mirror).

(2) 走 zǒu

The radical 走 is also a character, meaning "to walk". Characters with 走 are usually related to walking, e.g. 起 (qǐ, to start; get up); 越 (yuè, to exceed); 赶 (gǎn, catch up with); 超 (chāo, to surpass).

(3) 车 chē

The radical 车 is a simplified character of 車, which was derived from the pictographic character ![image], resembling a cart. This radical is usually put on the left side of a character. Characters with 车 are mostly related to vehicles, e.g. 转 (zhuǎn, to turn); 辆 (liàng, measure word for vehicles); 轮 (lún, wheel); 较 (jiào, to compare).

(4) 马 mǎ

The radical 马 is a simplified character of 馬 (horse), derived from the pictographic character ![image]. This radical is often put on the left side or bottom of a character. Characters with this radical are related to horses or action with a horse, like 驾 (jià, to drive, to sail), 驶 (shǐ, to drive, to sail). Sometimes, 马 can be used as a sound element, like 妈 (mā, mother), 吗 (ma, a question marker).

Exercise 3 ✍

> *The character 马 can be used as both a radical and a sound element to form characters. Write down as many characters as you can with 马 as a radical and sound element.*

As radical: ____   ____   ____
As sound element: ____   ____   ____   ____

四、语言点 Language Points

1. The prepositions 从 and 离

We learned the preposition 从 from previous lessons. 从 indicates the starting point of a location or a time, meaning "from" in English.

> **Subject + 从 + Location / Time + Verb**

> (1) 我爸爸妈妈都是从中国来的，而我是在美国出生的。
>   My parents are both from China but I was born in the U.S.
> (2) 我从网上知道北京昨天下了一场大雪，气温一下子降到摄氏零下 10 度。
>   I read on the Internet that it snowed heavily in Beijing yesterday and the temperature fell drastically to minus ten degrees Celsius.

19

(3) 她的室友叫王红，是从北京来的，她也参加了我们的聚会。

Her roommate, Wang Hong, is from Beijing. She also came to our party.

(4) 我是从中国来的游客，我想坐车去。

I am a tourist from China, and I want to take the bus there.

(5) 从这儿一直往前走，过了第一个十字路口，地铁站就在你的右手边。

Go straight forward from here, cross the first intersection, and the subway station is on your right.

(6) 她从晚上 7 点一直学习到 11 点半。

She studied in the evening from 7 to 11:30.

In this lesson, we will learn a similar preposition 离, which can be translated into "away from" in English. 离 indicates the temporal or spatial distance between two points.

Location / Time ＋ 离 ＋ Location / Time

(1) 中国城离这儿挺远的，您是走路去还是开车去？

Chinatown is far from here. Do you want to walk or drive there?

(2) 我们家离一家中国餐馆不太远。

My home is not far from a Chinese restaurant.

(3) 现在离圣诞节还有一个星期左右。

It is still about one week to Christmas.

(4) 现在离上课只有一刻钟时间了。

Now there are only 15 minutes before the class begins.

2. The phrase 对 … 来说

The phrase 对 … 来 说 is often used to serve as an adverbial in a sentence, meaning "to somebody" in English. Here are some examples:

(1) 笔试对我来说很容易，我考了一次就通过了。可是路试对我来说，真是太难了。

I feel that the written test was easy for me, which I passed on the first try. But the road test was too difficult for me.

(2) 对我来说，爸妈送给我的新汽车就是最好的生日礼物。

For me, the new car that my parents gave me is the best birthday gift.

(3) 对我来说，寄包裹最好用快递，邮费不太贵，而且特别快。

I think it is better to send a package by express mail; it is not very expensive and it is fast.

(4) <u>对你来说</u>，学中文难吗？

Is learning Chinese difficult for you?

3. The prepositions 往 and 向

When giving directions, both of the prepositions 往 and 向 may be translated into "toward", and they are interchangeable:

(1) 从这儿一<u>直</u><u>往</u>前走，过了第一个十字路口，地铁站就在你的右手边。

Go straight forward from here, cross the first intersection, and the subway station is on your right.

(2) 下车后，您先出站，再<u>向</u>左拐。

After getting off the subway, exit the station and then turn left.

(3) 沿着那条大街一<u>直</u><u>往</u>前走，过了两个红绿灯，就到中国城了。

Walk straight forward along that street, cross through two traffic lights and you will be in Chinatown.

4. The idiomatic expression 不好意思

The idiomatic expression 不好意思 is often used to introduce a seemingly awkward question. Here are some examples:

(1) <u>不好意思</u>，我还想问一下，中国城有公共洗手间吗？

Excuse me, may I ask you another question: is there a public restroom in Chinatown?

(2) <u>不好意思</u>，我没听清楚你的话，请你再说一遍，好吗？

Sorry I did not quite catch what you said. Could you please say it again?

(3) <u>不好意思</u>，我没带手机，我可以用一下你的手机吗？

Excuse me, may I borrow your cell phone? I don't have mine with me right now.

(4) <u>不好意思</u>，我的中文不太好，你可以说慢一点儿吗？

Sorry, my Chinese is not very good. Could you speak a little bit slower please?

5. The structural particle 地

The principal function of the structural particle 地 is to link an adverbial modifier to the verb or adjective it modifies. For example:

(1) 结果，我顺利地通过了路试，拿到了驾照。

As a result, I passed the road test without a hitch and got my driver's license.

(2) 听到这个好消息，爸爸妈妈都高兴地笑起来了。

Hearing the good news, Mom and Dad laughed.

(3) 那位女考官很客气地祝我生日快乐。

The female examiner politely wished me a happy birthday.

(4) 那位从中国来的游客不好意思地问李文哪里有洗手间。

The Chinese tourist, feeling somewhat embarrassed, asked Li Wen where there was a restroom.

6. The verb complement 见

In this lesson, we will learn 见 as a verb complement to indicate the result of the action, e.g. 看见 . Note the difference between the verb 看 (to look) and the verb compound 看见 (to see).

> ### Verb + 见 (to perceive) → Verb Complement Compound

看 (to look) + 见 (to perceive) → 看见 (to see) (similar to 看到)

听 (to listen) + 见 (to perceive) → 听见 (to hear) (similar to 听到)

碰 (to bump) + 见 (to perceive) → 碰见 (bump into) (similar to 碰到)

(1) 十点半，我到学校附近的咖啡店做作业，在那儿碰见了大卫。

I went to the coffee shop near school to do my homework at 10:30 and ran into David there.

(2) 下车后，您先出站，再向左拐，会看见一些中国商店的牌子。

After getting off the subway, exit the station and then turn left. You will see the signs of some Chinese stores.

(3) 我虽然听见他们在说话，可是听了半天也没听懂他们在说什么。

Although I heard them talking, hard as I tried I could not make out what they were saying.

Exercise 1 👂 ✎

Listen to the four short dialogs and answer the questions in Chinese characters. Pay attention to the idiomatic expression 不好意思.

Dialog 1 Question: 张老师的办公室在哪儿？	Answer:
Dialog 2 Question: 我点的清蒸鱼好了吗？	Answer:
Dialog 3 Question: 请问去中国城怎么走？	Answer:
Dialog 4 Question: 请问你的手机号码是多少？	Answer:

Exercise 2 📖 ✎

Read the following dialogs and fill in the blanks with the prepositions 从, 离, or 向/往.

1. A：你家 ＿＿＿＿＿＿＿ 学校远不远？

  B：不远，我 ＿＿＿＿＿＿＿ 家走到学校只要十二分钟。

2. A：姐姐，你什么时候回家？

  B：现在 ＿＿＿＿＿＿＿ 下班还有三刻钟，我想再过一个小时左右吧。

3. A：请问去食堂怎么走？

  B：＿＿＿＿＿＿＿ 这儿一直往前走，走到学校图书馆那儿再 ＿＿＿＿＿＿＿ 左拐就到了。

4. A：你知道 ＿＿＿＿＿＿＿ 旧金山飞到上海要多少小时吗？

  B：旧金山 ＿＿＿＿＿＿＿ 上海很远啊，差不多要十三个小时。

5. A：不好意思，你知道洗手间在哪里吗？

  B：从这儿一直 ＿＿＿＿＿＿＿ 前走就是。

6. A：你知道他是哪国人吗？

  B：他是 ＿＿＿＿＿＿＿ 伦敦来这儿的，他是英国人。

Exercise 3 ✎

Translate the following dialogs into Chinese characters using the phrase 对 … 来说.

1. A: What do you want to drink, coffee or tea?

  B: For me, either will do.

  ＿＿＿＿＿＿＿＿＿＿＿＿＿＿＿＿＿＿＿＿＿＿＿＿＿＿＿＿＿＿＿＿＿

  ＿＿＿＿＿＿＿＿＿＿＿＿＿＿＿＿＿＿＿＿＿＿＿＿＿＿＿＿＿＿＿＿＿

2. A: Was today's exam difficult?

   B: No. Actually, it was very easy for me.

   _____

   _____

3. A: What do you want to eat, fish or duck?

   B: For me, I do not mind what.

   _____

   _____

4. A: Have you visited New York City before?

   B: No, it's my first time. For me, it's a city worth seeing.

   _____

   _____

5. A: What kind of exercise is good for elderly people?

   B: Walking is good for them.

   _____

   _____

6. A: Why is today special for you?

   B: Because it is my birthday.

   _____

   _____

7. A: This new cell phone is really good.

   B: Yes. But it is too expensive for a college student.

   _____

   _____

Exercise 4 ✎

Translate the following sentences into Chinese using the structural particle 地.

1. Xiaohong quickly learned how to make dumplings. (很快地)

   _____

2. Today, I smoothly passed the driving test and got my driver's license. (顺利地)

   _____

3. Now John can fluently introduce his family members in Chinese. (流利地)

   _____

4. I happily told my parents that I got a 100 on my final exam. (高兴地)

   _____

5. Teacher Wang clearly answered my questions. (清楚地)

_____

6. My mom gets up early every morning. (早早地)

_____

7. She spoke with me very politely. (客气地)

_____

Exercise 5 ✎

Translate the following dialogs into Chinese using the verb complement.

Dialog 1

A: Can you see the Chinese characters written by the teacher?

B: I can see them.

_____

_____

Dialog 2

A: What are they talking about? Can you hear them?

B: I can hear them. They are talking about the weekend picnic.

_____

_____

Dialog 3

A: Whom did you run into at the store today?

B: I ran into Xiaohua and her mom.

_____

_____

Dialog 4

A: Whom did you see at the coffee shop?

B: I saw your elder brother and his girlfriend.

_____

_____

五、语言运用 Using the Language

Activity 1 📖 🗣

Xiao Zhang wrote in his blog about how he got his driver's license. Work in pairs. Each student reads one part of the blog. After reading, tell each other about the contents.

Part One

　　我从纽约来到加州后感觉到出入很不方便，我住的小城公共汽车很少。那时候出门能走路就走路，让朋友开车我也觉得不好意思。看来只有学开车考驾照了。我马上开始学习一本中文的驾驶手册。学好以后，我去考笔试。那一天，我很紧张，但是车管处的人笑着对我说，你通过了。

Part Two

　　考路试的那天，我不太紧张。我转弯、倒车、停车都做得不错。考完的时候，考官叫我把车停到路边，很客气地说："你通过了。"我高兴地说了声"谢谢"。现在我有驾照了！我的朋友们给我买了一个大蛋糕，庆祝我通过考试。我们都很开心。

Activity 2 👂 ✍

Listen to the following conversation and draw a simple map showing how the man arrives at the place he is looking for.

Activity 3 📖 🗣

1. Read the descriptions of the following photos of Chinatown in San Francisco and answer the questions orally in Chinese.

1. 这是旧金山中国城的大门。大门上边有"天下为公"四个字，意思是每个人应该为大家做好事。

Question:

这是什么？上边的字是什么意思？

2. 中国城有个北京商场，在 Grant 街，Washington 街和 Clay 街中间。

Question:

这个商场在什么地方？

3. 中国城里有家茶叶店。客人买茶叶以前，可以在这里免费喝一小杯茶，看看好不好喝。该店位于 Grant 街，在 Jackson 街和 Pacific 街中间。

Question:

这是什么地方？在哪儿？在这儿可以做什么？

4. 这家餐馆是中国城有名的饭馆之一。酒楼在 Washington 街，离希尔顿 (Hilton) 饭店不到一个路口。Washington 街的路口就在希尔顿饭店的对面。

Question:

这家餐馆怎么样？如果你住在希尔顿饭店，去这家餐馆方便不方便？

5. 中国城的路名有英文的也有中文的。不懂英文的中国游客来到这里也不会有问题。

Question:

如果中国游客不懂英文，在中国城会有问题吗？为什么？

6. 东风书店是一家中文书店。这里不但卖书，而且卖音乐光盘和电影光盘。东风书店在 Stockton 街和 Columbus 街的路口。

Question:

这是什么地方？卖什么？在哪儿？

Activity 4

What do you say?

1. You have lost your way. You ask someone how to get to a place.

2. You do not know whether Line 3 or Line 5 is the bus to take to the movie theater.

3. The movie theater that a man is looking for is three blocks away straight ahead, opposite the post office.

4. Tell someone that he/she needs to take the subway three stops and then change to Bus Line 1 and get off five stops away.

5. Tell your friend that he needs to take a written test before starting to learn how to drive.

6. Your turning and stopping were both OK, but your backing up did not pass the test.

Activity 5

Role Play

You are walking in the street and a stranger comes up to you because he/she has lost his/her way. He/she needs to go to a hotel. You know that the hotel is still far from where you both are. He/she needs to take a bus one block away on the right. After getting off the bus he/she needs to cross a street and make one turn. Give him/her the directions. The stranger should repeat the directions.

Work in pairs and speak in Chinese. One student should ask for directions, the other student should give the directions.

Sentences you may need to use:

旅馆离这儿还有点儿远。
汽车站在下一个路口。
你下车后，过马路，往……拐。
你走……就到了。

第二十课
Lesson Twenty

体育活动
Sports

一、导入 Lead-in

Exercise 1

Look at the pictures below and describe them in Chinese.

我喜欢所有的体育运动。

天冷时可以在室内游泳。

冬天的时候可以去滑雪。

秋天的时候最好去登山。

After learning this lesson, you will be able to:

1. Talk about one's favorite sports in different seasons of the year.

2. Talk about one's favorite basketball team and a basketball match.

3. Recognize new characters in this lesson, and know the common radicals ⺍, 辶, 纟 and 足.

4. Use the 越…越…structure, the expressions 根本, 加油 and adverbs 更 and 最.

二、课文 Texts

课文（一）Text (1)

体育运动

简体版

Xiaohua and Peter are talking about their favorite sports.

小华：彼得，你喜欢体育运动吗？

彼得：当然，几乎所有的体育运动我都喜欢。

小华：是吗？那你比较喜欢哪些运动？

彼得：我特别喜欢室外的运动。春天的时候，我喜欢到外边跑步、打棒球、打网球、踢足球。秋天的时候就去登山。

小华：我不太喜欢室外运动。特别是夏天那么热，根本不想出去。

彼得：夏天是游泳的好时候，我经常去海里游泳、潜水。

小华：到了冬天，天那么冷，有时候还下雪，室外运动就有麻烦了。

彼得：冬天可以去滑雪啊，雪下得越大越好！

小华：那倒是。不过，也可以在室内滑冰。

彼得：说了半天，你最喜欢的运动是什么？

小华：我最喜欢室内运动，例如打乒乓球、打羽毛球。我在中学时，还是学校羽毛球队的队员呢。

体育運動

飞跃——汉语初级教程学生用书 下册

繁体版

Xiaohua and Peter are talking about their favorite sports.

小華：彼得，你喜歡體育運動嗎？

彼得：當然，幾乎所有的體育運動我都喜歡。

小華：是嗎？那你比較喜歡哪些運動？

彼得：我特別喜歡室外的運動。春天的時候，我喜歡到外邊跑步、打棒球、打網球、踢足球。秋天的時候就去登山。

小華：我不太喜歡室外運動。特別是夏天那麼熱，根本不想出去。

彼得：夏天是游泳的好時候，我經常去海裏游泳、潛水。

小華：到了冬天，天那麼冷，有時候還下雪，室外運動就有麻煩了。

彼得：冬天可以去滑雪啊，雪下得越大越好！

小華：那倒是。不過，也可以在室內滑冰。

彼得：說了半天，你最喜歡的運動是什麼？

小華：我最喜歡室內運動，例如打乒乓球、打羽毛球。我在中學時，還是學校羽毛球隊的隊員呢。

Kèwén (yī) *Text (1)*

Tǐyù Yùndòng

拼音版

Xiaohua and Peter are talking about their favorite sports.

Xiǎohuá: Bǐdé, nǐ xǐhuan tǐyù yùndòng ma?

Bǐdé: Dāngrán, jīhū suǒyǒu de tǐyù yùndòng wǒ dōu xǐhuan.

Xiǎohuá: Shì ma? Nà nǐ bǐjiào xǐhuan nǎxiē yùndòng?

Bǐdé: Wǒ tèbié xǐhuan shìwài de yùndòng. Chūntiān de shíhou, wǒ xǐhuan dào wàibian pǎobù, dǎ bàngqiú, dǎ wǎngqiú, tī zúqiú. Qiūtiān de shíhou jiù qù dēngshān.

Xiǎohuá: Wǒ bú tài xǐhuan shìwài yùndòng. Tèbié shì xiàtiān nàme rè, gēnběn bù xiǎng chūqu.

Bǐdé: Xiàtiān shì yóuyǒng de hǎo shíhou, wǒ jīngcháng qù hǎi li yóuyǒng, qiánshuǐ.

Xiǎohuá: Dàole dōngtiān, tiān nàme lěng, yǒu shíhou hái xiàxuě, shìwài yùndòng jiù yǒu máfan le.

Bǐdé: Dōngtiān kěyǐ qù huáxuě a, xuě xià de yuè dà yuè hǎo!

Xiǎohuá: Nà dàoshì. Búguò, yě kěyǐ zài shìnèi huábīng.

Bǐdé: Shuōle bàntiān, nǐ zuì xǐhuan de yùndòng shì shénme?

Xiǎohuá: Wǒ zuì xǐhuan shìnèi de yùndòng, lìrú dǎ pīngpāngqiú, dǎ yǔmáoqiú. Wǒ zài zhōngxué shí, hái shì xuéxiào yǔmáoqiúduì de duìyuán ne.

生词（一）*New Words (1)*

	简体（繁體）	拼音	词性	解释
1	体（體）育	tǐyù	*n.*	sports; physical education 体育课 / 看体育新闻 / 开展体育活动 / 我们的体育老师个子很高。
2	运动（運動）	yùndòng	*n.*	sports 运动员 / 运动会 / 你喜欢运动吗？

简体（繁體）	拼音	词性	解释
3 几（幾）乎	jīhū	*adv.*	almost, nearly 我几乎忘了今天是你生日。/ 上次生病我几乎住了院。
4 所有	suǒyǒu	*pron.*	all 所有的学生都去锻炼了，教室里空无一人。/ 毕业以后，他把所有的书都卖了。
5 外边（邊）	wàibian	*n.*	outside 到外边去 / 窗户外边有一棵树。
6 棒球	bàngqiú	*n.*	baseball 棒球队 / 棒球比赛
7 踢	tī	*v.*	kick, play (football or soccer) 踢足球
8 足球	zúqiú	*n.*	soccer, football 踢足球 / 美式足球 / 足球赛
9 登山	dēngshān	*v.*	climb a mountain 登山队 / 登山运动员 / 我每个周末去登山。
10 根本	gēnběn	*adv.*	at all 我根本不会打棒球。/ 我根本不认识他。
11 游泳	yóuyǒng	*v.*	swim 我喜欢在海里游泳。/ 他游泳游得很快。
12 海	hǎi	*n.*	ocean, sea 大海 / 海边 / 海洋 / 海运
13 潜（潛）水	qiánshuǐ	*v.*	dive 潜水服 / 潜水员 / 我不会潜水。
14 越……越	yuè … yuè		the more…the more 抽烟越多，身体就越坏。/ 妈妈越是不让小明上网，小明越是要上。
15 滑冰	huábīng	*v.*	skate 花样滑冰 / 速度滑冰 / 这里天气不冷，要滑冰得去室内冰场。
16 例如	lìrú	*v.*	for example 川菜很辣，例如，麻婆豆腐就是很辣的菜。
17 乒乓球	pīngpāngqiú	*n.*	table tennis 打乒乓球 / 乒乓球比赛
18 羽毛球	yǔmáoqiú	*n.*	badminton 我喜欢打羽毛球。
19 队（隊）	duì	*n.*	team 运动队 / 队员 / 队友 / 队长
20 员（員）	yuán	*n.*	member, staff 球员 / 运动员 / 服务员 / 飞行员

Exercise 1 🎧 🗣

Listen to Text (1) and answer the questions orally in Chinese.

1. What type of sports does Peter like?

2. What different opinions do Peter and Xiaohua have about summer and winter?

3. What winter sports need not be outdoors?

4. What are Xiaohua's favorite sports?

Exercise 2 📖

Read Text (1) and decide whether the following statements are true or false.

1. 有很多体育活动彼得不喜欢。	(	)
2. 小华大部分时候都不喜欢到外边运动。	(	)
3. 彼得喜欢到海里游泳。	(	)
4. 小华打羽毛球打得不好。	(	)
5. 小华和彼得对滑雪的看法一样。	(	)

Exercise 3 📖 🗣

Work in pairs. Each student should read one of the following passages. Tell each other about the person in your passage.

Passage One

　　彼得是我的同学，他特别喜欢运动。春天他出去跑步，夏天他下海游泳，秋天他去登山，冬天他去滑雪。他的棒球打得特别好，他是学校棒球队的队员。彼得足球也踢得不错。

Passage Two

　　小华也是我的同学，她也喜欢体育运动。可是她的运动不分春夏秋冬，因为她都是在室内运动。所有的室内运动她都喜欢，她特别喜欢乒乓球、室内游泳和室内滑冰。她在我们班乒乓球打得最好。

Exercise 4 ✍

Write down the names of sports in characters that match the verbs given.

1. 滑：_____

2. 打：_____

3. 踢：_____

4. 潜：_____

5. 游：_____

6. 跑：_____

7. 登：_____

篮球迷

简体版

Li Wen writes about a basketball match in his journal.

　　我和约翰都喜欢打篮球，也喜欢看篮球比赛，同学们都说我俩是篮球迷。约翰喜欢芝加哥公牛队，我呢，喜欢休斯敦火箭队。不过，这没关系，我们还是好朋友。

　　今天晚上，火箭队和公牛队有一场比赛。白天的时候，我和约翰都认为自己喜欢的球队会赢。比赛开始以后，我大声地为火箭队加油。比赛场上，火箭队的每个球员都打得很出色。上半场结束，火箭队以59比51领先公牛队。下半场火箭队继续领先，公牛队也不断进球，比赛十分激烈。全场结束，火箭队以119比89赢了公牛队，我非常高兴。我本来想打个电话给约翰，告诉他这个结果。后来我没打，因为我想他一定看过比赛了，可能正在家里为公牛队难过呢。

飞跃——汉语初级教程学生用书 下册

籃球迷

繁体版

Li Wen writes about a basketball match in his journal.

我和約翰都喜歡打籃球，也喜歡看籃球比賽，同學們都說我倆是籃球迷。約翰喜歡芝加哥公牛隊，我呢，喜歡休斯敦火箭隊。不過，這沒關係，我們還是好朋友。

今天晚上，火箭隊和公牛隊有一場比賽。白天的時候，我和約翰都認為自己喜歡的球隊會贏。比賽開始以後，我大聲地為火箭隊加油。比賽場上，火箭隊的每個球員都打得很出色。上半場結束，火箭隊以 59 比 51 領先公牛隊。下半場火箭隊繼續領先，公牛隊也不斷進球，比賽十分激烈。全場結束，火箭隊以 119 比 89 贏了公牛隊，我非常高興。我本來想打個電話給約翰，告訴他這個結果。後來我沒打，因為我想他一定看過比賽了，可能正在家裏為公牛隊難過呢。

Kèwén (èr) *Text (2)*

Lánqiúmí

拼音版

Li Wen writes about a basketball match in his journal.

Wǒ hé Yuēhàn dōu xǐhuan dǎ lánqiú, yě xǐhuan kàn lánqiú bǐsài, tóngxuémen dōu shuō wǒ liǎ shì lánqiúmí. Yuēhàn xǐhuan Zhījiāgē Gōngniúduì, wǒ ne, xǐhuan Xiūsīdūn Huǒjiànduì. Búguò, zhè méi guānxi, wǒmen hái shì hǎopéngyou.

Jīntiān wǎnshang, Huǒjiànduì hé Gōngniúduì yǒu yì chǎng bǐsài. Báitiān de shíhou, wǒ hé Yuēhàn dōu rènwéi zìjǐ xǐhuan de qiúduì huì yíng. Bǐsài kāishǐ yǐhòu, wǒ dà shēng de wèi Huǒjiànduì jiāyóu. Bǐsài chǎng shang, Huǒjiànduì de měi gè qiúyuán dōu dǎ de hěn chūsè. Shàng bànchǎng jiéshù, Huǒjiànduì yǐ 59 bǐ 51 lǐngxiān

Gōngniúduì. Xià bàn chǎng Huǒjiànduì jìxù lǐngxiān, Gōngniúduì yě bùduàn jìnqiú, bǐsài shífēn jīliè. Quánchǎng jiéshù, Huǒjiànduì yǐ 119 bǐ 89 yíngle Gōngniúduì, wǒ fēicháng gāoxìng. Wǒ běnlái xiǎng dǎ gè diànhuà gěi Yuēhàn, gàosu tā zhège jiéguǒ. Hòulái wǒ méi dǎ, yīnwèi wǒ xiǎng tā yídìng kànguo bǐsài le, kěnéng zhèng zài jiā li wèi Gōngniúduì nánguò ne.

生词（二）New Words (2)

	简体（繁體）	拼音	词性	解释
1	篮（籃）球	lánqiú	n.	basketball 篮球明星 / 我们都爱看篮球比赛。
2	比赛（賽）	bǐsài	n.	match, contest 足球比赛 / 篮球比赛 / 中文演讲比赛
3	俩	liǎ	num.	the two of (put after plural pronoun) 你们俩谁去？ / 我们俩是好兄弟。 / 他们俩很要好。
4	白天	báitiān	n.	daytime 白天暖和, 晚上很冷。 / 夏天白天长, 冬天白天短。
5	认为（認為）	rènwéi	v.	believe, think 我认为中国足球还得再提高水平。
6	赢（贏）	yíng	v.	win, defeat 这场比赛谁赢了？ / 主队赢了客队。
7	大声（聲）	dàshēng	adv.	loudly 大声喊叫 / 大声说话 / 不要在图书馆里大声说话。
8	加油	jiāyóu	v.	cheer 为运动员加油 / 加油！
9	球员（員）	qiúyuán	n.	member of a ball game team 我们的球员打得很好。
10	出色	chūsè	adj.	excellent, brilliant 出色的成绩 / 这场比赛很出色。 / 他的学习很出色。
11	半场	bànchǎng	n.	half of the game 上半场 / 下半场
12	结（結）束	jiéshù	v.	finish 比赛结束了。 / 结束了大学的学习后, 他去了美国念研究生。

	简体（繁體）	拼音	词性	解释
13	以	yǐ	*prep.*	by, with 以三比零赢得比赛 / 以优异的考试成绩毕业
14	比	bǐ	*prep.*	to (in a score) 三比二 / 红队以三比二赢了比赛。
15	领（領）先	lǐngxiān	*v.*	be in the lead 比赛中，大学队一直领先。/ 百米赛中，小王领先其他人到达了终点。
16	继续（繼續）	jìxù	*v.*	continue 继续学习 / 继续工作
17	不断（斷）	búduàn	*adv.*	continuously 他不断地为火箭队加油。
18	进（進）球	jìnqiú	*v.*	score a goal 进了一个球 / 上半场没有进球。
19	十分	shífēn	*adv.*	very 春节的时候，商场里十分热闹。/ 听了他的话，我十分高兴。
20	激烈	jīliè	*adj.*	intense, fierce 激烈的比赛 / 激烈的战斗
21	过（過）	guo	*part.*	（particle after verb, indicating a past experience）你去过中国吗？/ 我学过中文，可以看懂这本中文书。
22	难过（難過）	nánguò	*adj.*	sad 考试没考好，他很难过。/ 她难过得哭了。/ 我心里很难过。
专有名词 Proper Nouns				
1	芝加哥	Zhījiāgē	*pn.*	Chicago
2	公牛队（隊）	Gōngniúduì	*pn.*	Chicago Bulls
3	休斯敦	Xiūsīdūn	*pn.*	Houston
4	火箭队（隊）	Huǒjiànduì	*pn.*	Houston Rockets

Exercise 5 🎧 🗣

Listen to Text (2) and answer the questions orally in Chinese.

1. What teams do John and I like respectively?

2. What did we watch this evening?

3. What was the score of the game?

4. Why didn't I call John?

Exercise 6 📖 ✍

There are two paragraphs in Text (2). Read Text (2) and summarize the main ideas of the two paragraphs in Chinese characters.

Paragraph 1:

_____

_____

Paragraph 2:

_____

_____

Exercise 7 ✍

Fill in the blanks with the given words.

高兴　　开始　　比赛　　加油　　时间　　喜欢　　篮球迷

我和约翰都是 _____。约翰喜欢芝加哥公牛队，我喜欢休斯敦火箭队。今天晚上，火箭队和公牛队有一场 _____。白天的时候，我和约翰都认为自己喜欢的球队会赢。比赛 _____ 以后，我们大声地为运动员们 _____。火箭队的球员打得很好，公牛队也打得不错。结果，火箭队和公牛队打了平手，谁也没有赢谁。我和约翰都非常 _____。我打了个电话给我女朋友告诉她比赛结果，因为她也 _____ 看篮球赛，可是今天没有 _____ 看。

Exercise 8 📖

Read the following statements followed by four responses and choose the most logical response to the statement.

1. 我听说你是个篮球迷。

　　a. 我和约翰都认为自己喜欢的球队会赢。

　　b. 我喜欢打篮球，也喜欢看篮球比赛。

　　c. 火箭队以 119 比 89 赢了公牛队。

　　d. 我想他一定看过比赛了。

2. 你觉得火箭队和公牛队哪个会赢?

　　a. 哪个队赢我都很高兴。

　　b. 冬天只能在室内打篮球。

　　c. 小明总是在网上玩篮球游戏。

　　d. 公牛队也不断进球。

3. 今天的比赛怎么样?

    a. 我呢,喜欢休斯敦的火箭队。

    b. 雪下得越大越好!

    c. 你喜欢在电视里看比赛吗?

    d. 一点儿也不激烈,没意思。

4. 你把比赛结果告诉约翰了吗?

    a. 还用我说吗? 他一定为自己喜欢的队难过呢。

    b. 一次比赛结果不能说明哪个队好。

    c. 中国乒乓球常常赢得比赛。

    d. 火箭队以 119 比 89 赢了公牛队。

三、汉字 Chinese Characters

1. New characters in this lesson

序号	拼音	简 / 繁	部件	构词
1	bàng	棒	木 + 奉（夫 + 十）	棒球 / 太棒了 / 非常棒
2	dēng	登	癶 + 豆	登山 / 登高 / 登顶
3	dòng	动 / 動	云 + 力	动手 / 动作 / 活动
4	duàn	断 / 斷	米 + ㄴ + 斤	不断 / 断层
5	duì	队 / 隊	阝 + 人	球队 / 军队 / 部队 / 队伍
6	gēn	根	木 + 艮	根本 / 根底 / 根据 / 树根
7	hǎi	海	氵 + 每（𠂉 + 母）	大海 / 海洋 / 海水 / 海军
8	hū	乎	乎	几乎 / 不外乎
9	huó	活	氵 + 舌（千 + 口）	活动 / 活跃 / 生活 / 快活
10	huǒ	火	火	火箭队 / 火车 / 火鸡
11	jī	激	氵 + 白 + 方 + 攵	激烈
12	jì	继 / 繼	纟 + 米 + ㄴ	继续
13	jiàn	箭	𥫗 + 前	火箭 / 射箭 / 弓箭
14	jìn	进 / 進	井 + 辶	进球 / 进口 / 进步
15	lán	篮 / 籃	𥫗 + 监（𠂉 + 皿）	篮球

16	lì	例	亻+列（歹+刂）	例如 / 例子 / 例题 / 例文
17	liǎ	俩	亻+两	我们俩
18	liè	烈	列（歹+刂）+灬	激烈 / 烈火
19	máo	毛	毛	羽毛球
20	pāng	乓	乓	乒乓球
21	pīng	乒	乒	乒乓球
22	qián	潜 / 潛	氵+夫+夫+日	潜水 / 潜水艇 / 潜伏
23	sài	赛 / 賽	宀+共+贝	比赛 / 赛场 / 赛车 / 赛跑
24	shēng	声 / 聲	士+尸	声音 / 大声 / 雷声 / 雨声
25	shù	束	束	结束 / 一束花
26	sī	斯	其+斤	休斯敦
27	tī	踢	𧾷+易（日+勿）	踢球 / 踢足球 / 用脚踢
28	xiū	休	亻+木	休斯敦 / 休息 / 休想
29	xù	续 / 續	纟+卖	继续 / 后续
30	yíng	赢 / 贏	亡+口+月+贝+凡	打赢 / 赢球 / 赢钱
31	yǒng	泳	氵+永	游泳 / 泳池 / 泳衣
32	yóu	油	氵+由	加油 / 汽油 / 石油
33	yǔ	羽	习+习	羽毛 / 羽毛球
34	yù	育	云+月	体育 / 智育 / 发育 / 生育
35	yuè	越	走+戉	越来越 / 超越 / 越过
36	yùn	运 / 運	云+辶	运动 / 运气 / 好运
37	zhī	芝	艹+之	芝加哥
38	zú	足	口+龰	足球 / 足球队 / 手足

Exercise 1 ✍

Copy the following single-component characters with correct stroke order in the spaces provided.

hū	乎	丿 乀 𠂉 丘 乎					

huǒ	火	、 丶 ゾ 火		
máo	毛	′ 二 三 毛		
pāng	兵	′ ′ ↑ ↑ 乒 兵		
pīng	乒	′ ′ ↑ ↑ 乒 乒		
shù	束	′ ′ 一 一 口 束 束		

Exercise 2 📖 ✍

Read the following sentences and choose the correct characters to fill in the blanks.

1. 他喜欢打篮球，在学校篮球 _____ 里他打得最好。(对 队 付)

2. 她篮球打得好，但是足球 _____ 得不好。(踢 剔 惕)

3. 今天比赛你们 _____ 了几个球？(进 迸 近)

4. 我喜欢室内运动，_____ 如打乒乓球、打羽毛球。(列 冽 例)

5. 夏威夷的海水又干净又暖和，是 _____ 水的人最喜欢的地方。(替 潜 浅)

6. 比赛一开始，我们就大 _____ 地为运动员们加油。(声 生 户)

7. 他大学毕业后，到美国继 _____ 读研究生。(须 续 绪)

8. 这场比赛十分激 _____。(列 烈 洌)

2. Common radicals (9)

(1) 灬 (火) huǒ

The radical 灬 is derived from the pictographic character 火 (火 , fire). This radical is usually written as 灬 when it is on the bottom of a character, but written as 火 when it is on the left side. Characters with this radical are mostly related to fire and burning, e.g. 点 (diǎn, light a fire, dot); 热 (rè, hot); 烧 (shāo, to burn); 烟 (yān, smoke, cigarette).

(2) 辶 zǒuzhīpáng

This radical is derived from the ancient character 辵 (辵) meaning "to walk, to advance"; thus, characters with this radical are usually related to this meaning, e.g. 进 (jìn, to advance, to enter); 过 (guò, to pass); 运 (yùn, to transport); 送 (sòng, to deliver, to send); 通 (tōng, get through).

(3) 纟（糸）jiǎosīpáng

This radical is derived from the pictographic character （糸）indicating a bundle of silk thread. Thus, characters with this radical are mostly related to silk or thread. When this radical is on the left side of a character, it is written as 纟, e.g. 线 (xiàn, thread); 纸 (zhǐ, paper); 红 (hóng, red); 经 (jīng, warp); 组 (zǔ, group). When it is on the bottom of a character, it is written as 糸, e.g. 繁 (fán, numerous); 紧 (jǐn, tight).

(4) ⻊ zúzìpáng

This radical is derived from the pictographic character （足 zú), symbolizing a man's leg and foot. Thus characters with this radical are usually related to the foot, e.g. 跑 (pǎo, to run); 跟 (gēn, to follow); 路 (lù, road); 踢 (tī, to kick); 跳 (tiào, to jump).

Exercise 3

Add different radicals to the following components to form different characters.

1. 井 ____ ____

2. 元 ____ ____ ____ ____

四、语言点 Language Points

1. The adverb 根本

The adverb 根本 is often used to modify a negative form, meaning "at all".

(1) 我不太喜欢室外运动。特别是夏天那么热，根本不想出去。
I do not like outdoor activities, especially in summer when it is so hot; I do not want to go out at all.

(2) 我根本没说过这话，你是从哪儿听来的？
I never said that. Where did you hear it?

(3) 她没学过中文，根本不会写汉字。
She never learned Chinese and cannot write characters at all.

(4) 他一有空就上网，根本不喜欢体育活动。
He goes online as soon as he has time and does not like sports at all.

2. The 越… 越… construction

The 越… 越… construction is similar to the structure "the more… the more…" in English:

Subject + 越 + Verb/Adjective + 越 + Verb/Adjective

(1) 冬天可以去滑雪啊，雪下得<u>越大越好</u>！
We can ski in winter. The bigger the snowfall, the better.

(2) 丽莎迷上了中国武术，她<u>越学越喜欢学</u>。
Lisa is now a fan of Chinese kung fu. The more she learns it the more she likes it.

(3) 我妈妈本来不知道可以<u>上网看中国电影</u>，现在她<u>越看越爱看</u>中国电影了。
My mother did not know that one can watch Chinese movies online, but now the more she watches Chinese movies the more she likes them.

(4) 丽莎学习中文快一年了，她的中文<u>越说越好</u>。
Lisa has been learning Chinese for almost a year. The more she speaks, the more her Chinese improves.

3. The adverb 最

In Lesson 11 we learned the adverb 更 which is equivalent to "more" in English, e.g. 去商店买得花更多的时间 (Shopping at a store takes more time.) In this lesson, we will learn the adverb 最, meaning "the most", to indicate the superlative degree in comparison.

(1) 你<u>最</u>喜欢的运动是什么？
What sports do you like the best?

(2) 我<u>最</u>喜欢室内运动，例如打乒乓球、打羽毛球。
I like indoor sports the most, like table tennis and badminton.

4. The idiomatic expression 加油

The original meaning of the compound verb 加油 is "add gas". It is also an idiomatic expression meaning "work with added vigor".

(1) 开车去旧金山以前，我得先给我的车<u>加油</u>。
Before driving to San Francisco, I have to fill up the tank of my car.

(2) 比赛开始以后，我大声地为火箭队<u>加油</u>。
When the game started, I cheered loudly for the Rockets.

(3) 期末考试快到了。同学们，<u>加油</u>！
The final exam is near. Please work harder, boys and girls!

(4) 老师说这个学期我的成绩一直不好，<u>应该加点儿油</u>了。
The teacher said my grades this semester have not been good, and I should work harder.

5. The preposition 以

Used in written language, the preposition 以 is equivalent to "with" in English, indicating the manner or degree of an action. Here are some examples:

> (1) 上半场，火箭队以 59 比 51 领先公牛队．
>
> In the first half, the Rockets were up against the Bulls 59 to 51.
>
> (2) 全场结束，火箭队以 119 比 89 赢了公牛队。
>
> When the game was over, the Rockets defeated the Bulls 119 to 89.
>
> (3) 昨天的比赛，我们班的乒乓球队以 3 比 0 赢了。
>
> My class table tennis team won the game yesterday 3 to 0.

Exercise 1

Listen to three short dialogs and answer the questions in Chinese characters. Pay attention to the adverb 根本.

Dialog 1 Question: 彼得昨天跟谁在一块儿吃饭？	Answer:
Dialog 2 Question: 小华在什么比赛中得了第一名？	Answer:
Dialog 3 Question: 比尔会做什么中国菜？	Answer:

Exercise 2

Complete the following sentences by using the structure 越…越… based on the information given in parentheses.

1. 我妈妈特别喜欢工作，她是 _____。(the busier, the happier)

2. 你看，外面的雨 _____，看来我们只好在室内打打羽毛球了。(it is raining harder and harder)

3. 我去年种的那棵小树 _____，已经比我高了。 (is growing taller and taller)

4. 彼得的汉语 _____，听起来和中国人说得差不多了。(is getting more and more fluent as he speaks)

5. 女大十八变，他妹妹 _____，像一个电影明星。(is getting prettier and prettier as she grows)

6. 中国有句老话"出门靠朋友"，朋友 _____。(the more, the better)

Exercise 3

Translate the following sentences into English paying attention to the underlined parts.

1. 我<u>根本没有想到</u>这儿的冬天这么冷。

_____

2. 他们<u>越说越高兴</u>，忘了上课的时间。

_____

3. 你们几个人谁跑得<u>最快</u>？谁跑得<u>最慢</u>？

_____

4. 我们学中文已经快一年了，觉得<u>越学越有意思</u>。

_____

5. 在昨天的比赛中，我们学校的篮球队<u>以 76 比 62</u> 赢了二中篮球队。

_____

6. 他说他是我小学的同学，可我<u>根本不记得他</u>。

_____

7. 在长跑比赛时，我们大声地为<u>运动员们</u>加油。

_____

Exercise 4

Work in pairs. Ask and answer the following questions in Chinese orally with the adverb 最.

1. 你们家谁最高？

2. 你们家谁做的饭最好吃？

3. 你们家每天谁起得最早？

4. 你们班谁最爱运动？

5. 你们班谁最喜欢喝咖啡？

6. 你们班谁最爱去图书馆看书？

7. 你们班谁的汉字写得最好看？

8. 你最喜欢吃哪国的饭？你最不喜欢吃哪国的饭？

9. 你最喜欢看什么球赛？你最不喜欢看什么球赛？

10. 你最喜欢什么运动？你最不喜欢什么运动？

11. 你最喜欢哪个球星？你最不喜欢哪个球星？

12. 你最喜欢上什么网站买东西？你最不喜欢上什么网站？

五、语言运用 Using the Language

Activity 1 📖 🗣

Read the following hand-written notice on the bulletin board of the school and discuss with your partner how you should respond to it if you are interested.

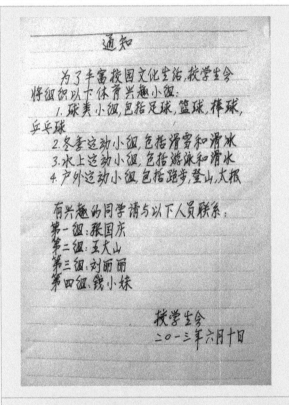

通　知

为了丰富校园文化生活，校学生会将组织以下体育兴趣小组：

1. 球类小组，包括足球、篮球、棒球、乒乓球
2. 冬季运动小组，包括滑雪和滑冰
3. 水上运动小组，包括游泳和滑水
4. 户外运动小组，包括跑步、登山、太极

有兴趣的同学请与以下人员联系：

第一组：张国庆

第二组：王大山

第三组：刘丽丽

第四组：钱小妹

校学生会

二〇一三年六月十日

Activity 2 👂 ✍

1. Listen to the following news briefs and write down in characters what sport each brief is about.

1. _____

2. _____

3. _____

4. _____

Activity 3 👂 ✍

Listen to the following conversation in pairs. Each person fills in the following chart with the information you heard. Compare your notes afterwards.

Hobbies of the man	
Hobbies of the woman	
Their plan for the weekend	

Activity 4 👂 🗣

Listen to this conversation and sum up the information about the man's likes, dislikes and the reason orally in Chinese.

Activity 5 📖 🗣

Read the following photo descriptions and answer the questions orally in Chinese.

1

为了学生的身体健康，某大学要求每个学生都参加一项体育活动。这是下课后大学生们在教室外面踢足球。

1. What is required of each student?
2. For what purpose is this requirement made?

2

张老师在加州中部工作。这里很少下雪。他听说旧金山东边不远的地方有个滑雪公园，就在一个长周末去那里滑了一天雪。

1. What is the climate in the place where Zhang works?
2. What did he do on the long weekend?

3

4

有些传统的中国功夫已经成了老百姓日常锻炼身体的活动。太极拳就是其中之一。现在在公园里，每天早上都能看到很多打太极的人。许多外国学生学的第一种中国武术，往往也是太极拳。

1. What has some Chinese kung fu turned into?
2. What is the style of kung fu foreign students tend to learn first?

在中国很多地方，登山是一种老老少少都喜爱的锻炼活动。在中国西南的一个城市里，每天早上都有上千的人到公园登山。上山的路上，可以看到猴子 (hóuzi, monkey) 在路边等着人们给它们东西吃。

1. What sport is loved by people of all ages?
2. How many people come to this mountain park every morning?

Activity 6 🗣

What do you say?

1. You want to invite a friend to a basketball game tonight and wonder if he is available.
2. You want to tell you friend that you like all sports except those related to water.
3. You called the ticket office of a stadium wondering if there are still tickets available for today's ball game.
4. Tell your friend that you like both indoor and outdoor sports by citing some examples.

Activity 7 🗣

Role Play

You want to find out if your new classmate likes similar sports. Talk with him/her and find out what sports he or she likes. Tell them about your favorite sports. After the conversation, report to the class what you have found out about your classmate.

Sentences and expressions you may need to use:

你喜欢什么运动?

我最喜欢的运动是……

我喜欢球类（lèi, category）运动。

我喜欢健身类运动。

我最爱在电视上看水上运动。

Activity 8 🗣✍

The following pictures represent a story of two friends going to watch a soccer game. Suppose you are one of them. Tell this story to your partner and then type it out on your computer. Your story should have a beginning, middle and an end.

第二十一课 **爱好**
Lesson Twenty-One **Hobbies**

一、导入 Lead-in

Exercise 1 📖 🗣

Look at the pictures below and describe them in Chinese.

王红的爱好是跳舞和摄影。

王红也喜欢逛商场。

她弟弟最喜欢踢足球。

After learning this lesson, you will be able to:

1. Ask and tell about one's hobbies and recreational activities.

2. Talk about one's likes and dislikes, narrate a personal past event.

3. Recognize new characters in this lesson, and understand the common radicals 目, 女, 彳 and 扌.

4. Use different types of questions, 先 … 再 … structure, and some descriptive complements correctly.

二、课文 Texts

课文〔一〕 Text (1)

你有什么爱好?

简体版

Wang Hong and Li Wen are talking about their hobbies.

王红: 李文,你平时有什么业余爱好?

李文: 我的爱好很多,我最喜欢的是打网球和踢足球,也很喜欢摄影。你呢?

Tips: how to ask about someone's hobbies

王红: 我也有不少爱好,我爱上网看微博、看新闻和听音乐。

李文: 有空的时候,我还喜欢玩儿电子游戏,在电视上看体育比赛。

王红: 我也经常看电视。可是我不喜欢看体育节目,我喜欢看电影和电视剧。

李文: 你喜欢什么样的电影?

王红: 我喜欢看爱情故事和科幻电影,不喜欢武打片。

李文: 平时你有什么样的娱乐活动呢?

王红: 娱乐活动嘛,我比较喜欢唱歌和跳舞,也喜欢弹钢琴和吉他。

李文: 我唱歌唱得不好,跳舞也跳得不怎么样,所以没有人约我参加舞会。可是我挺喜欢参加派对的。

王红: 其实跳舞不太难,以后我可以教你。先教你交谊舞,再教拉丁舞。

李文: 太好了。以后我也可以约女孩子去跳舞了。

你有甚麽愛好?

繁体版

Wang Hong and Li Wen are talking about their hobbies.

王紅: 李文, 你平時有什麼業餘愛好?

李文: 我的愛好很多, 我最喜歡的是打網球和踢足球, 也很喜歡攝影。你呢?

王紅: 我也有不少愛好, 我愛上網看微博、看新聞和聽音樂。

李文: 有空的時候, 我還喜歡玩兒電子游戲, 在電視上看體育比賽。

王紅: 我也經常看電視。可是我不喜歡看體育節目, 我喜歡看電影和電視劇。

李文: 你喜歡什麼樣的電影?

王紅: 我喜歡看愛情故事和科幻電影, 不喜歡武打片。

李文: 平時你有什麼樣的娛樂活動呢?

王紅: 娛樂活動嘛, 我比較喜歡唱歌和跳舞, 也喜歡彈鋼琴和吉他。

李文: 我唱歌唱得不好, 跳舞也跳得不怎麼樣, 所以沒有人約我參加舞會。可是我挺喜歡參加派對的。

王紅: 其實跳舞不太難, 以後我可以教你。先教你交誼舞, 再教拉丁舞。

李文: 太好了。以後我也可以約女孩子去跳舞了。

飞跃——汉语初级教程学生用书 下册

Kèwén (yī) *Text (1)*

Nǐ yǒu Shénme Àihào?

 拼音版

Wang Hong and Li Wen are talking about their hobbies.

Wáng Hóng: Lǐ Wén, nǐ píngshí yǒu shénme yèyú àihào?

Lǐ Wén: Wǒ de àihào hěnduō. Wǒ zuì xǐhuan de shì dǎ wǎngqiú hé tī zúqiú, yě hěn xǐhuan shèyǐng. Nǐ ne?

Wáng Hóng: Wǒ yě yǒu bù shǎo àihào, wǒ ài shàngwǎng kàn wēibó, kàn xīnwén hé tīng yīnyuè.

Lǐ Wén: Yǒu kòng de shíhou, wǒ hái xǐhuan wánr diànzǐ yóuxì, zài diànshìshang kàn tǐyù bǐsài.

Wáng Hóng: Wǒ yě jīngcháng kàn diànshì. Kěshì wǒ bù xǐhuan kàn tǐyù jiémù, wǒ xǐhuan kàn diànyǐng hé diànshìjù.

Lǐ Wén: Nǐ xǐhuan shénmeyàng de diànyǐng?

Wáng Hóng: Wǒ xǐhuan kàn àiqíng gùshi hé kēhuàn diànyǐng, bù xǐhuan wǔdǎpiàn.

Lǐ Wén: Píngshí nǐ yǒu shénmeyàng de yúlè huódòng ne?

Wáng Hóng: Yúlè huódòng ma, wǒ bǐjiào xǐhuan chànggē hé tiàowǔ, yě xǐhuan tán gāngqín hé jítā.

Lǐ Wén: Wǒ chànggē chàng de bù hǎo, tiàowǔ yě tiào de bù zěnmeyàng, suǒyǐ méiyǒu rén yuē wǒ cānjiā wǔhuì. Kěshì wǒ tǐng xǐhuan cānjiā pàiduì de.

Wáng Hóng: Qíshí tiàowǔ bú tài nán, yǐhòu wǒ kěyǐ jiāo nǐ. Xiān jiāo nǐ jiāoyìwǔ, zài jiāo lādīngwǔ.

Lǐ Wén: Tài hǎo le. Yǐhòu wǒ yě kěyǐ yuē nǚháizi qù tiàowǔ le.

生词（一）New Words (1)

	简体（繁體）	拼音	词性	解释
1	业余（業餘）	yèyú	*adj.*	amateur 业余爱好 / 业余歌手
2	爱（愛）好	àihào	*n.*	hobby 你有什么爱好？/ 我的爱好很广泛。
3	摄（攝）影	shèyǐng	*v.*	take a photograph 摄影家 / 摄影师 / 摄影展览
4	微博	wēibó	*n.*	microblog, miniblog 他天天在网上发微博。/ 微博不能写得很长。
5	电视（電視）	diànshì	*n.*	television 看电视 / 打开电视 / 关电视 / 今天晚上电视上有一个好电影。
6	节（節）目	jiémù	*n.*	program 音乐会的节目单 / 电视节目 / 广播节目 / 下一个节目是舞蹈。
7	剧（劇）	jù	*n.*	drama, play 京剧 / 戏剧 / 电视剧 / 广播剧 / 剧本
8	爱（愛）情	àiqíng	*n.*	love, romance 爱情片 / 爱情故事 / 两个人之间的爱情
9	科幻	kēhuàn	*n.*	science fiction 科幻小说 / 科幻电影
10	娱乐（娛樂）	yúlè	*n.*	entertainment 娱乐节目 / 娱乐活动 / 娱乐生活
11	活动	huódòng	*n.*	activity 举办活动 / 娱乐活动
12	嘛	ma	*part.*	（a modal particle）"你的中文很好。""那当然了，我是中文系毕业的嘛。"
13	跳舞	tiàowǔ	*v.*	dance 我每个周末都去跳舞。/ 中国城市的公园里常常有很多人跳舞。
14	弹（彈）	tán	*v.*	play (a musical instrument) 弹钢琴 / 弹吉他 / 我的同事弹得一手好钢琴。
15	钢（鋼）琴	gāngqín	*n.*	piano 钢琴师 / 钢琴家 / 给钢琴调音
16	吉他	jítā	*n.*	guitar 弹吉他 / 我弟弟是一名吉他手。
17	舞会（會）	wǔhuì	*n.*	dance party 办舞会 / 开舞会 / 化妆舞会
18	派对（對）	pàiduì	*n.*	party 开派对 / 举行派对 / 穿派对装
19	教	jiāo	*v.*	teach 教书 / 我在美国教中文。/ 你能教我游泳吗？

飞跃——汉语初级教程学生用书　下册

简体（繁體）	拼音	词性	解释
20 交谊（誼）舞	jiāoyìwǔ	*n.*	social dance 跳交谊舞 / 办交谊舞会
21 拉丁舞	lādīngwǔ	*n.*	Latin dance 拉丁舞比赛 / 拉丁舞很流行。/ 拉丁舞来自拉丁美洲。

Exercise 1

Listen to Text (1) and answer the questions orally in Chinese.

1. What hobbies does Li Wen have? List at least three of them.

2. What hobbies does Wang Hong have? List at least three of them.

3. Why do girls avoid dancing with Li Wen?

4. How does Wang Hong feel about dancing?

5. What will they teach each other?

Exercise 2

Read Text (1) and underline the incorrect parts of the following sentences.

1. 李文喜欢打网球和篮球。

2. 李文在体育馆看比赛。

3. 王红也喜欢看体育节目。

4. 李文喜欢弹钢琴。

5. 很多女孩子愿意跟李文跳舞。

6. 王红要教李文唱歌。

Exercise 3

Write down the objects in characters that match the verbs given.

1. 跳：_____

2. 唱：_____

3. 玩：_____

4. 弹：_____

5. 打：_____

6. 踢：_____

7. 看：_____

8. 听：_____

9. 约：_____

10. 参加：_____

Exercise 4

Translate the following sentences into Chinese.

1. My hobbies are playing tennis and watching sports on TV.

_____

2. Whenever Xiaohua has time, she plays games on the computer.

_____

3. For recreation, I normally write miniblogs online.

_____

4. No one ever invites me to dance.

_____

5. Can you teach me how to play tennis?

_____

6. Actually, I like watching love stories, not kung fu movies.

_____

课文（二）Text (2)

爱好不同

简体版

In his weekly journal, John writes about his recent conflicts with his girlfriend.

星期六早上八点，我还在睡觉呢，玛丽就打电话来找我了。她要我陪她去逛商场。我问她想买什么，她说也没想好要买什么，只是想去逛一逛。我本来不想去，可是想了想，还是去了。结果，从早上九点到中午十二点，我陪她逛了三个钟头，可她什么东西都没买。她还挺高兴的，可是，我却觉得很没意思。

下午，我刚开始上网玩儿电脑游戏，玛丽又给我打

电话了，她要我陪她去买衣服。我说今天上午你为什么不买呢，她说她要多看几家商店才能决定，还说我上网玩儿电脑游戏是浪费时间。这下子我生气了。我说，你有你的爱好，我也有我的爱好，我怎么就不能玩儿电脑游戏呢。玛丽也生气了，一下子就把电话挂了。我很难过，是不是爱好不同就很难成为男女朋友呢？

愛好不同

繁体版

In his weekly journal, John writes about his recent conflicts with his girlfriend.

星期六早上八點，我還在睡覺呢，瑪麗就打電話來找我了。她要我陪她去逛商場。我問她想買什麼，她說也沒想好要買什麼，祇是想去逛一逛。我本來不想去，可是想了想，還是去了。結果，從早上九點到中午十二點，我陪她逛了三個鐘頭，可她什麼東西都沒買。她還挺高興的，可是，我卻覺得很沒意思。

下午，我剛開始上網玩兒電腦遊戲，瑪麗又給我打電話了，她要我陪她去買衣服。我說今天上午你爲什麼不買呢，她說她要多看幾家商店才能決定，還說我上網玩兒電腦遊戲是浪費時間。這下子我生氣了。我說，你有你的愛好，我也有我的愛好，我怎麼就不能玩兒電腦遊戲呢。瑪麗也生氣了，一下子就把電話掛了。我很難過，是不是愛好不同就很難成爲男女朋友呢？

Àihào Bù Tóng

In his weekly journal, John writes about his recent conflicts with his girlfriend.

Xīngqīliù zǎoshang bā diǎn, wǒ hái zài shuìjiào ne, Mǎlì jiù dǎ diànhuà lái zhǎo wǒ le. Tā yào wǒ péi tā qù guàng shāngchǎng. Wǒ wèn tā xiǎng mǎi shénme, tā shuō yě méi xiǎnghǎo yào mǎi shénme, zhǐshì xiǎng qù guàng yi guàng. Wǒ běnlái bù xiǎng qù, kěshì xiǎng le xiǎng, háishì qù le. Jiéguǒ, cóng zǎoshang jiǔ diǎn dào zhōngwǔ shí'èr diǎn, wǒ péi tā guàngle sān gè zhōngtóu, kě tā shénme dōngxi dōu méi mǎi. Tā hái tǐng gāoxìng de, kěshì, wǒ què juéde hěn méi yìsi.

Xiàwǔ, wǒ gāng kāishǐ shàngwǎng wánr diànnǎo yóuxì, Mǎlì yòu gěi wǒ dǎ diànhuà le, tā yào wǒ péi tā qù mǎi yīfu. Wǒ shuō jīntiān shàngwǔ nǐ wèi shénme bù mǎi ne, tā shuō tā yào duō kàn jǐ jiā shāngdiàn cái néng juédìng, hái shuō wǒ shàngwǎng wánr diànnǎo yóuxì shì làngfèi shíjiān. Zhè xiàzi wǒ shēngqì le. Wǒ shuō, nǐ yǒu nǐ de àihào, wǒ yě yǒu wǒ de àihào, wǒ zěnme jiù bù néng wánr diànnǎo yóuxì ne. Mǎlì yě shēngqì le, yíxiàzi jiù bǎ diànhuà guà le. Wǒ hěn nánguò, shì bu shì àihào bù tóng jiù hěn nán chéngwéi nán-nǚpéngyou ne?

生词（二）*New Words (2)*

	简体（繁體）	拼音	词性	解释
1	陪	péi	*v.*	accompany 陪客人聊天 / 陪朋友逛街
2	却（卻）	què	*adv.*	but, yet 我请他寒假来海南，他却去东北了。/ 这个美国人不认识汉字，中文却说得很好。

简体（繁體）	拼音	词性	解释
3 决定	juédìng	*v.*	decide 我决定不考大学了。/ 这件事情我决定不下来。
4 浪费（费）	làngfèi	*v.*	waste 不要浪费时间。/ 你买这个东西是浪费钱。
5 这（這）下子	zhè xiàzi		this time; this act 这下子可把他气坏了。
6 怎么（麼）	zěnme	*pron.*	how, why 你不是大学毕业的吗，怎么会没有工作？
7 挂（掛）	guà	*v.*	hang up 挂电话 / 你怎么能挂我的电话呢！
8 同	tóng	*adj.*	same 同学 / 同志 / 同乡 / 同屋

Exercise 5 🎧 🗣✳

Listen to Text (2) and answer the questions orally in Chinese.

1. Why did Mary call John in the morning?

2. Did Mary have a definite shopping plan when she called John?

3. How did John feel that morning? Why?

4. How did Mary explain why she called again?

Exercise 6 📖

Read Text (2) and choose the correct answer to complete the following sentences.

1. 早上七点钟，约翰 _____。

   a. 给玛丽打电话   b. 在睡觉   c. 在看书

2. 逛街的时候，玛丽 _____。

   a. 知道买什么   b. 问约翰应该买什么   c. 没想好买什么东西

3. 对买东西，约翰 _____。

   a. 看法跟玛丽不一样   b. 看法跟玛丽一样   c. 没有兴趣

4. 约翰生气了，因为 _____。

   a. 玛丽说他的爱好不好   b. 玛丽又让他跟她去商店   c. 玛丽不想做他的女朋友

5. 玛丽生气了，因为 _____。

   a. 约翰说她不知道买什么东西

   b. 约翰只想着上网玩儿游戏

   c. 约翰让她给他买游戏

Exercise 7 📖 ✎

Read Text (2) again and summarize the main ideas of the two paragraphs in two or three sentences in Chinese.

1st paragraph	2nd paragraph

Exercise 8 ✎

Translate the following sentences into Chinese.

1. I was still sleeping when he called me.

_____

2. On Sundays I often accompany my girlfriend when she wants to go window shopping.

_____

3. My girlfriend said she had no idea what to buy.

_____

4. My wife said to me, "You have your job, and I have my job, why do you want me to cook everyday?"

_____

5. I do not like shopping. Why can't you go by yourself?

_____

6. When you go shopping, you should visit more stores to compare their prices.

_____

三、汉字 Chinese Characters

1. New characters in this lesson

序号	拼音	简 / 繁	部件	构词
1	bó	博	十＋尃（甫＋寸）	微博 / 博士 / 博学
2	gāng	钢（鋼）	钅＋冈	钢琴 / 钢铁

3	guà	挂（掛）	扌+圭（土+土）	挂电话 / 挂衣服
4	huàn	幻	幺+丁	科幻 / 幻想
5	jí	吉	士+口	吉他 / 吉利
6	jiāo	交	亠+父	交谊舞 / 交作业
7	jué	决	冫+夬	决定 / 决心
8	kē	科	禾+斗	科幻 / 科学
9	lì	历 / 歷	厂+力	历史 / 经历
10	ma	嘛	口+麻（广+林）	很好嘛 / 不错嘛
11	mù	目	目	节目 / 目的 / 目前
12	pài	派	氵+辰	派对 / 左派
13	péi	陪	阝+咅（立+口）	陪伴 / 陪朋友看电影
14	qín	琴	王+王+今	钢琴 / 小提琴
15	què	却（卻）	去+卩	却是 / 却没有
16	shì	视（視）	礻+见	电视 / 视像
17	tán	弹（彈）	弓+单	弹钢琴 / 弹吉他
18	tiào	跳	𧾷+兆	跳舞 / 跳水 / 跳绳
19	wēi	微	彳+岂（山+一+几）+攵	微博 / 微笑 / 微风
20	yí	谊（誼）	讠+宜（宀+且）	交谊舞 / 友谊
21	yú	娱（娛）	女+吴（口+天）	娱乐 / 娱乐场所 / 文娱
22	yú	余（餘）	人+示	业余 / 余下

Exercise 1 ✎

Copy the following single-component character with the correct stroke order in the spaces provided.

mù	目	丨 冂 冂 目 目						

Exercise 2 ✎

Read the following sentences and choose the correct characters to fill in the blanks.

1. 玛丽不愿意听约翰的电话，一下子就把电话 ＿＿＿＿＿ 上了。（挂　卦　褂）

2. 上中学的时候我买了一把 _____ 他，但是没有学会。（ 几　吉　击 ）

3. 小王的爱好是写 _____ 博，他特别喜欢在脸谱网写。（ 薇　微　澇 ）

4. 其实 _____ 舞不太难学，可以先学交谊舞，再学拉丁舞。（ 眺　挑　跳 ）

5. 今天电视里有 _____ 乐节目吗？（ 娱　愉　误 ）

6. 现在很多中国家长都要孩子从小就开始学弹钢 _____。（ 琴　亲　禽 ）

7. 这个周末李丽家有个 _____ 对，你去不去？（ 排　牌　派 ）

8. 我跳交 _____ 舞的时候，总是踩别人的脚。（ 宜　谊　易 ）

2. Common radicals (10)

(1) 目 mùzìpáng

This radical is derived from the pictographic character 👁, like an eye. Thus, characters with the 目 radical are usually related to eyes, e.g. 看 (kàn, look at), 眼 (yǎn, eye), 睛 (jīng, eyeball), 睡 (shuì, to sleep), 盲 (máng, blind).

(2) 女 nǚzìpáng

This radical is derived from the pictographic character 👤, resembling a kneeling woman. Characters with the radical 女 are usually related to females, e.g. 妈 (mā, mother), 姐 (jiě, elder sister), 妹 (mèi, younger sister), 婆 (pó, grandmother).

(3) 扌(手) tíshǒupáng

This radical is derived from the pictographic character 👋 (手 shǒu), indicating a hand. Thus, characters with this radical are usually related to hands or actions with hands, e.g. 打 (dǎ, to beat), 找 (zhǎo, look for), 指 (zhǐ, finger; point at), 把 (bǎ, to hold). When it is at the bottom of a character, it is written as 手, e.g. 拿 (ná, hold with hand).

(4) 彳 shuānglìrén

The radical 彳 is derived from a pictographic character resembling a cross road. Thus, characters with this radical are usually related to walking. This radical is always put on the left side of a character, e.g. 行 (xíng, to walk), 街 (jiē, street), 往 (wǎng, to go).

Exercise 3

Add radicals to the following components to form different characters.

1. 艮 _____　_____　_____　_____

2. 也 _____　_____　_____　_____

3. 子 _____　_____　_____　_____

四、语言点 Language Points

1. The descriptive complement (2)

In Lesson 14, we learned the descriptive complement as a part of a sentence. A descriptive complement is a phrase used after a verb or an adjective to describe how an action is carried out or how a state exists. In the previous lessons, the verbs with a descriptive complement are without an object, like 时间过得真快！ In this lesson, we will learn how a descriptive complement is formed when a verb carries an object. Here are the pattern and examples:

Subject + Verb + Object + the Repeated Verb + 得 + Complement

(1) 我唱歌唱得不好，跳舞也跳得不怎么样，所以没有人约我参加舞会。
I do not sing well, nor dance well. So no one invites me to dance parties.

(2) 他说中文说得好极了！（比较：他的中文说得好极了！）
He speaks Chinese extremely well.

(3) 约翰打篮球打得很好。（比较：约翰的篮球打得很好。）
John plays basketball very well.

(4) 丽莎打太极拳打得很不错。（比较：丽莎的太极拳打得很不错。）
Lisa plays taiji pretty well.

2. The 先 … 再 … structure

In Lesson 5, we learned that a Chinese sentence may have two or more verbs, and that the word order is used to show the relationship of the actions. In this lesson, we will learn how to use adverbs 先 and 再 to indicate the sequence of actions: "first…then…".

Subject + 先 + Verb1 + 再 + Verb 2

(1) 下车后，您先出站，再向左拐，您会看见一些中国商店的牌子。
After getting off the subway, go out of the station first and then turn left. You will see some Chinese store signs.

(2) 其实跳舞不太难，以后我可以教你。先教你交谊舞，再教拉丁舞。
Actually, dancing is not very difficult. I can teach you later. I will teach you ballroom dance first, and then Latin dance.

(3) 玛丽要约翰陪她先逛中国城，再到电影院看电影。

Mary wants John to go with her to Chinatown first, and then watch a movie in a movie theater.

(4) 今年圣诞节放假的时候，我们计划到中国旅行，先去北京，再到上海。

For this year's Christmas holiday, we plan to travel in China. We will first go to Beijing and then to Shanghai.

In the 先… 再… structure, 再 can be replaced by 然后. Note that 再 usually refers to a future action while 然后 can indicate both past and future actions. For example:

(1) 昨天是星期六，起床以后，我先洗澡，然后吃早餐。(past action)

It was Saturday yesterday. After getting up, I took a shower and then had break-fast.

(2) 今年圣诞节放假的时候,我们计划到中国旅行,先去北京,然后到上海。(future action)

For this year's Christmas holiday, we plan to travel in China. We will first go to Beijing and then to Shanghai.

3. The "V — V" construction

In Lesson 10, we learned the reduplication of a verb which indicates a short duration of an action, or an action in a casual way. In this lesson, we will learn the "V — V" construction, which has the same effect as the reduplication of a verb, and the "V —下" construction. For example:

看一看 = 看看 = 看一下
想一想 = 想想 = 想一下
逛一逛 = 逛逛 = 逛一下

Note the "V — V" construction only applies to monosyllabic verbs, but not disyllabic verbs. For example, we can say 学习学习 and 学习一下，but cannot say 学习一学习.

4. The time words 以前 and 以后

When attached to other time words or action words in forming time expressions, 以前 and 以后 means "before" and "after" respectively. Note that the word order in a Chinese time expression with 以前 and 以后 is the opposite from its counterpart in English.

以前		以后	
七点半以前	before 7:30	七点半以后	after 7:30
圣诞节以前	before Christmas	圣诞节以后	after Christmas
你来以前	before you come	你来以后	after you come

以前 and 以后 can also stand by themselves to indicate "in the past" and "later" respectively. Here are some examples from this lesson:

(1) 其实跳舞不太难，以后我可以教你。

Actually, dancing is not very dificult. I can teach you in future.

(2) 太好了！以后我也可以约女孩子去跳舞了。

Great! Later I can invite girls to dance.

(3) 以前我觉得中文很难，现在觉得不太难了。

Before, I felt Chinese was very difficult, but now I do not feel so.

(4) 他以前喜欢上网玩儿电脑游戏，没有时间陪女朋友逛街。

Before, he liked playing games online and had no time to go window shopping with his girlfriend.

5. Review:

(1) Question with 吗

a. 你的同学玛丽也是美国人吗？

Is your classmate Mary also an American?

b. 你们收信用卡吗？

Do you accept credit cards?

c. 不好意思，我还想问一下，中国城有公共洗手间吗？

Excuse me, may I ask another question: is there a public restroom in Chinatown?

(2) Affirmative-negative question

a. 你是不是学生？

Are you a student or not?

b. 不便宜啊！可不可以打个折？

So expensive! Can you give me a discount or not?

c. 要不要买保险？

Do you want to insure it or not?

d. 是不是昨天晚上上网睡得太晚了?

Is it because you stayed online too long last night and went to bed too late?

(3) Question with question word

a. 你的弟弟多大了?

How old is your younger brother?

b. 这位女孩是谁?

Who is this girl?

c. 地铁站在哪儿?

Where is the subway station?

d. 你最喜欢的运动是什么?

What is your favorite sport?

e. 今天上午你为什么不买呢?

Why didn't you buy it this morning?

f. 你喜欢什么样的电影?

What type of movies do you like?

(4) Alternative question

a. 要黑色的还是灰色的?

Do you want the black one or the gray one?

b. 你们想喝什么，红茶还是绿茶?

What do you want to drink? Black tea or green tea?

c. 中国城离这儿挺远的，您是走路去还是开车去?

Chinatown is pretty far from here. Are you walking or driving there?

(5) Question with 呢

a. 我很好。你呢?

I am very well, and you?

b. 我是在英国出生的。你呢?

I was born in Britain, and you?

c. 上了地铁以后，在哪一站下车呢?

Which stop should I get off after getting on the subway?

(6) Question with 吧

> a. 好久不见。最近学习很忙吧?
>
> Long time no see. You must have been busy with your study?
>
> b. 你们的身体还好吧? 望多多保重!
>
> You are in good health, I hope? Take good care of yourself.

Exercise 1

Listen to the three short dialogs and answer the questions in Chinese, paying attention to the 先 … 再 … structure.

Dialog 1 Question: 小红是不是喜欢先喝汤再吃饭?	Answer:
Dialog 2 Question: 汤姆每天回到家是先休息一会儿再开始做作业吗?	Answer:
Dialog 3 Question: 大卫每天什么时候喝茶?	Answer:

Exercise 2

Read the following sentences and fill in the blanks with 以前 or 以后 .

1. 你来 _____ 给我打个电话，我去车站接你。

2. 去北京 _____ 我会跟你们保持联系的。

3. _____ 我有时间的时候一定会做几个中国菜给你吃。

4. _____ 他是一名医生，现在是一所大学的老师。

5. 你要是真想学习中国书法，_____ 我会请一位老师教你。

6. 你俩大学毕业 _____ 有什么打算，读研究生还是找工作?

7. 我和小华的姐姐 _____ 在同一家银行工作。后来我考上了大学，她出了国。

8. _____ 我每个星期都给父母打电话，这学期太忙，每两个星期才打一次。

Exercise 3

Translate the following Dialogs into Chinese using the "V — V" construction. Type the characters on your computer.

Dialog 1

A: Xiaohua, I don't understand this sentence. Do you know what it means?

B: I don't understand it either. Let me think and I'll tell you later.

Dialog 2

A: David, what do you like to do during weekends?

B: I like to go to a coffee shop to chat with my friends.

Dialog 3

A: Mary, what do you want to buy when you go to the mall today?

B: I don't want to buy anything. I just want to walk around the mall and relax.

Dialog 4

A: Teacher Wang, how can one learn a new word very quickly?

B: You need to listen to it, say it out, and write it down. You also need to put it into use.

Exercise 4 ✎

Complete the following sentences with the descriptive complement by following the example below.

Example: 他唱歌唱得不太好 。(not so well)

1. 王红跳舞 _____。(very well)

2. 约翰打篮球 _____。(pretty well)

3. 李文跑步 _____。(very slowly)

4. 他妹妹滑冰 _____。(very beautifully)

5. 小华打乒乓球 _____。(very well)

6. 丽莎打太极拳 _____。(pretty well)

7. 彼得踢足球 _____。(not very well)

8. 李文打网球 _____。(not well)

Exercise 5

Match the questions in column I with the appropriate replies in Column II.

Column I	Column II
(　　) 1. 你现在有时间吗？	a. 绿茶。
(　　) 2. 你家都有些什么人？	b. 是的，我和朋友一起去的。
(　　) 3. 你想喝咖啡还是绿茶？	c. 不好意思，我们只收现金。
(　　) 4. 到了中国城，我们在哪儿见面呢？	d. 爸爸、妈妈、弟弟和我。

（　）5. 你今天晚上去跳舞了吧？	e. 科幻电影。
（　）6. 我们去伦敦的机票你订了没有？	f. 对不起，我现在没有时间。
（　）7. 你最喜欢看什么样的电影？	g. 是的，我已经给它吃药了。
（　）8. 你的老家有多少人口？	h. 就在中国城大门那儿。
（　）9. 你们这儿收不收信用卡？	i. 还没呢。
（　）10. 你们家的小狗是不是病了？	j. 有十几万。

Exercise 6 📖 ✍

Read the following sentences and write a question regarding the underlined parts.

1. 那个男孩是<u>我弟弟</u>。

_____

2. 我爷爷今年 <u>75 岁</u>了。

_____

3. 我的老家在<u>纽约</u>。

_____

4. 我喜欢<u>会中国武术</u>的人。

_____

5. 我最喜欢的运动是<u>打网球</u>。

_____

6. 我昨天<u>病了</u>，没来上课。

_____

7. 我是中国人，<u>我想你也是中国人</u>。

_____

8. 玛丽今天没来上课，我不知道<u>她是不是病了</u>。

_____

9. 这里有红茶也有绿茶，我不知道<u>你们想喝什么</u>。

_____

10. 我想知道<u>中国城有没有公共洗手间</u>。

_____

五、语言运用 Using the Language

Activity 1 📖 🗣

Read the following article and discuss the three reasons why the author likes one of his hobbies the most.

　　我有许多爱好，比如看书、打网球、看电视、上网。打网球是我最喜欢的。

　　我为什么喜欢打网球呢？第一，我打网球的时候认识了很多朋友。我每个周末都去网球场打网球，跟朋友们在一起我很高兴。第二，打网球让我身体健康。我以前常常生病，开始打网球以后，我的身体越来越好了。第三，打网球让我学习更好了。

Activity 2 👂 🗣

At a match making agency, you overheard a man and a woman introducing themselves to each other. Listen and answer the following questions orally in Chinese.

1. What are the hobbies of the man and the woman?

2. How do they feel about each other?

3. Do they plan to meet again? How do you know?

Activity 3 📖

Read the following photo descriptions and match the numbers with the pictures.

1. 我们班的女同学在新年的晚会上跳舞。

2. 早上，有很多人在公园里锻炼。

3. 我女朋友特别喜欢买漂亮的衣服，还总是让我陪她去。

4. 我喜欢逛这家商场，因为这里有很多小店，东西都很便宜。

a

b

c

d

Activity 4 🦻 🗣

Listen to the passage and answer the questions below in English.

1. What is the survey about?
2. List, minimally, the five most favored activities of the people being surveyed.
3. How many students spend the weekend off the campus?
4. What do those who prefer to stay in their dorms do?

Activity 5 ✍

Look at the following pictures representing one day of a college student's weekend. Type out a brief description for each of his activities on your computer.

早上：体育馆，游泳

下午：图书馆，看书、复习

晚上：有时跟朋友去看画展

晚上：有时去唱卡拉 OK

Activity 6 🗣

Role Play

You are a reporter for the school newspaper. You need to write an article about student hobbies. Conduct an interview for the article. Your partner will play the role of a student.

Sentences you may need to use:

你有什么爱好？

你放学后常常做什么？

你周末喜欢做什么？

你的爱好对学习有帮助吗？

你课余 (kèyú, after class) 时间是怎么过的？

第二十二课 暑假
Lesson Twenty-Two **Summer Vacation**

一、导入 Lead-in

Exercise 1

Look at the pictures below and describe them in Chinese.

坐飞机旅游又方便又舒服。

去中国旅游当然得去北京看看。

去旅游不能错过香港这个购物天堂。

上海是个现代化的大城市。

After learning this lesson, you will be able to:

1. Talk about summer vacation travel plans and itineraries.

2. Talk about major cities and famous scenic or historical spots in China and the United States.

3. Recognize new characters in this lesson, and know about the common radicals 山, 广, 石 and 阝.

4 Use the 除了 ... 以外 structure and common Chinese particles correctly.

二、课文 Texts

课文（一）*Text (1)*

去中国旅游

Mary and John are making plans for their trip to China.

玛丽：约翰，咱们暑假去中国的飞机票订了没有？

约翰：还没呢，咱们先计划一下。你想去哪儿呢？

玛丽：除了北京以外，我哪儿都没去过。

约翰：我们先去上海吧，上海是个现代化的大城市，去
中国旅游当然得去上海看看。

Tips: how to tell a travel plan step by step

玛丽：然后呢？

约翰：可以去苏州和杭州，苏州有著名的园林，杭州有
美丽的西湖，都值得看看。

玛丽：嗯，我想去香港看看，听说香港的衣服又漂亮又
便宜。

约翰：是啊，香港这个购物天堂你怎么能错过呢！我们
可以先到广州，然后从广州坐火车去香港。

玛丽：听说中国的兵马俑很有名，是在哪个城市呢？

约翰：兵马俑在西安。西安是个历史古都，当然也不能
错过。我们可以从香港坐飞机去西安，最后再从
西安去北京。

玛丽：太棒了！那就这样定了，你赶快订飞机票和旅馆吧！

去中國旅遊

Mary and John are making plans for their trip to China.

瑪麗：約翰，咱們暑假去中國的飛機票訂了沒有？

約翰：還沒呢，咱們先計劃一下。你想去哪兒呢？

瑪麗：除了北京以外，我哪兒都沒去過。

約翰：我們先去上海吧，上海是個現代化的大城市，去中國旅遊當然得去上海看看。

瑪麗：然後呢？

約翰：可以去蘇州和杭州，蘇州有著名的園林，杭州有美麗的西湖，都值得看看。

瑪麗：嗯，我想去香港看看，聽說香港的衣服又漂亮又便宜。

約翰：是啊，香港這個購物天堂你怎麼能錯過呢！我們可以先到廣州，然後從廣州坐火車去香港。

瑪麗：聽說中國的兵馬俑很有名，是在哪個城市呢？

約翰：兵馬俑在西安。西安是個歷史古都，當然也不能錯過。我們可以從香港坐飛機去西安，最後再從西安去北京。

瑪麗：太棒了！那就這樣定了，你趕快訂飛機票和旅館吧！

Kèwén (yī) *Text (1)*

Qù Zhōngguó Lǚyóu

拼音版

Mary and John are making plans for their trip to China.

Mǎlì: Yuēhàn, zánmen shǔjià qù Zhōngguó de fēijīpiào dìngle méiyǒu?

Yuēhàn: Hái méi ne, zánmen xiān jìhuà yíxià. Nǐ xiǎng qù nǎr ne?

Mǎlì: Chúle Běijīng yǐwài, wǒ nǎr dōu méi qùguo.

Yuēhàn: Wǒmen xiān qù Shànghǎi ba, Shànghǎi shì ge xiàndài-
huà de dàchéngshì, qù Zhōngguó lǚyóu dāngrán děi qù
Shànghǎi kànkan.

Mǎlì: Ránhòu ne?

Yuēhàn: Kěyǐ qù Sūzhōu hé Hángzhōu, Sūzhōu yǒu zhùmíng de
yuánlín, Hángzhōu yǒu měilì de Xīhú, dōu zhíde kànkan.

Mǎlì: Ǹg, wǒ xiǎng qù Xiānggǎng kànkan, tīngshuō Xiānggǎng de
yīfu yòu piàoliang yòu piányi.

Yuēhàn: Shì a, Xiānggǎng zhège gòuwù tiāntáng nǐ zěnme néng
cuòguò ne! Wǒmen kěyǐ xiān dào Guǎngzhōu, ránhòu cóng
Guǎngzhōu zuò huǒchē qù Xiānggǎng.

Mǎlì: Tīngshuō Zhōngguó de bīngmǎyǒng hěn yǒumíng, shì zài
nǎge chéngshì ne?

Yuēhàn: Bīngmǎyǒng zài Xī'ān. Xī'ān shì ge lìshǐ gǔdū, dāngrán
yě bù néng cuòguò. Wǒmen kěyǐ cóng Xiānggǎng zuò fēijī qù
Xī'ān, zuìhòu zài cóng Xī'ān qù Běijīng.

Mǎlì: Tài bàng le! Nà jiù zhèyàng dìng le, nǐ gǎnkuài dìng fēijīpiào
hé lǚguǎn ba!

生词（一）New Words (1)

	简体（繁體）	拼音	词性	解释
1	暑假	shǔjià	*n.*	summer vacation 放暑假 / 暑假实习
2	除了……以外	chúle … yǐwài		besides; apart from 除了小王以外，小李也去看电影了。
3	现(現)代	xiàndài	*n.*	modern time 现代化 / 中国现代文学
4	化	huà	*suff.*	（suffix indicating a change, similar to –ize in English）城市化 / 工业化 / 年轻化
5	城市	chéngshì	*n.*	city 城市生活比较方便。/ 我喜欢住在大城市里。

	简体（繁體）	拼音	词性	解释
6	著名	zhùmíng	adj.	famous 著名历史人物 / 著名的文学家
7	园（園）林	yuánlín	n.	garden, park 苏州园林 / 园林艺术
8	美丽（麗）	měilì	adj.	beautiful 美丽的风景 / 美丽的姑娘
9	值得	zhíde	v.	be worthy 北京有很多地方值得看。
10	嗯	ǹg	intj.	（a sound indicating awareness or agreement）"你穿这双鞋吧。""嗯，好的。"
11	听说（聽說）	tīngshuō	v.	hear about 我听说他在北京学中文。
12	天堂	tiāntáng	n.	paradise, heaven 人们把苏州和杭州比作人间天堂。
13	错过（錯過）	cuòguò	v.	miss 别错过火车。/ 我错过了那次机会。
14	火车（車）	huǒchē	n.	train 火车站 / 火车头 / 中国的火车交通很发达。
15	兵马（馬）俑	bīngmǎyǒng	n.	Terracotta Warriors and Horses 西安的兵马俑很值得一看。
16	历（歷）史	lìshǐ	n.	history 历史课 / 中国近代的历史
17	古都	gǔdū	n.	ancient capital 北京是一个古都。/ 世界上很多古都都在河流旁边。
18	棒	bàng	adj.	superb, excellent 李小龙的功夫棒极了。
19	定	dìng	v.	decide "这件事定下来没有？""还没定呢。"
	专有名词 Proper Nouns			
1	上海	Shànghǎi	pn.	Shanghai
2	苏（蘇）州	Sūzhōu	pn.	Suzhou
3	杭州	Hángzhōu	pn.	Hangzhou
4	西湖	Xīhú	pn.	West Lake
5	香港	Xiānggǎng	pn.	Hong Kong
6	广（廣）州	Guǎngzhōu	pn.	Guangzhou
7	西安	Xī'ān	pn.	Xi'an

Exercise 1 🎧

Listen to Text (1) and decide whether the following statements are true or false.

1. 玛丽去过中国。	(	)
2. 关于上海，约翰喜欢的是买东西。	(	)
3. 苏州和杭州的风景都很好。	(	)
4. 他们想看看香港的海上风景 (scenery)。	(	)
5. 他们要在旅游商店买兵马俑。	(	)
6. 他们到中国以后再找旅馆。	(	)

Exercise 2 📖 🗣

Read Text (1) and answer the questions orally in Chinese.

1. 玛丽和约翰的飞机票订了没有？
2. 他们计划先到哪儿？为什么？
3. 他们为什么要去苏州和杭州？
4. 西安是一个怎么样的城市？
5. 去西安以后他们还要到哪儿去？

Exercise 3 🎧 📖

You will hear five statements followed by three responses. Choose the most logical response to each statement.

1. a. 香港这个购物天堂你怎么能错过呢！
   b. 那把旅馆也一块儿订了吧。
   c. 听说中国的兵马俑很有名。
2. a. 大城市人多车多，我不喜欢。
   b. 西安是个历史古都。
   c. 我们可以坐飞机去西安旅游。
3. a. 没有。上次去中国本来要去的，后来没时间了。
   b. 兵马俑非常有意思，它每天都开放。
   c. 西安是一个历史古都，兵马俑就在西安。
4. a. 南京我去过好几次，每次都买了很多便宜的东西。
   b. 我们先从上海坐飞机去香港。
   c. 上海购物的好地方很多，不一定要去南京路。
5. a. 那当然，"上有天堂，下有苏杭"嘛。
   b. 李文是让旅行社订的机票和旅馆。
   c. 苏州和杭州不在同一个省。

Exercise 4 ✎

Fill in the blanks with the following words and then translate the sentences into English.

历史　西湖　漂亮　除了　错过　现代化　暑假　赶快

1. 每年 _____ 我都到南方去旅游。

_____

2. _____ 北京以外，中国哪个城市我都没去过。

_____

3. 我喜欢住在 _____ 的城市，生活很方便。

_____

4. 你这件衣服很 _____，在哪儿买的？

_____

5. 杭州人小王爱画老家 _____ 的风景。

_____

6. 那个地方没什么可看的，_____ 了也没关系。

_____

7. 中国有四五千年的 _____，值得去一趟。

_____

8. 上课时间到了，你 _____ 走吧，不然要迟到了。

_____

课文（二）*Text (2)*

谈暑假计划

简体版

Lin Hua writes to her parents in Taiwan about her summer plans in the United States.

Tips: a proper way to start a letter to parents

亲爱的爸爸妈妈：

你们好！今天我的考试全部结束了。我的几门课考得都不错，终于可以松一口气了。

过两天就要放暑假了。现在机票比较贵，今年暑假我不打算回台湾了。因为明年我就要毕业了，我打算暑假的时候找一份实习的工作。我的专业是翻译，我们这里有一两家翻译公司正在招人，我已经给他们寄去了我的简历。这个暑假，我打算用一半的时间打工，一半的时间和同学们一起去旅游。我们计划先到洛杉矶，然后去拉斯维加斯和大峡谷。游完大峡谷以后，我们再开车去盐湖城和黄石公园。我想我这个暑假会比较累，但一定很有意思。

你们的身体还好吧？望多多保重！

Tips: a proper way to end a letter to parents

女儿：林华
六月十三日

談暑假計劃

Lin Hua writes to her parents in Taiwan about her summer plans in the United States.

繁体版

親愛的爸爸媽媽：

你們好！今天我的考試全部結束了。我的幾門課考得都不錯，終于可以鬆一口氣了。

過兩天就要放暑假了。現在機票比較貴，今年暑假我不打算回臺灣了。因爲明年我就要畢業了，我打算暑假的時候找一份實習的工作。我的專業是翻譯，我們這裏有一兩家翻譯公司正在招人，我已經給他們寄去了我

飞跃——汉语初级教程学生用书 下册

的簡歷。這個暑假，我打算用一半的時間打工，一半的時間和同學們一起去旅游。我們計劃先到洛杉磯，然後去拉斯維加斯和大峽谷。游完大峽谷以後，我們再開車去鹽湖城和黃石公園。我想我這個暑假會比較累，但一定很有意思。

你們的身體還好吧？望多多保重！

女兒：林華

六月十三日

Kèwén (èr) *Text (2)*

Tán Shǔjià Jìhuà

拼音版

Lin Hua writes to her parents in Taiwan about her summer plans in the United States.

Qīn'ài de bàba māma:

Nǐmen hǎo! Jīntiān wǒ de kǎoshì quánbù jiéshù le. Wǒ de jǐ mén kè kǎo de dōu búcuò, zhōngyú kěyǐ sōng yì kǒu qì le.

Guò liǎng tiān jiù yào fàng shǔjià le. Xiànzài jīpiào bǐjiào guì, jīnnián shǔjià wǒ bù dǎsuan huí Táiwān le. Yīnwèi míngnián wǒ jiù yào bìyè le, wǒ dǎsuan shǔjià de shíhou zhǎo yí fèn shíxí de gōngzuò. Wǒ de zhuānyè shì fānyì, wǒmen zhèli yǒu yì-liǎng jiā fānyì gōngsī zhèngzài zhāorén, wǒ yǐjing gěi tāmen jìqule wǒ de jiǎnlì. Zhège shǔjià, wǒ dǎsuan yòng yíbàn de shíjiān dǎgōng, yíbàn de shíjiān hé tóngxuémen yìqǐ qù lǚyóu. Wǒmen jìhuà xiān dào Luòshānjī, ránhòu qù Lāsīwéijiāsī hé Dàxiágǔ. Yóuwán Dàxiágǔ yǐhòu, wǒmen zài kāichē qù Yánhúchéng hé Huángshí Gōngyuán. Wǒ xiǎng wǒ zhège shǔjià huì bǐjiào lèi, dàn yídìng hěn yǒu yìsi.

Nǐmen de shēntǐ hái hǎo ba? Wàng duōduō bǎozhòng!

nǚ'ér: Lín Huá

liù yuè shísān rì

生词（二）New Words (2)

	简体（繁體）	拼音	词性	解释
1	谈（談）	tán	v.	talk 谈暑假计划 / 我想跟你谈一谈。
2	亲爱（親愛）	qīn'ài	adj.	dear 亲爱的祖国 / 亲爱的老师
3	全部	quánbù	n.	all 我全部的钱都在这里了。/ 我认识他，但是不了解他的全部经历。
4	门（門）	mén	m.	(measure word for a school course) 一门课 / 一门科学
5	松（鬆）	sōng	v.	let loose 松手 / 请你把手松开。
6	气（氣）	qì	n.	air, breath 吸气 / 呼气 / 松一口气
7	明年	míngnián	n.	next year 明年我打算去中国旅游。
8	份	fèn	m.	share, portion 一份工作 / 一份收入
9	实习（實習）	shíxí	v.	practice what has been taught in class; to be an intern 大学生们将到一些公司实习。/ 他只是一名实习大夫。
10	专业（專業）	zhuānyè	n.	specialized field; major 专业课 / 我的专业是英语。
11	翻译（譯）	fānyì	n./v.	translation/ translate 翻译专业 / 翻译学校
12	招	zhāo	v.	recruit 招生 / 招工 / 招兵 / 招人
13	简历（簡歷）	jiǎnlì	n.	résumé 一份简历 / 好的简历对找工作很重要。
14	打工	dǎgōng	v.	work a temporary job 我在姐夫的公司打工。/ 他离开老家到大城市打工。
15	计划（計劃）	jìhuà	v.	plan 你这个周末计划做什么？
16	累	lèi	adj.	tired, exhausted 他每天都很累。/ 这是个很累的工作。
17	望	wàng	v.	hope, wish 望你保重身体！/ 望你早日回来。

	简体（繁體）	拼音	词性	解释
18	保重	bǎozhòng	v.	take good care 天冷了，请多多保重！
专有名词 Proper Nouns				
1	洛杉矶（磯）	Luòshānjī	pn.	Los Angeles
2	拉斯维（維）加斯	Lāsīwéijiāsī	pn.	Las Vegas
3	大峡（峽）谷	Dàxiágǔ	pn.	Grand Canyon
4	盐（鹽）湖城	Yánhúchéng	pn.	Salt Lake City
5	黄石公园（園）	Huángshí Gōngyuán	pn.	Yellowstone National Park

Exercise 5 🦻

Listen to Text (2) and decide whether the following statements are true or false.

1. 林华还有一门课没有考。	(	)
2. 林华觉得她的考试没有问题。	(	)
3. 林华的父母要来看她，所以她不去台湾了。	(	)
4. 已经有两家公司告诉林华她可以去工作了。	(	)
5. 林华的暑假不都是用在旅行上。	(	)
6. 林华觉得暑假很可能没有什么意思。	(	)

Exercise 6 📖 🗨

Read Text (1) and answer the questions orally in Chinese.

1. 暑假什么时候开始？

2. 林华考试考得怎么样？

3. 最近的飞机票价怎么样？

4. 林华打算暑假做什么工作？

5. 林华给哪些公司寄去了她的简历？

6. 林华计划暑假到哪些地方去旅游？

Exercise 7 ✍

Complete the following sentences using the words listed below. Use each word once.

保重　　学期　　打工　　专业　　找到　　结束

1. 我们学校的中文课程一共有两个 _____ 。

2. 考试 _____ 以后我要跟朋友们去旅游。

3. 这份工作是我的老师帮我 _____ 的。

4. 他的 _____ 是翻译。毕业以后他在联合国当翻译。

5. 现在到公司 _____ 也得看学历。

6. 天冷了，请您们多多 _____ 身体。

Exercise 8 ✎

Translate the following paragraph into Chinese. Type it out on your computer.

The semester has ended and I passed all the exams with good grades. My parents said I should learn to drive in a driving school because I will start looking for an internship soon, and my dad will give me his car. In the first half of the summer vacation, I will learn to drive. Then I will look for a job. I plan to send my resumes to two companies. I also plan to travel with my friends. We are thinking of going to Las Vegas. I will be busy, but my vacation will be very fun.

三、汉字 Chinese Characters

1. New characters in this lesson

序号	拼音	简 / 繁	部件	构词
1	ān	安	宀 + 女	西安 / 安全 / 安好
2	bīng	兵	丘 + 八	兵马俑 / 兵种 / 官兵
3	chú	除	阝 + 余	除了 / 除非 / 除去
4	dài	代	亻 + 弋	现代化 / 年代 / 时代
5	fān	翻	番 + 羽（习 + 习）	翻译 / 翻车 / 翻身
6	fèn	份	亻 + 分（八 + 刀）	一份工作 / 一份饭
7	gǎng	港	氵 + 巷	香港 / 海港 / 港口 / 港湾
8	guǎng	广（廣）	广	广州 / 广东 / 广场 / 广大
9	háng	杭	木 + 亢（亠 + 几）	杭州 / 苏杭
10	hú	湖	氵 + 胡（古 + 月）	西湖 / 湖泊 / 淡水湖 / 湖水
11	huà	划（劃）	戈 + 刂	计划 / 规划
12	jī	矶（磯）	石 + 几	洛杉矶

13	jì	计 (計)	讠＋十	计划 / 计算机 / 计时 / 计工
14	lèi	累	田＋糸	很累 / 累坏了
15	luò	洛	氵＋各 (夂＋口)	洛杉矶
16	ǹg	嗯	口＋恩 (因＋心)	嗯，挺好！/ 嗯，不错！
17	shān	杉	木＋彡	洛杉矶 / 杉树
18	shí	石	石	黄石公园 / 石山 / 石头 / 矿石
19	shǐ	史	史	历史 / 史书 / 史记
20	shǔ	暑	日＋者 (耂＋日)	暑假 / 暑期 / 大暑天 / 中暑
21	sōng	松	木＋公	松口气 / 放松
22	sū	苏 (蘇)	艹＋办	苏州 / 苏醒
23	tán	谈 (談)	讠＋炎 (火＋火)	谈话 / 谈爱好 / 谈天说地
24	wéi	维 (維)	纟＋隹	拉斯维加斯 / 维护
25	xiá	峡 (峽)	山＋夹	大峡谷
26	xiāng	香	禾＋日	香港 / 香花 / 香水 / 菜很香
27	yán	盐 (鹽)	土＋卜＋皿	盐湖城 / 海盐 / 食盐 / 盐水
28	yì	译 (譯)	讠＋睪 (又＋幸)	翻译 / 译文 / 英译中
29	yǒng	俑	亻＋甬 (マ＋用)	兵马俑 / 木俑 / 石俑
30	zhāo	招	扌＋召 (刀＋口)	招人 / 招工 / 招呼 / 招手
31	zhí	值	亻＋直	值得 / 不值 / 值日 / 值班
32	zhòng	重	千＋里	保重 / 重要 / 重量
33	zhù	著	艹＋者	著名 / 著作
34	zhuān	专	专	专业 / 专门 / 专一 / 专心专意

Exercise 1 ✎

Copy the following single-component characters with the correct stroke order in the spaces provided.

| guǎng | 广 | 丶 一 广 | | | | | | |
| shí | 石 | 一 プ ズ 石 石 | | | | | | |

shǐ	史	丶 口 口 史 史				
zhòng	重	一 二 千 千 舌 舌 盲 重 重				
zhuān	专	一 二 专 专				

Exercise 2 📖 ✍

Read the following sentences and choose the correct characters to fill in the blanks.

1. 除了小王没去过洛杉 _____ 以外，我们都去过。(矶　机　饥)

2. 我的专业是 _____ 译。我能做英译汉，也能做汉译英。(番　翻　藩)

3. 暑假快到了，我们订一个旅行计 _____ 吧。(华　话　划)

4. 这个暑假我要到很多地方旅游，我想我会很 _____。(类　果　累)

5. 去中国旅游以前，最好看一点儿中国历 _____ 的书。(吏　史　实)

6. 你能不能 _____ 一下毕业以后的计划？(谈　毯　痰)

7. _____ 了北京以外，我没有去过别的城市。(蜍　除　徐)

8. 大 _____ 谷和黄石公园都值得一看。(侠　狭　峡)

2. Common radicals (11)

(1) 山 shānzìpáng

This radical is derived from the pictograph 山山 which resembles a mountain. Characters with the 山 radical are usually related to mountains and rocks, e.g., 峡 (xiá, gorge), 岩 (yán, rock), 岗 (gǎng, mound), and 岛 (dǎo, island).

(2) 石 shízìpáng

This radical is derived from the pictographic character 㕛, symbolizing a stone below a cliff. Thus, characters with this radical are usually related to stones or rocks, e.g., 碗 (wǎn, bowl), 碟 (dié, small plate), and 矶 (jī, rock protruding over water).

(3) 广 guǎngzìtóu

This radical is derived from 广 which looks like a house with a roof. Therefore, characters with 广 are mostly related to shelters and houses, e.g., 店 (diàn, store), 床 (chuáng, bed), 座 (zuò, seat), 府 (fǔ, mansion) and 庭 (tíng, hall).

飞跃——汉语初级教程学生用书　下册

(4) 阝 zuǒ'ěrpáng and 阝 yòu'ěrpáng

These two radicals look exactly the same, although they were derived from different pictographs. The 阝 (zuǒ'ěrpáng) is always put on the left side of the characters like 院(yuàn, yard), 阳(yáng, sun), and 陆(lù, land); 阝 (yòu'ěrpáng) always on the right side, such as 那 (nà, that), 都(dōu, all), and 邮(yóu, to post).

Exercise 3 📖 ✎

How many characters can you form with the following character components?

夂　王　木　禾　钅　马　灬　辶　纟　足　目　女
彳　广　石　阝　且　几　井　艮　力　口　主　人

四、语言点 Language Points

1. The construction 除了... (以外), 都...

This construction is used to exclude something after 除了 and emphasize what is stated with 都, meaning "except..."

> 除了... (以外), Subject ＋ 都...

> (1) <u>除了</u>北京<u>以外</u>，我哪儿都没去过。
>   I have been to no other places except Beijing.
> (2) <u>除了</u>张红<u>以外</u>，谁都没去过中国。
>   No one has been to China, except Zhang Hong.
> (3) <u>除了</u>玛丽<u>以外</u>，全班同学都不喜欢逛街。
>   None of the people in this class, except Mary, like to go window shopping.
> (4) 我们家<u>除了</u>妈妈，每个人都有一台电脑。
>   All of the members of my family, except my mother, have a computer.

2. Review: types of predicates

There are different types of predicates in Chinese. The following are the most common types of predicates that we learned in this book.

Subject	Predicate	Meaning
我	Verb + Object 叫江小华	I am called Jiang Xiaohua.
王先生和王太太	Adjective 也很好	Mr. and Mrs. Wang are also fine.
今天	Noun 星期一	Today is Monday.
您	Predicate Phrase 工作忙吗	Are you busy at work?

3. Review: aspects of an action

In Lesson 6, we learned the grammatical term "aspect" (tài, 态) which refers to the particular status of an action or event. Aspects of an action in Chinese are shown by aspectual particles and some adverbs. The following is a summary of the six aspects that we have learned so far with their aspectual particles.

Completion Aspect

The completion aspect indicates an action is/was/will be completed with the aspectual particle 了 attached to a verb.

> (1) 我们买了很多糖，还买了一个很大的南瓜，做了一个南瓜灯，放在家门口。
> We bought a lot of candy and a big pumpkin. We made a jack-o-lantern and put it at the door.
> (2) 我本来不太会做中国菜，今天也做了一个红烧肉。
> I do not know how to cook Chinese food well, but today I cooked braised pork.

Progressive Aspect

The progressive aspect indicates an action is in progress. The progress aspect is primarily shown by putting the adverb 在 before the verb. The aspectual particle 着 attached to a verb can also indicate a progressive action.

> (1) 我给你打了三次电话，都占线。你在跟谁说话呢？
> I called you three times and the line was busy. Who were you talking to?
> (2) 张老师正跟学生说着话呢。
> Mr. Zhang is talking to his students now.

Continuous Aspect

The continuous aspect indicates a state or event continues with the aspectual particle 着 attached to a verb.

> (1) 我们几个同学凑钱给林华买了一个生日蛋糕，上面用中英文写着"生日快乐"。
>   My classmates and I chipped in to buy a birthday cake for Lin Hua, on which was written in Chinese and English, "Happy Birthday".
>
> (2) 他们还放了一张祝母亲节快乐的贺卡，贺卡上写着我的名字。
>   They also attached a Mother's Day card with my name on it.

Experiential Aspect

The experiential aspect indicates a past experience of a person or a thing. It is shown by attaching the aspectual particle 过 to a verb.

> (1) 这我知道，咱们做过好几回了。
>   I know, we have done this many times.
>
> (2) 除了北京以外，我哪儿也没去过。
>   I have been to no other places except Beijing.

Short-duration Aspect

The short-duration aspect indicates a short or casual action. It is shown by the reduplication of the verb, or putting 一下 after the verb. If the verb is monosyllabic, adding 一 between the reduplicated verbs may indicate the short-duration aspect, too.

> (1) 我来看一下日历。
>   Let me take a look at the calendar.
>
> (2) 真的吗？那我得上网去试试！我还真想找找我的老同学！
>   Really? Then I would like to try it online. I really want to find my former class-mates.
>
> (3) 今天不要上学了，请大夫检查一下。
>   Do not go to school today, you should go see a doctor instead.
>
> (4) 她说也没想好要买什么，只是想去逛一逛。
>   She said she had no idea what to buy. She just wanted to go have a look.

Imminent Aspect

The imminent aspect indicates that an action or an event is about to happen. It is shown by the（快／就）要 + Verb + 了 construction.

> (1) 情人节<u>就要</u>到<u>了</u>。
> Valentine's Day is near.
> (2) 过两天<u>就要</u>放暑假<u>了</u>。
> Summer vacation will begin in two days.
> (3) 快走吧，<u>要</u>下雨<u>了</u>！
> Hurry up! It is going to rain.

4. Review: common particles in Chinese

In this book, we have learned three types of particles in Chinese: structural particles, aspectual particles, and modal particles.

Structural Particles

Structural particles are used to indicate the structural or grammatical relationship between components of a sentence. The most common structural particles are 的, 地 and 得.

The principal function of 的 is to link the attributive word or phrase to the noun it modifies. It is also used in 是…的 pattern and 的 phrase.

> (1) 你<u>的</u>老家在哪儿?
> Where is your hometown?
> (2) 我是在美国出生<u>的</u>，我<u>的</u>老家在纽约。
> I was born in the United States. My hometown is New York.
> (3) 您得穿大号<u>的</u>。看看这件行不行?
> You must wear size L. Try this one.

The principal function of 地 is to link an adverbial modifier to the verb or adjective it modifies.

> (1) 结果，我顺利<u>地</u>通过了路试，拿到了驾照。
> As a result, I passed the road test smoothly and got my driver's license.
> (2) 比赛开始以后，我大声<u>地</u>为火箭队加油。
> When the game started, I cheered loudly for the Rockets.

The principal function of 得 is to link a complement to a verb or an adjective.

(1) 时间过得真快！

How time flies!

(2) 是不是昨天晚上上网睡得太晚了？

Is it because you stayed online too long last night and went to bed too late?

(3) 现在她的太极拳打得很不错，汉语也说得很流利。

Now her *taiji* is good and her Chinese is very fluent.

Aspectual Particles

The most important aspectual particles are 了, 着 and 过.

了 is attached to a verb indicating an action was/is/will be completed.

(1) 爸爸点了三道菜：北京烤鸭、清蒸鱼，还有蒙古牛肉。

My father ordered three dishes: Beijing roast duck, steamed fish as well as Mongolian beef.

(2) 弟弟点了一盘春卷。

My little brother ordered a plate of spring rolls.

过 is attached to a verb to indicate a past experience.

(1) 这我知道，咱们做过好几回了。

I know, we have done this many times.

(2) 丽莎看过很多中国电影。

Lisa has seen many Chinese movies.

着 is attached to a verb or adjective to indicate a progressive action, a continuous state, and an accompanying action of another verb.

(1) 一个服务员推着点心车过来。

A waitress came over pushing a cart of dim sum.

(2) 我们几个同学凑钱给林华买了一个生日蛋糕，上面用中英文写着"生日快乐"。

My classmates and I chipped in to buy a birthday cake for Lin Hua, on which was written in Chinese and English "Happy Birthday".

Modal Particles

Modal particles are used to add a mood, spirit, or tone to an utterance. "Mood" includes such diverse qualities as interrogation, affirmation, request, command, emphasis, and exclamation. The common modal particles are 了, 吗, 呢, 吧, 啊, 啦, and 喂.

The particle 了 can serve as an aspectual particle and modal particle. As a modal particle, 了 is used at the end of a sentence to express the speaker's certain moods, such as affirmation for a change, urging, or exclamation.

(1) 你的弟弟多大了?
How old is your younger brother?
(2) 我下午第一节有课，不跟你多说了。
I have class in the first period in the afternoon, so I can't chat with you anymore.
(3) 你晚上开车得小心点儿，别太快了。
Drive carefully in the evening. Don't go too fast.
(4) 太棒了！那就这样定了！
Excellent! It's decided then.

The principal function of 吗 is to form a yes-no question.

(1) 你的同学玛丽也是美国人吗?
Is your classmate Mary also an American?
(2) 林华，你好！找我有事吗?
Hi, Lin Hua! What did you want to see me for?

The modal particle 呢 can be used to form different types of questions. It can also be used to indicate that an action is underway. For example:

(1) 我是学生。你呢?
I am a student. And you?
(2) 我的老家在伦敦，我是在英国出生的。你呢?
My hometown is London. I was born in Britain. How about you?
(3) 我们几点钟吃饭呢?
When shall we have dinner?
(4) 星期六早上八点，我还在睡觉呢，玛丽就打电话来找我了。
Mary called me while I was still sleeping at 8:00 am on Saturday morning.

The modal particle 吧 is used to make suggestions, requests, polite commands, or a presumption in a question.

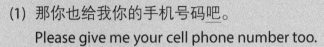

(1) 那你也给我你的手机号码吧。
Please give me your cell phone number too.

(2) 哥，还是要那件灰色的吧。
Brother, you'd better take the gray one.

(3) 好久不见。最近学习很忙吧?
Long time no see. You must have been busy with your study recently?

The modal particle 啊 can express different moods, such as interrogation, urging, emotion and affirmation.

(1) 后天就是长周末了，你们想到哪儿去玩儿啊?
The long weekend begins the day after tomorrow. Where do you want to go to have some fun?

(2) 啊，你不舒服?
What? You feel uncomfortable?

The principal usage of 呀 is to form a question and to express a strong feeling.

(1) 什么呀! 他是我哥!
What are you talking about! He is my elder brother!

(2) 我们到底去哪儿呀?
Where on earth shall we go?

The modal particle 啦 is used to express the mood of interrogation, exclamation, and affirmation, etc.

当然啦! 父母、兄弟、姐妹、朋友都得送。
Of course, I have to give gifts to my parents, brothers, sisters and friends.

The model particle 喂 is used when calling someone or answering a telephone call.

(1) 喂，约翰，我是玛丽。我给你打了三次电话，都占线。
Hello, John. This is Mary. I called you three times but the line was busy every time.

(2) "喂，哪位? " "是彼得吗? 我是林华。"
"Hello, who's speaking?" "Is it Peter? This is Lin Hua."

Exercise 1 🎧 ✍

Listen to three short dialogs and answer the following questions with the 除了…（以外），都… structure.

Dialog 1

小明今天买了什么好吃的东西?

_____。

Dialog 2

玛丽去过美国哪些城市?

_____。

Dialog 3

约翰每天早上都练习跑步吗?

_____。

Exercise 2 ✍

Follow the example and rewrite the following sentences with the 除了…（以外），都… structure.

Example:　星期天我不在学校，其他时间我都在。
　　　　　除了星期天（以外），我其他时间都在学校。

1. 我星期二晚上没有空，别的晚上都有空。

_____。

2. 他的房间只有床和桌子，什么别的家具都没有。

_____。

3. 他只去过旧金山，美国西部别的城市他都没去过。

_____。

4. 小陈是开车去的，我们都是坐公共汽车去的。

_____。

5. 彼得不喜欢吃饺子，其他同学都喜欢吃饺子。

_____。

飞跃——汉语初级教程学生用书　下册

Exercise 3

Complete the following sentences with 着, 了, 过 and 的, 地, 得.

1. 我计划明天早上吃 _____ 早饭就去图书馆做作业。

2. 情人节前一天，玛丽收到约翰的情人卡，上面写 _____ "我爱你。"

3. 我总是喜欢唱 _____ 歌开车，这样一点儿也不觉得累。

4. 彼得已经去 _____ 中国三次了，可是他还想再去。

5. 现在是七点一刻，你赶快走呀，要迟到 _____！

6. 那个英国女孩的中文说 _____ 好极了！

7. 公牛队和火箭队的比赛十分激烈，约翰大声 _____ 为公牛队加油。

8. 林华是在台湾出生 _____，她的父母兄弟都在台湾。

9. 她跳交谊舞跳 _____ 不怎么样，还说要教我呢！

10. 那件黑色的上衣大了一点儿，我还是要那件灰色 _____ 吧。

11. 我在大学学 _____ 一年的中文。不过，很多词我都忘了。

12. 这个星期我太忙了，周末我要好好 _____ 休息休息。

五、语言运用 Using the Language

Activity 1

Look at the pictures and tickets and listen to the corresponding conversations. Then answer the questions orally in Chinese.

Conversation 1

Mr. Zhou tells a female colleague about his trip.

Questions:

1. When did Zhou go on a trip? For what?

2. How did he get his ticket?

3. How much did the ticket cost?

Conversation 2

Wang Ming just returned from a trip to Kunming.

Questions:

1. What did Wang do in Kunming?

2. How did he feel on his return trip?

3. Why did he feel that way?

Conversation 3

A man tells a woman about his trip to Yunnan.

Questions:

1. What are the three places that he visited?

2. Where did he enjoy beautiful scenery?

3. Where did he buy his plane ticket?

22

Activity 2 📖 👁️

Look at the following pictures, then answer the questions in each picture by reading the Chinese descriptions.

北京的前门大街在天安门广场南边，以前每天街上车来人往，非常热闹。几年前，北京市把它变成了步行街，不走汽车了。现在每天都有中外游客来这里旅游，看新建的老式房子。但是这条街没有以前那么热闹了。

Questions:

1. What was the street like in the old days?

2. What is it mainly used for now?

1. Qianmen Street, Beijing

厦 (xià) 门市是中国福建省海边的一个有名的城市，在台湾省的对面。那里有美丽的风景，每年都有很多国内外的游客去那里旅游。这是厦门市鼓浪屿龙头山上的一块大石。

Questions:

1. Where is Xiamen City located?

2. What kind of people go there every year?

2. Xiamen City, China

夏威夷 (Hawaii) 是美国有名的旅游点。那里有美丽的大海。游客可以白天去海里游泳，晚上在城里逛商店，吃当地的美食，看夏威夷舞。这是夏威夷美丽的海滩。

Questions:

1. What is Hawaii famous for?

2. What can tourists do in Hawaii?

3. Waikiki Beach, Hawaii

蒙特雷 (Monterey) 是美国加州的一个历史古城，有二百四十多年的历史了。这里常常有老式汽车展。各种各样的老式汽车像新的一样漂漂亮亮的。这些老汽车不但可以看，也可以买，但是每次都是看的人多，买的人少，因为太贵了！

Questions:

1. What kind of town is Monterey?

2. What can people do at the antique car show?

4. Monterey, California

Activity 3 📖🗣✳

Answer the following questionnaire and then tell your partner your preferences.

1. 旅行的时候你喜欢怎么买飞机票或者火车票？
   a. 自己到售票处买   b. 打电话给旅行社预订
   c. 自己上网预定   d. 找朋友帮忙

2. 你觉得下面城市中，哪些可以错过？
   a. 上海   b. 北京   c. 西安   d. 杭州   e. 苏州   f. 香港

3. 你去中国旅游主要是为了 _____。
   a. 看风景   b. 购物   c. 学习历史和文化

4. 如果你的学校让你到中国去一边工作，一边学习，你想在哪工作？
   a. 飞机场   b. 大饭店   c. 旅行社   d. 图书馆

Activity 4 📖🗣✳

Read the following signs aloud and answer the questions.

旅游客运	超大件行李檢查
1. What is this sign for?	**2.** Do you come to this place if your luggage is regular size?
諮詢服務台	網際網路服務
3. What do people do here?	**4.** What can you do here?
出境報到櫃檯 出境报到柜台	公共電話
5. What passengers is this counter for?	**6.** When should you be interested in this sign?
洗手間	地铁天安门东站
7. When should you be interested in this sign?	**8.** Where are you now?

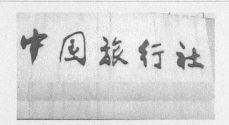

9. Who should be interested in this place?

10. What can you do here?

Activity 5

Role Play

You plan to travel to China during the summer vacation. You do not know what places to go. Call a travel agency and ask them to recommend some places for you. Your partner will play the role of the travel agent. You can use Text (1) as reference.

Sentences you may need to use:

我暑假要到中国旅游。

你们有中国旅游的项目 (xiàngmù program) 吗?

请你告诉我有哪些值得去的地方。

Activity 6

Look at the pictures and read the following description of a tourism program. Then answer the questions below orally in Chinese.

New words:

观光	guānguāng	to tour
节目	jiémù	program
游览	yóulǎn	go sightseeing
博物馆	bówùguǎn	museum
艺术	yìshù	art
剧院	jùyuàn	theater
杂技	zájì	acrobatics
演出	yǎnchū	performance

1. 上海浦东新区

2. 上海外滩

3. 南京路步行街

4. 南京路上的观光车

5. 上海博物馆

6. 上海大剧院

上海观光一日游

价格：228元/人（餐费自理）

游览景点：上海浦东新区，上海外滩，南京路步行街，上海博物馆，上海大剧院
供应标准：空调旅游车，全程导游服务

"上海一日游"是上海旅行社新的旅游节目。参加这个节目的游客，先参观浦东新区。参观完新区后，游客将乘坐旅游巴士回到上海老市区，游览有名的上海外滩。然后，游客有一个半小时的时间逛一逛上海的购物天堂南京路步行街。不喜欢步行的游客可以乘坐观光车。参观完南京路以后，导游将带游客前往上海博物馆参观。上海博物馆是一个大型的古代艺术博物馆。在这里，游客可以了解中国的古代文化。一日游的最后一站是上海大剧院。在这里，游客将观看上海杂技团演出。

Questions:

1. 上海一日游的价钱包括吃饭的费用吗?

2. 游客可以在南京路做什么?

3. 上海博物馆主要展览什么?

4. 上海大剧院可以看到什么节目?

附 录
Appendix

生词总表 Glossary

序号	简体（繁體）	拼音	词性	解释	课号
1	学（學）期	xuéqī	n.	term, semester	12
2	选（選）	xuǎn	v.	select, choose	12
3	听（聽）力	tīnglì	n.	listening ability; listening comprehension	12
4	阅读（閱讀）	yuèdú	n.	reading	12
5	口语（語）	kǒuyǔ	n.	spoken language	12
6	文化	wénhuà	n.	culture	12
7	饮（飲）食	yǐnshí	n.	food and drinks	12
8	节（節）日	jiérì	n.	festival	12
9	风（風）俗	fēngsú	n.	folk customs	12
10	习惯（習慣）	xíguàn	n.	habit	12
11	等等	děngděng	part.	so on and so forth; etc.	12
12	功夫	gōngfu	n.	kung fu; martial art skills	12
13	太极（極）拳	tàijíquán	n.	taichi	12
14	什么（甚麼）的	shénmede	part.	etc.	12
15	学（學）分	xuéfēn	n.	credit	12
16	考试（試）	kǎoshì	n./v.	take an examination	12
17	期中	qīzhōng	n.	mid-term	12
18	期末	qīmò	n.	end of semester	12
19	平时（時）	píngshí	n.	at normal times	12
20	测验（測驗）	cèyàn	n.	test	12
21	将来（將來）	jiānglái	n.	future	12
22	汤（湯）姆	Tāngmǔ	pn.	Tom	12
23	而	ér	conj.	whereas	12
24	所以	suǒyǐ	conj.	therefore	12
25	听（聽）	tīng	v.	listen, hear	12
26	懂	dǒng	v.	understand	12

序号	简体（繁體）	拼音	词性	解释	课号
27	简单（簡單）	jiǎndān	*adj.*	simple	12
28	可是	kěshì	*conj.*	but	12
29	汉（漢）字	Hànzì	*n.*	Chinese character	12
30	为（為）了	wèile	*conj.*	in order to	12
31	让（讓）	ràng	*v.*	let	12
32	上学（學）	shàngxué	*v.*	attend school	12
33	其实（實）	qíshí	*adv.*	actually	12
34	挺	tǐng	*adv.*	very	12
35	好玩儿（兒）	hǎowánr	*adj.*	fun, interesting	12
36	不但……还（還）……	búdàn... hái...	*conj.*	not only… but also	12
37	舞蹈	wǔdǎo	*n.*	dance	12
38	书（書）法	shūfǎ	*n.*	penmanship, calligraphy	12
39	画（畫）	huà	*v.*	draw, paint	12
40	画儿（畫兒）	huàr	*n.*	picture, painting	12
41	自从（從）	zìcóng	*prep.*	since	12
42	高中	gāozhōng	*n.*	senior high school	12
43	开设（開設）	kāishè	*v.*	open; set up (a course in school)	12
44	大学（學）	dàxué	*n.*	university	12
45	汉语（漢語）	Hànyǔ	*n.*	the Chinese language	12
46	先修课（課）	xiānxiūke	*n.*	Advanced Placement Classes in high school	12
47	茶	chá	*n.*	tea	13
48	红（紅）茶	hóngchá	*n.*	black tea	13
49	绿（綠）茶	lǜchá	*n.*	green tea	13
50	冰	bīng	*n.*	ice	13
51	水	shuǐ	*n.*	water	13
52	服务员（務員）	fúwùyuán	*n.*	waiter, waitress	13
53	请（請）	qǐng	*v.*	please (do something)	13
54	壶（壺）	hú	*m./n.*	pot	13
55	稍	shāo	*adv.*	a little	13
56	推	tuī	*v.*	push	13
57	点（點）心	diǎnxin	*n.*	snack; dim sum	13
58	过来（過來）	guòlai	*v.*	come over	13
59	包子	bāozi	*n.*	steamed bun with fillings	13

序号	简体（繁體）	拼音	词性	解释	课号
60	饺(餃)子	jiǎozi	n.	dumpling	13
61	春卷	chūnjuǎn	n.	spring roll	13
62	样(樣)	yàng	n.	kind, variety, type	13
63	碟	dié	n./m.	small plate	13
64	碗	wǎn	n./m.	bowl	13
65	筷子	kuàizi	n.	chopsticks	13
66	信用卡	xìnyòngkǎ	n.	credit card	13
67	非常	fēicháng	adv.	unusually, very	13
68	下	xià	n.	next	13
69	练习(練習)	liànxí	v.	practice	13
70	不错(錯)	búcuò	adj.	not bad; pretty good	13
71	马(馬)克	Mǎkè	pn.	Mark	13
72	昨天	zuótiān	n.	yesterday	13
73	新年	xīnnián	n.	New Year	13
74	全	quán	adj.	all	13
75	餐馆(餐館)	cānguǎn	n.	restaurant	13
76	年夜饭(飯)	niányèfàn	n.	Chinese New Year's Eve dinner	13
77	有名	yǒumíng	adj.	famous, well-known	13
78	外面	wàimian	n.	outside	13
79	久	jiǔ	adj.	long time	13
80	钟头(鐘頭)	zhōngtóu	n.	hour	13
81	结(結)果	jiéguǒ	conj.	as a result	13
82	分钟(鐘)	fēnzhōng	n.	minute	13
83	点(點)	diǎn	v.	order	13
84	道	dào	m.	(measure word for a dish)	13
85	菜	cài	n.	dish of non-grain food	13
86	烤鸭(鴨)	kǎoyā	n.	roast duck	13
87	清蒸	qīngzhēng	v.	steam in broth	13
88	鱼(魚)	yú	n.	fish	13
89	牛肉	niúròu	n.	beef	13
90	肉	ròu	n.	meat	13
91	盘(盤)	pán	n./m.	plate	13
92	过(過)年	guònián	v.	celebrate the Chinese New Year	13

序号	简体（繁體）	拼音	词性	解释	课号
93	时（時）	shí	*n.*	time; when	13
94	家家户户	jiājiā-hùhù		each and every family	13
95	拿	ná	*v.*	hold in hand	13
96	菜单（單）	càidān	*n.*	menu	13
97	甜	tián	*adj.*	sweet	13
98	酸	suān	*adj.*	sour	13
99	味道	wèidào	*n.*	flavor, taste	13
100	结帐（結帳）	jiézhàng	*v.*	pay a bill	13
101	蒙古	Měnggǔ	*pn.*	Mongolia	13
102	趟（趟）	tàng	*m.*	(measure word for a trip)	14
103	邮（郵）局	yóujú	*n.*	post office	14
104	寄	jì	*v.*	mail, send	14
105	信	xìn	*n.*	letter	14
106	包裹	bāoguǒ	*n.*	package	14
107	张（張）	zhāng	*m.*	(measure word for certain objects)	14
108	卡	kǎ	*n.*	card	14
109	盒	hé	*m.*	box	14
110	巧克力	qiǎokèlì	*n.*	chocolate	14
111	慢	màn	*adj.*	slow	14
112	快递（遞）	kuàidì	*n.*	express delivery	14
113	邮费（郵費）	yóufèi	*n.*	postage	14
114	保险（險）	bǎoxiǎn	*n.*	insurance	14
115	需要	xūyào	*v.*	need	14
116	另外	lìngwài	*conj.*	besides, moreover	14
117	包括	bāokuò	*v.*	include	14
118	礼（禮）品	lǐpǐn	*n.*	gift	14
119	公司	gōngsī	*n.*	company	14
120	母亲（親）	mǔqīn	*n.*	mother	14
121	鲜（鮮）花	xiānhuā	*n.*	fresh flowers	14
122	订购（訂購）	dìnggòu	*v.*	order	14
123	祝	zhù	*v.*	wish	14
124	贺（賀）卡	hèkǎ	*n.*	greeting card	14
125	写（寫）	xiě	*v.*	write	14

序号	简体（繁體）	拼音	词性	解释	课号
126	必须（須）	bìxū	a.v.	must	14
127	签（簽）名	qiānmíng	n.	signature	14
128	别人	biéren	pron.	other people	14
129	替	tì	prep.	for; in someone's place	14
130	悄悄话	qiāoqiāohuà	n.	whisper	14
131	情人节（節）	Qíngrénjié	pn.	Valentine's Day	14
132	过（過）	guò	v.	pass	14
133	身体（體）	shēntǐ	n.	body, health	14
134	想念	xiǎngniàn	v.	miss	14
135	场（場）	cháng	m.	measure word for rain, snow, etc.	14
136	一下子	yíxiàzi	adv.	all of a sudden	14
137	降	jiàng	v.	fall, decline, land	14
138	注意	zhùyì	v.	pay attention to	14
139	着凉（著涼）	zháoliáng	v.	catch a cold	14
140	就要	jiù yào		be going to	14
141	种（種）	zhǒng	m.	kind, type	14
142	一定	yídìng	adv.	necessarily, surely	14
143	音乐（樂）	yīnyuè	n.	music	14
144	光盘（盤）	guāngpán	n.	compact disc	14
145	服务（務）	fúwù	n.	service	14
146	人员（員）	rényuán	n.	personnel	14
147	邮（郵）寄	yóujì	v.	mail	14
148	老	lǎo	adv.	always	15
149	上	shang	n.	on, upon	15
150	资（資）料	zīliào	n.	material, data	15
151	暴力	bàolì	n.	violence	15
152	黄色	huángsè	adj.	pornographic	15
153	就	jiù	adv.	only	15
154	网购（網購）	wǎnggòu		online shopping	15
155	咱（们）	zán(men)	pron.	we (including both the speaker and listeners)	15
156	好	hǎo	adv.	quite	15
157	回	huí	m.	(measure word for an action)	15
158	查	chá	v.	check, search	15

飞跃——汉语中级教程学生用书 上册

序号	简体（繁體）	拼音	词性	解释	课号
159	地图（圖）	dìtú	*n.*	map	15
160	订（訂）	dìng	*v.*	reserve, order	15
161	旅馆（館）	lǚguǎn	*n.*	hotel	15
162	飞机（飛機）	fēijī	*n.*	airplane	15
163	票	piào	*n.*	ticket	15
164	世界	shìjiè	*n.*	world	15
165	各地	gè dì		all parts of (a country, world); various regions	15
166	新闻（聞）	xīnwén	*n.*	news	15
167	网（網）站	wǎngzhàn	*n.*	website	15
168	中小学（學）	zhōng-xiǎoxué	*n.*	primary and middle school	15
169	谷歌	Gǔgē	*pn.*	Google	15
170	雅虎	Yǎhǔ	*pn.*	Yahoo	15
171	百度	Bǎidù	*pn.*	Baidu	15
172	优（優）酷	Yōukù	*pn.*	Youku (a Chinese video sharing site)	15
173	脸谱（臉譜）	Liǎnpǔ	*pn.*	Facebook	15
174	日子	rìzi	*n.*	day, date	15
175	数学（數學）	shùxué	*n.*	mathematics	15
176	及格	jígé	*v.*	pass a test	15
177	生气（氣）	shēngqì	*v.*	be angry	15
178	患	huàn	*v.*	contract (a disease)	15
179	网瘾（網癮）	wǎngyǐn	*n.*	Internet addiction	15
180	整天	zhěngtiān	*n.*	all day long	15
181	电脑（電腦）	diànnǎo	*n.*	computer	15
182	成绩（績）	chéngjì	*n.*	grades	15
183	夸奖（誇獎）	kuājiǎng	*v./n.*	praise	15
184	听话（聽話）	tīnghuà	*adj.*	obedient	15
185	从来（從來）	cónglái	*adv.*	always; at all times	15
186	网页（網頁）	wǎngyè	*n.*	web page	15
187	经（經）常	jīngcháng	*adv.*	often	15
188	购（購）物	gòuwù	*v.*	go shopping	15
189	漂亮	piàoliang	*adj.*	pretty, beautiful	15
190	总（總）是	zǒngshì	*adv.*	always	15
191	功课（課）	gōngkè	*n.*	homework	15

序号	简体（繁體）	拼音	词性	解释	课号
192	而且	érqiě	*conj.*	in addition	15
193	向	xiàng	*prep.*	from	15
194	上床	shàngchuáng	*v.*	go to bed	15
195	起来（來）	qǐlái	*v.*	(after a verb or adjective) indicate the beginning and continuation of an action	15
196	舒服	shūfu	*adj.*	comfortable; feeling well	16
197	头（頭）	tóu	*n.*	head	16
198	疼	téng	*adj.*	aching	16
199	咳嗽	késòu	*v.*	cough	16
200	难（難）受	nánshòu	*adj.*	difficult to bear; uncomfortable	16
201	发烧（發燒）	fāshāo	*v.*	have a fever	16
202	可能	kěnéng	*adv.*	maybe; it is possible that	16
203	感冒	gǎnmào	*v.*	catch a cold	16
204	家庭	jiātíng	*n.*	family, household	16
205	约（約）	yuē	*v.*	make an appointment	16
206	看病	kànbìng	*v.*	visit a doctor	16
207	药（藥）	yào	*n.*	medicine	16
208	及时（時）	jíshí	*adv.*	in time; timely	16
209	大夫	dàifu	*n.*	doctor	16
210	检（檢）查	jiǎnchá	*v.*	examine, check	16
211	请（請）假	qǐngjià	*v.*	ask for leave	16
212	好久	hǎojiǔ	*adj.*	for a long time	16
213	急	jí	*adj.*	urgent	16
214	请（請）教	qǐngjiào	*v.*	seek advice	16
215	狗	gǒu	*n.*	dog	16
216	它	tā	*pron.*	it	16
217	散步	sànbù	*v.*	take a walk	16
218	健康	jiànkāng	*adj.*	healthy	16
219	突然	tūrán	*adv.*	suddenly	16
220	病	bìng	*v./n.*	fall ill illness	16
221	看起来（來）	kàn qǐlái		seem	16
222	厉（厲）害	lìhài	*adj.*	severe	16
223	鼻子	bízi	*n.*	nose	16
224	烫（燙）	tàng	*adj.*	burning hot	16

飞跃——汉语中级教程学生用书　上册

序号	简体（繁體）	拼音	词性	解释	课号
225	不要紧（緊）	bú yàojǐn		it doesn't matter	16
226	赶（趕）快	gǎnkuài	*adv.*	at once; quickly	16
227	跟……一样（樣）	gēn … yíyàng		same as	16
228	应该（應該）	yīnggāi	*a.v.*	should	16
229	宠（寵）物	chǒngwù	*n.*	pet	16
230	医（醫）院	yīyuàn	*n.*	hospital	16
231	医疗（醫療）	yīliáo	*n.*	medical service	16
232	主意	zhǔyi	*n.*	idea	16
233	回信	huíxìn	*n./v.*	a letter in reply/reply a letter	16
234	贝贝（貝貝）	Bèibei	*pn.*	name of the dog in the text	16
235	生日	shēngrì	*n.*	birthday	17
236	便饭	biànfàn	*n.*	simple meal	17
237	麻烦（煩）	máfan	*v.*	bother, trouble	17
238	打算	dǎsuàn	*v./n.*	plan	17
239	拿手菜	náshǒucài	*n.*	specialty (dish)	17
240	红烧（紅燒）肉	hóngshāoròu	*n.*	pork braised in brown sauce	17
241	尝（嚐）	cháng	*v.*	taste	17
242	啤酒	píjiǔ	*n.*	beer	17
243	饮（飲）料	yǐnliào	*n.*	drink, beverage	17
244	葡萄酒	pútaojiǔ	*n.*	wine	17
245	刚（剛）	gāng	*adv.*	just, barely	17
246	瓶	píng	*m.*	bottle	17
247	加州	Jiāzhōu	*pn.*	California (U. S.)	17
248	参（參）加	cānjiā	*v.*	participate	17
249	聚会（會）	jùhuì	*n.*	party	17
250	住	zhù	*v.*	live, stay	17
251	室	shì	*n.*	room	17
252	厅（廳）	tīng	*n.*	living room	17
253	公寓	gōngyù	*n.*	apartment	17
254	宫保鸡（雞）丁	gōngbǎojīdīng	*n.*	Kung Pao chicken	17
255	泡菜	pàocài	*n.*	pickled vegetables	17
256	麻婆豆腐	mápódòufu	*n.*	Mapo tofu	17
257	酸辣汤（湯）	suānlàtāng	*n.*	sour and spicy soup	17

序号	简体（繁體）	拼音	词性	解释	课号
258	西红（紅）柿	xīhóngshì	n.	tomato	17
259	炒	chǎo	v.	stir-fry	17
260	凑	còu	v.	put together; amass	17
261	蛋糕	dàngāo	n.	cake	17
262	上面	shàngmian	n.	on top of	17
263	点着（點著）	diǎnzháo	v.	light; set fire to	17
264	蜡烛（蠟燭）	làzhú	n.	candle	17
265	唱	chàng	v.	sing	17
266	歌	gē	n.	song	17
267	许（許）	xǔ	v.	make a wish	17
268	愿（願）	yuàn	n.	hope, wish	17
269	吹	chuī	v.	blow	17
270	灭（滅）	miè	v.	extinguish; put out	17
271	肯	kěn	a.v.	willing to	17
272	希望	xīwàng	v.	wish for; hope	17
273	毕业（畢業）	bìyè	v.	graduate	17
274	四川	Sìchuān	pn.	Sichuan Province	17
275	电（電）影院	diànyǐngyuàn	n.	cinema; movie theater	18
276	录（錄）像带（帶）	lùxiàngdài	n.	video cassette	18
277	租	zū	v.	rent	18
278	直接	zhíjiē	adv.	directly	18
279	收费（費）	shōufèi	v.	charge a fee	18
280	如果	rúguǒ	conj.	if; in case	18
281	坐	zuò	v.	sit, take	18
282	真正	zhēnzhèng	adj.	genuine, real	18
283	爆米花	bàomǐhuā	n.	popcorn	18
284	空儿（兒）	kòngr	n.	spare time; free time	18
285	免费（費）	miǎnfèi	v.	free of charge	18
286	明星	míngxīng	n.	star, celebrity	18
287	演	yǎn	v.	perform	18
288	清楚	qīngchu	adj.	clear	18
289	爱（愛）	ài	v.	love, like	18
290	卡通	kǎtōng	n.	cartoon	18

序号	简体（繁體）	拼音	词性	解释	课号
291	片	piàn	*n.*	movie	18
292	故事	gùshi	*n.*	fiction, story	18
293	喜剧（劇）	xǐjù	*n.*	comedy	18
294	迷	mí	*n./v.*	fan/become very interested in	18
295	好些	hǎoxiē	*adj.*	a lot of	18
296	武术（術）	wǔshù	*n.*	Chinese martial arts	18
297	锻炼（鍛煉）	duànliàn	*v.*	do physical exercise	18
298	了（瞭）解	liǎojiě	*v.*	understand; learn something about	18
299	拳	quán	*n.*	fist; a set of movements of fist fighting	18
300	流利	liúlì	*adj.*	fluent	18
301	花木兰（蘭）	Huā Mùlán	*pn.*	Hua Mulan, legendary woman warrior; protagonist of the Chinese fiction movie Hua Mulan; protagonist of the Hollywood cartoon Mulan	18
302	少林寺	Shàolín Sì	*pn.*	The Shaolin Temple; a Chinese fiction movie	18
303	李小龙（龍）	Lǐ Xiǎolóng	*pn.*	Bruce Lee	18
304	游客	yóukè	*n.*	traveler, tourist	19
305	走	zǒu	*v.*	walk, go	19
306	离（離）	lí	*v.*	away from	19
307	远（遠）	yuǎn	*adj.*	far	19
308	地铁（鐵）	dìtiě	*n.*	subway	19
309	往	wǎng	*prep.*	toward	19
310	十字	shízì		cross-shaped	19
311	路口	lùkǒu	*n.*	intersection	19
312	右手	yòushǒu	*n.*	right hand	19
313	边（邊）	biān	*n.*	side	19
314	市场（場）	shìchǎng	*n.*	market	19
315	大街	dàjiē	*n.*	street	19
316	出	chū	*v.*	come out	19
317	左	zuǒ	*n.*	left	19
318	拐	guǎi	*v.*	turn	19
319	看见（見）	kànjiàn	*v.*	see	19
320	牌子	páizi	*n.*	sign	19

序号	简体（繁體）	拼音	词性	解释	课号
321	沿	yán	*prep.*	along, following	19
322	红绿灯（红綠燈）	hónglǜdēng	*n.*	traffic lights	19
323	不好意思	bù hǎo yìsi		excuse me; pardon me	19
324	公共	gōnggòng	*adj.*	public	19
325	洗手间（間）	xǐshǒujiān	*n.*	toilet, lavatory	19
326	厕（廁）所	cèsuǒ	*n.*	toilet, lavatory	19
327	不客气（氣）	bú kèqi		not at all; don't mention it	19
328	通过（過）	tōngguò	*v.*	pass	19
329	路试（試）	lùshì	*n.*	road test	19
330	终于（終於）	zhōngyú	*adv.*	at last; eventually	19
331	驾驶（駕駛）	jiàshǐ	*v.*	drive	19
332	执（執）照	zhízhào	*n.*	license	19
333	驾（駕）照	jiàzhào	*n.*	driver's license	19
334	笔试（筆試）	bǐshì	*n.*	written test	19
335	对（對）……来说（來說）	duì … lái shuō		as far as…is concerned	19
336	容易	róngyì	*adj.*	easy	19
337	难（難）	nán	*adj.*	difficult	19
338	紧张（緊張）	jǐnzhāng	*adj.*	nervous	19
339	考官	kǎoguān	*n.*	examiner	19
340	中年	zhōngnián	*n.*	middle-age	19
341	女士	nǚshì	*n.*	lady, madam	19
342	转弯（轉彎）	zhuǎnwān	*v.*	turn	19
343	倒车（車）	dàochē	*v.*	back up	19
344	停车（車）	tíngchē	*v.*	stop a car	19
345	顺（順）利	shùnlì	*adj.*	smooth	19
346	辆（輛）	liàng	*m.*	(measure word for vehicles)	19
347	汽车（車）	qìchē	*n.*	automobile	19
348	体（體）育	tǐyù	*n.*	sports; physical education	20
349	运动（運動）	yùndòng	*n.*	sports	20
350	几（幾）乎	jīhū	*adv.*	almost, nearly	20
351	所有	suǒyǒu	*pron.*	all	20
352	外边（邊）	wàibian	*n.*	outside	20
353	棒球	bàngqiú	*n.*	baseball	20

序号	简体（繁體）	拼音	词性	解释	课号
354	踢	tī	v.	kick, play (football or soccer)	20
355	足球	zúqiú	n.	soccer, football	20
356	登山	dēngshān	v.	climb a mountain	20
357	根本	gēnběn	adv.	at all	20
358	游泳	yóuyǒng	v.	swim	20
359	海	hǎi	n.	ocean, sea	20
360	潜（潛）水	qiánshuǐ	v.	dive	20
361	越……越	yuè … yuè		the more…the more	20
362	滑冰	huábīng	v.	skate	20
363	例如	lìrú	v.	for example	20
364	乒乓球	pīngpāngqiú	n.	table tennis	20
365	羽毛球	yǔmáoqiú	n.	badminton	20
366	队（隊）	duì	n.	team	20
367	员（員）	yuán	n.	member, staff	20
368	篮（籃）球	lánqiú	n.	basketball	20
369	比赛（賽）	bǐsài	n.	match, contest	20
370	俩	liǎ	num.	the two of (put after plural pronoun)	20
371	白天	báitiān	n.	daytime	20
372	认为（認為）	rènwéi	v.	believe, think	20
373	赢（贏）	yíng	v.	win, defeat	20
374	大声（聲）	dàshēng	adv.	loudly	20
375	加油	jiāyóu	v.	cheer	20
376	球员（員）	qiúyuán	n.	member of a ball game team	20
377	出色	chūsè	adj.	excellent, brilliant	20
378	半场	bànchǎng	n.	half of the game	20
379	结（結）束	jiéshù	v.	finish	20
380	以	yǐ	prep.	by, with	20
381	比	bǐ	v.	to (in a score)	20
382	领（領）先	lǐngxiān	v.	be in the lead	20
383	继续（繼續）	jìxù	v.	continue	20
384	不断（斷）	búduàn	adv.	continuously	20
385	进（進）球	jìnqiú	v.	score a goal	20
386	十分	shífēn	adv.	very	20

序号	简体（繁體）	拼音	词性	解释	课号
387	激烈	jīliè	*adj.*	intense, fierce	20
388	过（過）	guo	*part.*	(particle after verb, indicating a past experience)	20
389	难过（難過）	nánguò	*adj.*	sad	20
390	芝加哥	Zhījiāgē	*pn.*	Chicago	20
391	公牛队（隊）	Gōngniúduì	*pn.*	Chicago Bulls	20
392	休斯敦	Xiūsīdūn	*pn.*	Houston	20
393	火箭队（隊）	Huǒjiànduì	*pn.*	Houston Rockets	20
394	业余（業餘）	yèyú	*adj.*	amateur	21
395	爱（愛）好	àihào	*n.*	hobby	21
396	摄（攝）影	shèyǐng	*v.*	take a photograph	21
397	微博	wēibó	*n.*	microblog, miniblog	21
398	电视（電視）	diànshì	*n.*	television	21
399	节（節）目	jiémù	*n.*	program	21
400	剧（劇）	jù	*n.*	drama, play	21
401	爱（愛）情	àiqíng	*n.*	love, romance	21
402	科幻	kēhuàn	*n.*	science fiction	21
403	娱乐（娛樂）	yúlè	*n.*	entertainment	21
404	活动	huódòng	*n.*	activity	21
405	嘛	ma	*part.*	(a modal particle)	21
406	跳舞	tiàowǔ	*v.*	dance	21
407	弹（彈）	tán	*v.*	play (a musical instrument)	21
408	钢（鋼）琴	gāngqín	*n.*	piano	21
409	吉他	jítā	*n.*	guitar	21
410	舞会（會）	wǔhuì	*n.*	dance party	21
411	派对（對）	pàiduì	*n.*	party	21
412	教	jiāo	*v.*	teach	21
413	交谊（誼）舞	jiāoyìwǔ	*n.*	social dance	21
414	拉丁舞	lādīngwǔ	*n.*	Latin dance	21
415	陪	péi	*v.*	accompany	21
416	却（卻）	què	*adv.*	but, yet	21
417	决定	juédìng	*v.*	decide	21
418	浪费（費）	làngfèi	*v.*	waste	21
419	这（這）下子	zhè xiàzi		this time; this act	21

序号	简体（繁體）	拼音	词性	解释	课号
420	怎么（麼）	zěnme	*pron.*	how, why	21
421	挂（掛）	guà	*v.*	hang up	21
422	同	tóng	*adj.*	same	21
423	暑假	shǔjià	*n.*	summer vacation	22
424	除了……以外	chúle … yǐwài		besides; apart from	22
425	现（現）代	xiàndài	*n.*	modern time	22
426	化	huà	*suff.*	(suffix indicating a change, similar to –ize in English)	22
427	城市	chéngshì	*n.*	city	22
428	著名	zhùmíng	*adj.*	famous	22
429	园（園）林	yuánlín	*n.*	garden, park	22
430	美丽（麗）	měilì	*adj.*	beautiful	22
431	值得	zhíde	*v.*	be worthy	22
432	嗯	ng	*intj.*	(a sound indicating awareness or agreement)	22
433	听说（聽說）	tīngshuō	*v.*	hear about	22
434	天堂	tiāntáng	*n.*	paradise, heaven	22
435	错过（錯過）	cuòguò	*v.*	miss	22
436	火车（車）	huǒchē	*n.*	train	22
437	兵马（馬）俑	bīngmǎyǒng	*n.*	Terracotta Warriors and Horses	22
438	历（歷）史	lìshǐ	*n.*	history	22
439	古都	gǔdū	*n.*	ancient capital	22
440	棒	bàng	*adj.*	superb, excellent	22
441	定	dìng	*v.*	decide	22
442	上海	Shànghǎi	*pn.*	Shanghai	22
443	苏（蘇）州	Sūzhōu	*pn.*	Suzhou	22
444	杭州	Hángzhōu	*pn.*	Hangzhou	22
445	西湖	Xīhú	*pn.*	West Lake	22
446	香港	Xiānggǎng	*pn.*	Hong Kong	22
447	广（廣）州	Guǎngzhōu	*pn.*	Guangzhou	22
448	西安	Xī’ān	*pn.*	Xi'an	22
449	谈（談）	tán	*v.*	talk	22
450	亲爱（親愛）	qīn’ài	*adj.*	dear	22
451	全部	quánbù	*n.*	all	22

序号	简体（繁體）	拼音	词性	解释	课号
452	门（門）	mén	m.	(measure word for a school course)	22
453	松（鬆）	sōng	v.	let loose	22
454	气（氣）	qì	n.	air, breath	22
455	明年	míngnián	n.	next year	22
456	份	fèn	m.	share, portion	22
457	实习（實習）	shíxí	v.	practice what has been taught in class; to be an intern	22
458	专业（專業）	zhuānyè	n.	specialized field; major	22
459	翻译（譯）	fānyì	n./v.	translation/translate	22
460	招	zhāo	v.	recruit	22
461	简历（簡歷）	jiǎnlì	n.	résumé	22
462	打工	dǎgōng	v.	work a temporary job	22
463	计划（計劃）	jìhuà	v.	plan	22
464	累	lèi	adj.	tired, exhausted	22
465	望	wàng	v.	hope, wish	22
466	保重	bǎozhòng	v.	take good care	22
467	洛杉矶（磯）	Luòshānjī	pn.	Los Angeles	22
468	拉斯维（維）加斯	Lāsīwéijiāsī	pn.	Las Vegas	22
469	大峡（峽）谷	Dàxiágǔ	pn.	Grand Canyon	22
470	盐（鹽）湖城	Yánhúchéng	pn.	Salt Lake City	22
471	黄石公园（園）	Huángshí Gōngyuán	pn.	Yellowstone National Park	22

责任编辑：薛彧威
中文编辑：史文华
封面设计：王薇薇

图书在版编目（CIP）数据

飞跃. 汉语初级教程学生用书. 下册 / 林柏松主编，李蓓，于岚编者. --
北京：华语教学出版社，2013
ISBN 978-7-5138-0561-2

Ⅰ. ①飞⋯ Ⅱ. ①林⋯ ②李⋯ ③于⋯ Ⅲ. ①汉语－对外汉语教学－教材
Ⅳ. ①H195.4

中国版本图书馆CIP数据核字(2013)第217750号

飞跃——汉语初级教程学生用书　下册

主编　林柏松　编者　李　蓓　于　岚
＊
©华语教学出版社有限责任公司
华语教学出版社有限责任公司出版
（中国北京百万庄大街24号　邮政编码100037）
电话: (86)10-68320585, 68997826
传真: (86)10-68997826, 68326333
网址：www.sinolingua.com.cn
电子信箱：hyjx@sinolingua.com.cn
新浪微博地址：http://weibo.com/sinolinguavip
北京京华虎彩印刷有限公司印刷
2014年（16开）第1版
ISBN 978-7-5138-0561-2
定价：119.00元